PENGUIN BOOKS

Michael Kirby

Daryl Dellora is an award-winning documentary filmmaker. He is the recipient of an Australian Human Rights Award for his film *Mr Neal is Entitled to Be an Agitator*, about the life of High Court justice Lionel Murphy, and a Gold Plaque at the Chicago International Television Festival for *The Edge of the Possible* – a film about Sydney Opera House architect Jørn Utzon.

Daryl has been an Australian Film Commission documentary fellow, and in 2005 was awarded a residency at the Rockefeller Foundation Bellagio Study Centre. He wrote and directed the film *Michael Kirby: Don't forget the justice bit* (2010) for ABC-TV, has made films about the Governor-General of Australia and the High Court, and has worked for Film Australia and SBS-TV. Daryl co-produced the 2006 feature film *Hunt Angels* (winner of the AFI Award for Best Documentary) and was an executive producer of *Celebrity: Dominick Dunne* (2008).

He is a director of the film production company Film Art Doco and filmartmedia.com, and lives in Melbourne. *Michael Kirby: Law, Love & Life* is his first book.

Daryl Dellora

Michael Kirby

Law, Love & Life

PENGUIN BOOKS

PENGUIN BOOKS

UK | USA | Canada | Ireland | Australia
India | New Zealand | South Africa | China

Penguin Books is part of the Penguin Random House group of companies
whose addresses can be found at global.penguinrandomhouse.com.

First published by Penguin Group (Australia), 2012
This edition published by Penguin Group (Australia), 2013

Design by John Canty © Penguin Group (Australia)
Front cover photograph by John Tsiavis
Typeset in Garamond
Printed and bound in Australia by Griffin Press, an accredited ISO AS/NZS 14001
Environmental Management Systems printer.

National Library of Australia
Cataloguing-in-Publication data:

Dellora, Daryl.
Michael Kirby: law, love & life / Daryl Dellora.
9780143569152 (pbk.)
Kirby, M. D. (Michael Donald), 1939–
Judges-Australia-Biography.
Lawyers-Australia-Biography.

340.092

penguin.com.au

Contents

Contents

Introduction

Shortly after Michael Kirby's father, Don Kirby, died in November 2011, a truckload of papers and letters arrived from the Kirby family home in Concord and was deposited in Michael's chambers in Macquarie Street. Don had been an inveterate hoarder of anything relating to the most famous member of the Kirby clan: letters to and from Michael, every conceivable document that bore some significance, invitations from the Queen, postcards, photographs, press clippings – all going right back to his school days. This is material designed to elevate the blood pressure of a biographer. Perhaps buried in these boxes somewhere is *the* letter, or *the* official document that reveals once and for all the 'true story' about some compelling drama, maybe *the* most important drama in a life. When I opened a package of letters, many written in blue fountain pen, in Michael Kirby's distinctive flowing hand, I knew I had found just such a treasure. Here was private correspondence that Don had kept hidden for more than forty years, even from the closest members of his family.

I first met Michael Kirby on 29 April 1991 at 4.30 p.m. sharp. On arrival at the Metro film complex in the old Paddington Town Hall, the then president of the NSW Court of Appeal was not overly impressed. 'Rather tatty place, isn't it?' he said as he walked down the dusty, unpainted corridor to the studio space buried in the heart of the building. I was directing a film about the life of former High Court justice Lionel Murphy for ABC-TV, and by that time I had made a number of films and worked in a range of studios. They were all pretty tatty; Metro wasn't the tattiest or the most elegant. As Kirby entered the studio itself he probably felt more comfortable: his chair, with red leather upholstery and black arms, was elevated. A hand-painted, grey textured canvas hung behind the chair and was draped under it. A number of lights were carefully focussed on this tableau, as was the crew of ten or so people, and as he sat down, the image that flickered up on the television monitor was delicately modelled. The whole scene had a touch of the regal about it.

There was a backstory to Kirby's agreement to appear in our film. He was happy to offer his observations on the life of a great Australian and friend, who he had known well, but he was a little concerned about being filmed in front of a painted backdrop. Correspondence ensued, in which he suggested that his contribution should be offered in front of the customary shelves of law reports in his chambers. Every one of the many television crews that had interviewed him in the past had done it that way. It was touch and go for a while as to whether he would agree to appear at all, until it was finally clear that every other interviewee, including Gough Whitlam, David Lange, Neville Wran, Don Dunstan and Jim McClelland, had all agreed to the painted backdrop. They were all VIPs – two former prime ministers, two former premiers and another judge – and they had agreed. He would be the odd man out if he stuck to his own special prerequisite. In the end, he acceded to our request, both to conform to the precedent established in this particular case but also because he eventually accepted the legitimate demands of the creative process.

Throughout Michael Kirby's life he has, with only a few notable exceptions, successfully balanced two conflicting propositions. He saw himself as a conservative legal figure (his own Aunt Glory even thought him 'reactionary'), and carried himself with a kind of princely air that belied his humble origins. He modestly claimed to be no better or worse than his judicial colleagues and was always proudly nonpartisan. He counted among his friends Liberal icons like Malcolm Fraser, Alexander Downer, Tony Abbott, Nick Greiner, John Dowd and Chris Puplick, as well as Labor greats such as Neville Wran, Lionel Murphy, Barry Jones and Gareth Evans. But balanced against this was the important proviso: Michael Kirby was never afraid to be the odd man out. At the right moment he would speak out against the tide; in fact he saw it as his duty to do so, and never shirked that duty.

For the best part of the decade following that first meeting, I watched Kirby's career with interest from Melbourne. When he was elevated to the High Court in 1996, I again approached him, this time with a request that he be the subject of a documentary. He was not inclined to do so at that time. He was a part of a bench on the highest court in the land, and thought it inappropriate to promote himself above his six sister and brother judges. No doubt they didn't see him as genuinely having that concern; by then he was already a household name in Australia, and not reluctant to comment publicly on a diverse range of topics. Many of his legal colleagues thought it enormously amusing that he even spoke authoritatively about the use of breastmilk substitutes in Zimbabwe. Why would he, a gay man, have any credentials to speak on such an issue? In adopting this stance, they also ridiculed a serious problem that was claiming the lives of thousands of infants in the developing world every year.

In 2008, the year before Kirby's retirement from the High Court of Australia, I approached him once more with the idea of a documentary film about his life, and this time he agreed. Although we would begin filming before he had retired, the finished program would only go to air after he was no longer on the Court, and therefore he could speak with a candour that might not have been possible when he was still a High Court judge. We were fortunate that Johan van Vloten, Kirby's partner of forty years, also agreed to participate in the film. It was the first and only time Johan had appeared in such a public way, discussing their relationship and life together. My work on that project, *Michael Kirby: Don't forget the justice bit*, has led to this book. It is not the book of the film, but it builds on the work done in that production. Johan's observations about his partner, in particular, provided a unique perspective for the film, and I have used much more from that funny and engaging interview in this book.

Here I have taken as my starting point the idea that Kirby's own words should be paramount. On top of the interviews I conducted with him, there are hundreds of his speeches, articles and other writings, along with his books, many other interviews and, of course, a massive archive of his legal judgements. The one thing that became abundantly clear during the film production was that Michael Kirby was the consummate narrator of the story of his own life. Beside him and set against his version of events are the many contributions from his family, friends, colleagues and critics, his partner not the least among them all.

Michael Kirby was born six months before the declaration of World War II, and in the following seven decades he has seen Australia change in remarkable ways. It is now a nation that is unrecognisable when set against the world of the late 1930s. Kirby himself remains somewhat quaintly old-fashioned in many of his fundamental values, yet at the same time he is insistently modern (never postmodern) in so much of his outlook. Throughout his life, he has drawn criticism from many quarters. As a student politician, he was derisively labelled 'the Vicar of Bray' by his left-wing opponents, seen as willing to change his views depending on the circumstances just to remain in office. Later, on the High Court, he was attacked as an 'activist judge' by conservative commentators who claimed he determined his judgements according to his desired outcome rather than the requirements of the law. Although determinedly Anglican, he has been in many battles with his church and with other denominations, rejecting the still common attitude that equates homosexuality with 'intrinsic evil'. And, finally, his progressive approach to the Australian Constitution – his view of it as a living, breathing document, evolving with the people and the nation it defines – sit uncomfortably beside his undiminished loyalty to the Queen. One thing is certain: there is a dialectic operating in Michael Kirby's life. The resulting synthesis is revealed through the pages of this book.

1

The Yellow Jacket

> Of course I'm optimistic. How could you be an Australian who's seen a nation that was rather self-satisfied solve or partly solve issues of Aboriginal land rights, issues of gay rights, issues of white Australia, and increasingly become a multicultural, multinational society, a much more interesting and vibrant society. I've seen many things improve in Australia in my lifetime and if you've seen that, then you know it can be done.
>
> *Michael Kirby*

Forty-six thousand photographs. Many carefully displayed under clear plastic in spiral-bound photo albums – 123 of them. Hundreds more still in their yellow, black and blue envelopes, Kodak, Agfa, Fuji, exactly as they were when retrieved from the chemist after developing and printing. Michael Kirby has been taking photographs for more than forty years, including almost every day of his professional life. It is unlike any other amateur photo collection, not just in its sheer volume, but also because it is unusually consistent in one major respect: the subject matter. Almost every one of these tens of thousands of photographs features people. Page after page of anonymous conference delegates, occasionally broken by a shot of Queen Elizabeth II or Nelson Mandela or a Nobel laureate. Young associates snapped in chambers on their last day of work, only to reappear years later as distinguished academics, lawyers, MPs or United Nations representatives. In their own way, the photos document a professional life through the people and the places that define it.

From 1996 to 2009 Michael Kirby served as a justice on the highest court in the Australian judicial system. His first judicial appointment, to the Arbitration Commission, had come in 1974 at the tender age of thirty-five, but by 1996 he was by far and away the best-known judge in Australia. Not all Australians would have known he was a judge of the High Court, or perhaps even what that institution was, but almost all would recognise the deep, mellifluous, somehow comforting tone of his voice when they heard it in one of his many radio or television appearances. He was uniquely accessible in a profession that generally tries to remain aloof – certainly from the masses. Kirby was the most outspoken and active judge the High Court had ever seen.

But looking back at this collection of moments, album after album of them piled high on trolleys, it is almost as if those thirteen years on the High Court were a quiet time, compared with the life that had come before. 'Well, maybe I'm trying to capture life before it all disappears,' Kirby notes wistfully.

> It's unfolding day by day and I'm trying to stop it for a moment and capture the moment and capture the people. It's probably my endeavour to rescue events from the inexorable pace of time. Maybe in the future, especially in the future of the High Court, internal photographs that are taken informally, a view of the court that has never before emerged, will be quite useful. Probably very embarrassing to some of the justices, but never to me because I'm behind the camera. My great-aunts in Ireland were portraitists, and I sometimes think composing a photograph and getting the balance in a photograph and centring or putting the subject in an appropriate position is a sort of endeavour for me to give an artistic expression. But artist will I never be, singer will I never be.

The stage, the spotlight, the roar of the crowd, that did have enormous appeal to Kirby and he sought it out. In 2002 he helped open the World Gay Games at the Sydney Football Stadium at Moore Park to rapturous applause from the thousands attending. In 2006 he even got out in his jogging shorts (and brown suede Hush Puppies) to run through the suburban streets of Sydney in the Queen's Baton Relay for the Commonwealth Games. If there was an audience of twenty or an audience of 20 000, Michael Kirby would be up on the platform with microphone in hand.

'Tread softly, tread softly.' Kirby's voice wasn't melodic, it was rhythmic and slightly distorted by the PA. But all eyes were fixed on him. Hip-hop performer Elf Tranzporter leant towards the

High Court judge and put his arm around him. They looked good together up on the stage, the judge belting out a rap of Yeats and the hip-hop artist creating the rhythm track, both holding microphones, an incongruous version of Mick and Keith. The crowd was enthralled, cheering and clapping wildly. The appearance of 68-year-old Justice Michael Kirby of the High Court of Australia at the 2007 Victorian Arts Law Week function had been determined well in advance, but the routine itself was far more spontaneous. He had agreed on the day to do an impromptu act with Elf Tranzporter. The only pre-planned part of it was his dress. He appeared on the stage at first apparently garbed in the traditional dark blue suit of a judge. Initially, he'd feigned surprised indignation at the act he was supposed to perform. 'Why didn't they tell me?' he said. 'I'd prepared a most wonderful address on the inter-relationship between the Constitution and the implied right to free expression and the law on copyright.' Laughter from the crowd. 'This is something new . . . something new for the High Court . . . and we are going to get with it and get it on.'

And with that, he'd got it off – well, his suit coat, at least, revealing a garish yellow jacket underneath. 'It's a little number we are going to put in the High Court. They're all going to be wearing it next week! . . . And I'm going to have to get ready for the time in two years when I leave the High Court and I am going to become the Jerry Springer of Australia! So, here we go, out into the multitude.'

Kirby stepped down into the excited crowd and calmed them. The room fell silent and he began his recitation of the W. B. Yeats poem, 'He Wishes for the Cloths of Heaven':

Had I the heavens' embroidered cloths,
Enwrought with the golden and silver light,
The blue and the dim and the dark cloths
Of night and light and the half-light,
I would spread the cloths under your feet:
But I, being poor, have only my dreams;
I have spread my dreams beneath your feet;
Tread softly because you tread on my dreams.

The crowd seemed a little stunned, perhaps wondering if they had somehow missed the punchline. But then Elf Tranzporter began his beatbox rhythm track and Kirby jumped back on the stage, now singing along: 'Had I the heavens' embroidered . . . tread softly, tread softly, tread softly, tread softly.' The young audience revelled in it.

Kirby had worked the crowd beautifully. The 300 assembled lawyers and artists were in the palm of his hand, but they weren't going to escape until Kirby had turned their minds to some matters of human rights. He now reprised a part of the speech he had delivered at the opening ceremony of the Gay Games. Kirby added some new material to reflect the theme of that year's Arts Law Week, which was sponsored by Multicultural Arts Victoria.

> But to come, there will be inclusion and fusion not exclusion. Fusion not exclusion. Under different stars, at the opening of a new millennium, in an old land and a young nation, we join together in the hope and conviction that the future will be kinder and more just than the past. At a time when there is so much fear and danger, anger and destruction, tonight represents

> an alternative vision struggling for the soul of humanity. Acceptance. Diversity. Inclusiveness. Participation. Tolerance. Joy. Ours is the world of love, questing to find the common links that bind all people. We are here because, whatever our identity, we believe that the days of exclusion are numbered. The days of fusion are come . . . Enjoy yourselves. And by our lives, let us be an example of respect for human rights. Fusion not exclusion. And not just for minorities. For everyone.

The next day, Michael Kirby made it once more into pages of the nation's newspapers, this time for being the first High Court judge in the history of the Commonwealth to have performed a rap. As he said himself during the performance: 'This is a very important night, I don't see Sir Owen Dixon coming here and doing this, I don't see Sir Wilfred Fullagar coming here and doing this!' Dixon, perhaps the most respected of all High Court judges and his colleague Fullagar, both Victorians, were, of course, now long dead.

Only a few months before this, Kirby had been listed by *The Bulletin* magazine as one of Australia's top ten creative minds, alongside Aboriginal academic Pat Dodson, restaurateur Gay Bilson, philosopher Peter Singer and physicist Paul Davies. And the same year he was included as one of the hundred most influential Australians in a list that recognised Germaine Greer, Patrick White, Kylie Minogue and Robert Menzies. These accolades were becoming commonplace for Justice Michael Kirby. In 2002, *Who Weekly* had even put him up there with Halle Berry, Natalie Portman, Hugh Jackman and Denzel Washington in its annual round-up of the world's twenty-five most beautiful people.

From the moment Labor prime minister Paul Keating had quite unexpectedly appointed him to the High Court of Australia in 1996 to the day he left in February 2009, Michael Kirby was the most recognisable judge in Australia and a most unusual man. Openly gay, the first judge of any final national constitutional court in the world to have come out while still in office, Kirby had been controversial and outspoken – even, at times, to his own personal cost. As the first chairman of the new Australian Law Reform Commission (ALRC), from 1975 to 1984, Kirby was no stranger to media attention. In fact, from the outset he saw it as his duty to bring the law to the people. More importantly, he actually wanted meaningful input from the people themselves, especially those who would be immediately affected by the laws in question.

Most Australians were mystified by the legal process and in awe of lawyers and, particularly, judges. Indeed, in Australia in 1975 the law was a closed community, almost exclusively male, white, Anglo-Saxon, Protestant, straight (at least outwardly – homosexuality was still criminalised in most states) and extremely conservative. In nearly thirty-five years on the bench, Kirby was, in his judgements and public statements, to challenge many of these stereotypes. If there was a complex or difficult moral or ethical question, people quickly came to expect Michael Kirby to be outspoken about it. Unlike most of the politicians, Kirby was admired for not running away from the hard questions. He was careful to avoid conflict with issues that were before his court, or might in the future come before his court, and for the most part this was a successful strategy, but he would not shy away from difficult or controversial matters when it came to fundamental principles.

There was one regret in a long and extraordinary career on the bench: he came to the High Court too late to be part of the famous and lauded Court under Chief Justice Sir Anthony Mason. It was the Mason Court that heard the *Mabo* case and Kirby would have dearly liked to have been a part of that judgement.

If Melbourne barrister Barbara Hocking, the 'intellectual architect' of *Mabo*, had not completed her Master of Laws on the topic of native title land rights, it is unlikely that Eddie Mabo, who heard Hocking address a conference, would have set out his action in the way he did, or sought her out as the first counsel to be briefed on his claim. Hocking presented, eloquently and for the first time, the moral and legal issues at the heart of *Mabo*: the simple thought that Aboriginal people and their land claims must be treated equally, under Australian law, to every other landholder. That Indigenous Australians did not own their lands was a wrong that had long been relegated to the category of unfortunate and unfair but, by 1980, it had been settled Australian law for 200 years. At the time, no Australian politician was prepared to even acknowledge the wrong, let alone try to do something about it.

Michael Kirby was fascinated as the *Mabo* case finally emerged from the High Court twelve years later, and he was as shocked by the outcome as most other Australians. The judges could not simply put it into the too-hard basket, as every colonial administration and parliament had done since white settlement. The Court had a duty to decide the matter that was before it and that is what they did. Eddie Mabo died in January 1992 and the High Court found in his favour in June of the same year. All he had asked was that his traditional lands be recognised as belonging to his clan at the time of white settlement – that native title was real and that the proposition of terra nullius (land belonging to no one) was a fiction in the Australian context.

Like Hocking, Kirby saw it as his duty to speak up when his voice was needed. Whether it was for the rights of HIV/AIDS sufferers, the human rights of the Cambodian or Tibetan people, or the rights of prisoners and other disenfranchised Australians, including refugees and Aborigines, he was outspoken again and again.

Kirby wasn't always right – far from it. All judges make mistakes. Nevertheless, there were fundamental principles, as he saw it, that could not be compromised. The importance and relevance of international human rights law was one such principle, certainly one of the most important for him.

One case that Kirby sat on, in particular, illustrated this more than any other. A Palestinian man born in Kuwait, Ahmed Ali Al-Kateb, had sought political asylum in Australia but had been held in immigration detention for years. Israel would not allow Palestinians to return to Gaza once they left and no other country would take him, so he was stuck in Australia. He was classified under Australian and international law as stateless. In 2004 the Howard Government was arguing before the High Court that Mr Al-Kateb could, if necessary, be held in immigration detention, literally, for the rest of his life. Kirby strongly disagreed and invoked his understanding of international human rights law to support his view that someone who is escaping persecution and has committed no crime ought not be put in jail, potentially for the rest of their life, on the whim of an immigration minister. As it turned out, the Government won the case; Mr Al-Kateb and the other two or three stateless people in

Australian immigration detention centres could now be doomed to a life behind bars unless the minister decided to release them into the community. Mr Al-Kateb was eventually released by the minister but the unfairness entrenched in the law remained.

The yellow jacket was pulled out of the closet once more. In the month he retired from the High Court, February 2009, Kirby addressed a black-tie function at the Great Hall at Sydney University. Few knew the significance of the tiny glimpse of yellow that could be seen under the cuff of his black jacket. After the formalities and some introductory words there was an audible gasp from those assembled when Kirby removed his tuxedo jacket to reveal the yellow one beneath.

The dignitaries present included the chancellor of the university and New South Wales governor Marie Bashir, the vice-chancellor and several knights of the realm, the leader of the Opposition, the attorney-general and many other politicians and judges. But the most important guest as far as Kirby was concerned was Mr Al-Kateb himself.

> Two weeks ago, on 7 February, [he] was made a citizen of Australia. Now Ahmed Ali Al-Kateb is here with us tonight. He is a person who used every legal endeavour, as was his right, and he went through the hierarchy of the Australian courts, as is rather unusual. I'm told that his ceremony of admission to Australian citizenship was marred a little by the fact that the official who was present at the time was, shall we say, not entirely sober. But I want to tell you, Ahmed, I want to tell you that you are now a citizen of a free and fair country that

> lives by the rule of law, that the judges who decided against you were doing what they believed the law to require, that the judges who decided for you were doing what they believed the law to require. That it is part of the price of a rule-of-law society that you have to have decision-makers, that they act according to their conscience and to their understanding of the law [. . .]
>
> You have been accepted into our midst as an honoured citizen and I want, on behalf of everyone present, to say welcome to our citizenship. Congratulations and we honour you as an Australian citizen.

At the end of his address Kirby dived into the crowd in his self-appointed role as Australia's Jerry Springer. Dazzling in the yellow jacket, he shook Mr Al-Kateb by the hand and asked and answered questions about a bill of rights, terrorism, global and Aboriginal affairs. He may have ended a long career as a judge but it seemed that Michael Kirby wouldn't be going anywhere soon. And despite a few minor protestations that the yellow jacket had passed its use-by date, it too was in for a lot more action.

> The yellow jacket is just something that I have worn from time to time. My partner, Johan, says I've worn it too often. It has to be pensioned off. It's to show that all lawyers are, in a sense, double personalities. That you have your own inner soul, and your inner being, and your personal life and your loves and friendships, but you have to play a role in the administration of justice, and so this is a very physical and dramatic way of

demonstrating that underneath everyone's dark suits is a bright golden outfit, which they're just waiting to get into.

But the yellow jacket meant a lot more than this. Throughout his whole life Kirby had been guided by some basic moral principles that came directly from his Anglican Christian beliefs. He didn't trumpet his religion; in fact, for the most part it remained a private side of his life. He neither hid it nor wore it on his sleeve, it was just part of him and always would be. But there was something else, something fundamental to him and to everything he did, whether in his private life or publicly, and unlike any other prominent public figure Michael Kirby was prepared to speak openly and regularly about it. It was something that came from his religion but was in no way exclusive to it. When the yellow jacket came out, when he literally took on a different aura, when every pair of eyes in the room were fixed on him, this was the time to act. Kirby stood out, at that moment, from all around him and he spoke from the heart.

> I have a view that the foundation of human rights, international human rights, is love. Why do we respect human dignity? Why do we uphold the right to civil and political rights or economic, social and cultural rights? We do so because we can see enough in other people to understand that their lives are sufficiently similar to our own that we should 'do unto others as we would have them do unto us'. The golden rule is actually through all the religions. It's the common feature of all the human belief systems and all the spiritual explanations.
>
> So, if you think in those terms and you ask, what is the

absolute bedrock of human rights, of our legal system, of striving to have order? Why are we here today and tomorrow, and what does our life mean? Well, love has a lot to do with it and we can't leave love out of it. If you've had a life like mine, with a loving family and loving parents, siblings, good friends, and then a loving companion over such a long time, then you're very lucky. The foundation of so much of that is love and I've never been ashamed to say so.

2

A Lucky Life

Where, after all, do universal human rights begin? In small places, close to home – so close and so small that they cannot be seen on any maps of the world. Yet they are the world of the individual person; the neighbourhood he lives in; the school or college he attends; the factory, farm, or office where he works. Such are the places where every man, woman, and child seeks equal justice, equal opportunity, equal dignity without discrimination. Unless these rights have meaning there, they have little meaning anywhere. Without concerted citizen action to uphold them close to home, we shall look in vain for progress in the larger world.

Eleanor Roosevelt

Wednesday, 8 September 1943 delivered a glorious Sydney spring morning. The motorcade of the first lady of the United States of America, Mrs Eleanor Roosevelt, swept down Parramatta Road on her way from Victoria Barracks, where she had had morning tea, 'one of the pleasant customs here', with men recently returned from the Middle East campaign and women from the Auxiliary Military Services. She was on her way to lift the spirits of the boys at the US Army's 118th General Hospital, at Herne Bay in western Sydney. The three soldiers seated opposite her in the limousine had all been wounded in New Guinea, and she took their names and addresses so that she could write to their families back home. Everywhere she went, thousands of Australians turned out to line the streets. Men, women and children left their factories, businesses, schools and homes and all were waving handkerchiefs. Three thousand women had greeted her at the Sydney Town Hall the night before and as one they'd roared a thunderous 'Coo-ee!' on her arrival. Hundreds of NSW police officers and Australian and US Provost men had to hold the huge crowds at bay.

Michael was four and a half at the time, and attending St Andrew's Kindergarten on the corner of Parramatta and Concord roads. The children were often marched out onto Parramatta Road to see dignitaries drive past, including the governor-general. 'Concord Road was pretty quiet in those times,' he says now. 'I remember the khaki trucks going along the road with the big red cross in a circle of white, on their way to the Repatriation General Hospital at Concord. At one stage I have a dim recollection that Mrs Roosevelt came past our school. But perhaps that is a trick of the memory.' But American first ladies don't come to town that often. In fact, one had never been to Sydney's western suburbs before, or, indeed, to Australia. It would be twenty-three years before another US first lady, in the form of Lady Bird Johnson, would come that way again, this time as part of a presidential visit that became famous for all the wrong reasons.

For Michael Kirby, Eleanor Roosevelt's visit was important. She was a driving force behind the United Nations Organization and the development of the Universal Declaration of Human Rights, a landmark achievement that stands to this day as a basic foundation of all international human rights law. The later Justice Michael Kirby would turn again and again to the Universal Declaration of Human Rights, the first lady's most enduring legacy. This dreamlike image of the US motorcade and its distinguished passenger, and all that it stood for, has stayed with him all his life, both as one of his earliest childhood memories and as a guiding light.

Over nearly three decades, from his first memories of Eleanor Roosevelt to his admission to the Bar as a 28-year-old barrister, Michael Donald Kirby remained firmly ensconced in the family home at Sydney Street, Concord. It was a happy, secure and comfortable life with devoted, loving parents. As the eldest child, he watched his siblings grow up around him, he nurtured and supported them and he saw them leave home and start their own independent lives. But he never felt the need to follow.

Michael was born on 18 March 1939 and twin brothers arrived two years later: Donald William and David Charles. David Charles died of pneumonia at eighteen months of age, when Michael was three. It was a family tragedy that affected everyone in different ways. David Charles's twin, Donald, was inconsolable. When another son was born a year or so later, parents Jean and Don decided to call him David. As it turned out, Donald and his younger brother David were also to become inseparable.

Michael was less than impressed when his new brother was born. 'Why do we want another boy?' he asked his parents. 'We've got a houseful of boys.' He made it plain he wanted a sister. On this, like on so many things, he was as one with his mother; Jean too wanted a girl. When Diana was born in 1946, everyone was happy. Their father Don was inclined to spoil his only daughter and if there ever were disagreements between the siblings, his second son, Donald, invariably sided with his little sister. Don Kirby recognised the difference in temperament in his children and in particular the special bond between Donald and Diana: '[Donald] was a Celt with ginger-red hair, and she was also a Celt, and from the early days they were so close and he defended her,' Don recalls. 'Of course the others would torment her; she was a stranger in the midst.'

From the earliest age, Michael was an extremely self-motivated child – in part through necessity, but mostly because that was just his nature. Books were everywhere in the Kirby household and Michael was an avid reader and writer. Shakespeare, Yeats, Dickens and especially history were his passions. Michael's father Don liked to take the family to plays when he could. 'We took them to *The Taming of the Shrew* and they loved it. I got long-playing records for them to listen to and it kind of seeped into their brains.'

The Kirby household was a lively place, and there was always a lot of animated discussion and argument. This was especially so during parliamentary elections like the one in 1946, when the Chifley Labor Government was returned. 'At the table at night-time we used to listen to different commentaries and political elections and all of that,' Don says. 'Michael wouldn't have been more than about six. He would be sitting on the floor on his legs and he would be writing down what they were getting, the results of the election. And I'd say, "Put him down, he's going to win, I think."

Whereas Jean had a quiet opinion. She always voted the opposite, we suspected, of what we did.'

The overwhelming memories of this time for Michael Kirby are of a happy, loving family life.

> I had wonderful siblings, two brothers and a sister, and it was a pretty lucky childhood, indeed, a pretty lucky life, really. We lived together, we ate together, we talked together and we reinforced our bonds with each other, and that is still the case; we are still a close family.

Don Kirby worked for a hardware store in York Street called Pauls, then he set up his own manufacturing business. He built woodworking machines: bandsaws, jointers, and other light machinery, and his fortunes as a small businessman wavered. In the Menzies Government credit squeeze of 1951 he had to close his doors and move the business into the garage of the Kirby home. David Kirby recognised in his father a genial exterior that hid a steely determination and an authority that none of the children ever crossed.

> He was a person that you never defied as a child. I don't remember him ever hitting me, but he had such integrity when he gave a direction, and he lowered his voice an octave or two, you did what you were told to do. There were no questions. And Michael, no less than the rest of us, was obedient to my father's commands. My mother was an entirely different person. She was passionate, explosive, Irish, emotional, highly intellectual in a sense that when you spoke to her, you had the

> feeling of this searchlight intelligence that really understood very quickly what was going on, and what you were saying. She was a joy to talk to.

These were also hard years for the Kirbys; they never had much money, never took holidays, never had a car and only occasionally went out to entertainment. Jean Kirby was in and out of hospital with serious and at times life-threatening complaints, including complications from neurodermatitis, so doctors and hospitals seemed to be frequent factors in their lives and a constant drain on the household expenses. As a result, Don depended on the support of his extended family, including his grandmother and mother Norma. For a short period, when Jean was hospitalised for three months, Michael and Donald, then about eight and six respectively, had to be sent off to a children's home while Diana stayed with Norma and David with friends. It was an awful experience for the two boys and Michael never forgot it. But it was short-lived; when Don Kirby saw the daily squalor they had to endure and the fear in their eyes, he immediately removed them.

As the eldest, Michael knew that he needed to take on increased responsibilities at different times in order to take the pressure off his parents. Don remembers Michael as ordered, methodical and self-directed. 'On occasion when Jean wasn't well and had to go to doctors and specialists, we would come home and find the table set and a menu laid out in his writing. And he had it cooked and ready.'

When he was only eight years old, Michael had become acutely aware of his own mortality and did something quite unusual. He had lived through the horror of the war years, the daily newspaper headlines and radio broadcasts of millions of civilian deaths, of destruction and atrocities. He had lost his young brother to pneumonia and seen his mother gravely ill, so in a logical, thoughtful way, and perhaps in his first legal act, Michael decided to prepare his 'Last Will And Last Testiment'. It was an interesting document for many reasons, and a very poignant one. The name he used was Michael Donald Sheridan Kirby. 'Sheridan' was his own addition, quite deliberately reflecting two important matters of heritage. First and perhaps most significantly, especially in the context of the overall document, it gave a special place to his mother's ancestry, which otherwise would not have been recognised at all. Second, it made specific reference to a particular figure, the Irish playwright and Whig parliamentarian Richard Brinsley Sheridan, who was thought to be one of his mother's forebears. In this way Michael laid claim, through a direct blood link, to a rich historical, literary and political legacy taking him right to the heart of the British Empire – the Parliament at Westminster itself.

Rather than just a technical legal document, albeit rudimentary and with an eight-year-old's fragile grasp of grammar and punctuation, what the young boy had written was poetic and heartfelt: 'It is my last will that My brothers Donald William Kirby and David Kirby should each get 3 sixtenths of My Entire wealth my Sister shall enherit my books desk and wirless'. And for Don Kirby, 'my father who was always most kind and understanding Always admired my Encyclopedias he shall get them and as he is very much in need of a new case shall get mine to do as he pleases with it.' It ends: 'And my love be with you allways I sign this with Knowlege of a pure sane and obediant hart M Kirby'. It was countersigned 'doctor Joan Fotheringham [the family doctor] mental surgen BB Edwards solisator JFR Barracks witness J Barron [his school chums]'.

The seventh line of the will was a clause referring to his mother, and it was as if the whole document had somehow been constructed around this central compelling statement. It was guaranteed to bring a tear to the eye of any parent. He had distributed all his worldly goods, and now the most important gift of all was bestowed: 'My most beloved and Kind Mother shall get my love as it would be impossible to repay her any other way.'

Michael had a habit of behaving in ways that, to say the least, were extremely unusual for a child of his age. His brother David knew Michael was exceptional and unique. 'Well, there was Michael, and then there was the rest of us, who were normal kids, really. I mean, he read books, we played games. We occasionally read books, or more often than not, comics. He was different.' But preparing his own will really took his father by surprise: 'He was eight and a half and I found it on his desk. And I said to him later, "When are you planning to die?" He laughed.'

Michael was witness to the disorder left when his grandfather died without a will in 1947. Jean was distressed, and on top of this stood to miss out on any inheritance when her sister claimed the estate. It was Michael's job, as he saw it, to protect his mother, who was the most vulnerable member of the family. His ordered mind immediately clicked into action. He could not do anything about his grandfather's oversight but he could make sure his mother was a beneficiary, the most important one, in his own will.

From St Andrew's Kindergarten, Michael went on to Strathfield

North Primary School, where he was always a high achiever. There was subtle and not so subtle pressure, especially from Jean, to be number one. 'On one occasion I came second in the class under Mrs Godwin. When I told my mother, she asked who had come first. "Bobby Chong," I announced. My mother let me know that next time I was expected to come first. It was not imperious and certainly not punitive. Simply expectations of excellence.'

There was nothing special about Strathfield North Primary but Michael relished his time there and enjoyed just being another ordinary Australian student. They all sat side by side, the lower-middle classes and the dirt poor; there was no discrimination and no religion. 'In those days, some came to school without shoes from The Home, a nearby orphanage and refuge for underprivileged children. Some, like me, were sent off to school with peanut butter or cheese sandwiches, wearing ties. That was the minority.'

Michael was always surrounded by strong women, his 'aunts' Lillian and Gloria (an early feminist and close friend of Jessie Street) were fixtures in the household, and especially their sister, Michael's grandmother, Norma. When Jean Kirby gave birth to Diana in 1946, there were serious complications. The baby was fine but again Jean became very ill. She was only thirty years old, with four children: Michael was seven, Donald five, David three, and now a newborn. The Second World War had only just ended and Australians were still suffering food shortages and other hardships, which extended well into the 1950s. Don Kirby's mother, Norma, played a crucial role of support and assistance to Jean. Although working during the week herself, on her day off she would take the bus to Concord and spend the day helping Jean with the housework. On many other occasions she would take a young Michael to stay at Tempe, where she lived with her second husband, Jack Simpson. To Michael, he was always simply Uncle Jack.

Both Norma and Jack smoked and drank alcohol and gambled. Michael was accustomed to parents who never smoked and who never drank; his father might take one glass of wine at Christmas or on a special occasion. The radio at Don and Jean's never left the ABC, while Michael remembers the trots and the dogs blaring at the Tempe house. 'The place was different because it was on the main street and there was a tram line that went past it. I complained bitterly to my father that I couldn't sleep properly there and he just told me not to be a brat and to go to sleep.' Michael got used to it – never liked it, but got used to it. 'I'm afraid to this day I'm a bit of a wowser and I still don't drink very much alcohol. I have never gambled and never smoked, so all in all it probably reinforced my prejudices against these evils of the working class.' But it never diminished his respect or love for his grandmother and Uncle Jack. He never forgot the sound of the nearby factory or the neighbours' voices through the walls, the smell of potatoes cooked in their jackets and the taste of loquats.

It was an intellectual household and a working-class one. Jack Simpson was a New Zealander and a veteran of the Great War. He had been in the first landing at Gallipoli and then at the Somme, where he was awarded the Military Medal for bravery in the field. When he returned after the war he became disillusioned. There was little or no support for ex-servicemen and many fell by the wayside during the Great Depression in the 1920s and '30s. Jack Simpson joined the Australian Communist Party, as many ex-Catholics did. 'It became like his religion – he just switched from Catholicism to communism.' Michael's mother, on the other hand, had no time for communism.

> My mother was the product of this Northern Irish upbringing. She never drank alcohol in her life and she always looked down on gambling or horseracing or radio broadcasts. And she was always a lady and she had high values. But they didn't worry about Jack; they rather liked Jack as a person, but they divorced him, as a person, from the communist associations. My father took it all with a grain of salt; of course he loved his mother and therefore supported her. And Jack was very, very fond of my father's mother. And he was a very fine man.

Norma was well-read and the house at Tempe was full of books, communist tracts in particular. Many small, soft-cover pamphlets printed by Progress Publishers, the Soviet foreign languages press, lined the walls of the modest terrace house: the complete works of V. I. Lenin, works of Marx and Engels. But to the young Michael, it appeared as though they had never been opened, and perhaps he was right. Even though Jack Simpson rose to the office of national treasurer of the Australian Communist Party, he seemed throughout this time to be a rather sad figure, always suffering from the horrible effects, both physical and mental, of his military service. The strident anti-communism in Australia and the increasing news of Stalinist repression in Russia all took its toll on the rather fragile

Uncle Jack and by 1952 he had resigned from the party, completely disheartened.

In the federal election of 1949, Michael, then ten years old, helped Jack paste up Communist Party posters around the back streets of Sydney. It was a vain effort: no communist candidates came close to success. Robert Menzies had consolidated the anti-Labor vote and energised the new Liberal Party of Australia. He rode an international wave of anti-communism and encouraged fears that the Australian Labor Party itself was under the influence of communists. In this new world of the cold war, the old and loved Labor figures like Prime Minister Ben Chifley somehow seemed out of date – a link to the war years that people now wanted to forget. Menzies promised a stop to Chifley's bank nationalisation program and an end to post-war austerity measures like petrol rationing, and that sealed his election victory. Even so, the Liberal–Country Party Coalition won just 51 per cent of the two-party preferred vote. Under the massive country gerrymander then in force, this translated to over 60 per cent of the seats. Fourteen months later, Ben Chifley died.

For the Kirby family, 1950 ushered in a period of fear and persecution, specifically for Michael's Uncle Jack. Menzies tried three times over the next two years to ban the Communist Party. He first secured the passage of legislation under which anyone would go to jail for five years if found to be a member. In fact, even 'fellow travellers' could be charged – in this way actual membership was not required to be proved; the legislation ushered in a crime of guilt by association. It was aimed squarely at the union movement. Any unionist who went to a meeting, for example, where many of those attending were communists, could be tarred with the same brush, even if they themselves were not members of the party. Under this legislation, the onus of proof was reversed. It was up to the person charged to show that he or she was not a communist or 'fellow traveller'. There were grave and well-founded fears that many members of the Labor Party would be caught in this net. Indeed, Menzies, speaking in parliament, rather ominously pointed to the Opposition benches and declared that he could think of at least one Labor senator who would be caught, and a member of the House who might only escape 'by the skin of his teeth'. Uncle Jack Simpson, treasurer of the Communist Party, arranged to go into hiding, and to take with him the Communist Party books and finances.

The new Labor Party leader of the Opposition, Dr H.V. Evatt, immediately led the challenge to the legislation in the High Court. The case that followed, *Australian Communist Party v. The Commonwealth* (1951), was to be Dr Evatt's greatest legal victory and lead to his greatest political victory. In a five-to-one verdict, the High Court found that the Menzies legislation to ban the Communist Party was unconstitutional because it relied on special powers only available during times of war. Michael did not, then, understand the full import of the High Court decision, but he knew it had delivered enormous comfort to the family.

> My first recollection of the High Court of Australia, being then eleven, was that that body had lifted a cloud that hung over my Uncle Jack and rescued him from the disadvantages that were imposed on communists by the *Communist Party Dissolution Act 1950*. When we got the news, it was a good day in our

> family's life and I can remember the feeling of relief, because it meant that my Uncle Jack didn't have to go into hiding and take the funds of the Communist Party up to Tamworth, or wherever they were going to hide them. No doubt they would have hidden them under a bed, because that's where all the reds were – under the bed!

The relief didn't last long. Menzies' third bite at the cherry was to attempt to change the Australian Constitution itself. In September 1951 he presented a referendum to ban the Communist Party. Again, Dr Evatt took up the challenge. He barnstormed the country, arguing the 'no' case. The whole issue was bitterly divisive. The Labor Party became hopelessly split and even members of the same families never spoke to each other again, brother pitted against sister. People who had been friends all their lives crossed the street rather than share the same footpath. It was a signal civil libertarian issue. The government, Dr Evatt would claim, was trying to criminalise Australians for how and what they thought, rather than how they acted.

When the result came in, it could barely have been any tighter. The national vote was 49.44 per cent in favour, 50.56 per cent against. A majority of states also had to be in favour for the referendum to pass; again the country was split – of the six states, only Queensland, Western Australia and Tasmania supported the Bill.

> I was ten in 1949 when Mr Menzies was elected. And he came in with the mandate to ban the Communist Party that was spreading around the world. They were the terrorists of the

time. So I had somehow, as a very young boy, to reconcile in my mind this hatred that existed in the media, in the press, about communists with this very friendly, avuncular new member of the family who was a decent man – even if he did gamble and drink a beer on a Saturday afternoon. And reconciling those things in my mind led me to be deeply suspicious about stereotypes and about attempts to put labels on people and to reach conclusions about them, and to take away their civil liberties.

My father was quite interested in national politics. His view of politics was quite different from my mother's; my mother always voted for Mr Menzies and my father always voted for Dr Evatt, and that was the world of politics into which I came. It sort of gave me both sides of the picture and I suspect I've always had an ambivalence about each side. I've never really believed that one side has all the wisdom in politics or in anything else.

The year 1949 also marked the beginning of Michael's high-achieving academic career. It was clear from an early age that Michael was extremely intelligent and it was in that year he was streamed with the gifted children moving from Strathfield North Primary School to Summer Hill Opportunity School. There was another trait that was immediately apparent in the young Michael Kirby: like his father, he had a steely determination and a resolve that was most uncommon, especially in a young boy. Once he made his mind up to achieve some goal, there was nothing that would stop him from achieving it. Added to that was an enormous capacity to work long hours and to approach each task with a careful and methodical purpose.

Don Kirby saw this marked trait in his son from the day he started kindergarten. 'He was just focused on something and it was there. And he loved the work. He loved it.' Don was given a desk when Michael was about fourteen. 'I put it in the spare room, and he thought it was his. And I didn't tell him it was mine. He was glued to that desk from that minute on. He was just dedicated to hard labour. You know, all his contemporaries would be going off to parties, and he'd be sitting at his desk with his table light on, studying away. He was really controlled.'

While his brother David was playing, climbing trees and generally mucking about with the others, Michael would be locked in his study. 'He would come out at a certain time. Usually he would time his breaks to coincide with the news. You know, he wasn't prepared to waste a minute. He would listen to the news, sometimes the BBC news. He would get a pot of tea and biscuits and various things and then go back in, and then he'd study for another several more hours. He was a most unusual person.'

Michael would very occasionally involve himself in the games that David and the others were playing, and his brother recalls he did this in a unique way:

> Well, the only communal activity I really remember Michael ever engaging in was one in which he naturally became the president – the Star Club. It consisted of a group of kids from the neighbourhood, who participated in various events, such as billycarts around a garden plot that was quite close to our

> house. Billycart races, scooter races, bike races, running races, different distances, and Michael was there as the judge, on the finishing line, and determining who won, and handing out the awards, which were cardboard cut-out stars, and we all participated. He didn't participate, except to be the judge.

At the end of 1950, Michael knew he would be going to the selective Fort Street Boys' High School. The imposing building on the hill had held an attraction for him ever since he first saw it. He had worked all his short life with the thought increasingly in the back of his mind that one day he would join the big boys at Fort Street, and 1950 had been a year of especially hard work. But he never forgot the person who was most responsible for that achievement. On Christmas Day he wrote a special letter of thanks to his mother, Jean. Like the Last Will and Testament of three years before, it was recognition for the person who had sacrificed so much for all her children. Michael got each of them to sign it.

The Boys & Girl
26 Sydney Street
Concord

Dear Mum,
Just a little Christmas thought in appreciation of all the things you have done for us this year. Throughout the year you have always helped us when we needed help, comforted us when we needed comfort and generally kept the house in order.

On behalf of, Donald, David, Diana, Rodger [the family dog] and my humble self I wish you the merriest of Christmases and a hapy, prosperouse, eventfull New Year.

Between us we have secretly brought you a present – I (that is we) hope it brings you hours of enjoyment. Also is enclosed 10/- to spend as you will

Thanking You for Everything

[signed, with Michael signing for Diana]

Michael

David Kirby

Donald

Diana Kirby

Fort Street Boys' High School was situated high on Taverners Hill, Parramatta Road, in Petersham. The red-brick and sandstone building – the Old Building, as they called it – was an imposing sight with its grand Romanesque arches and precise white tuck pointing. The girls were still at the original 1849 site on Observatory Hill, at the foot of the Sydney Harbour Bridge in the Rocks. There was only one school in the country that had a pedigree that went back further than Fort Street, and that was the exclusive private King's School at Parramatta, which dated from 1831. Sydney Grammar School came later, opening in 1857. There was a time when no bench of the High Court of Australia was without a Grammar old boy.

Fort Street was an enduring symbol of the early egalitarianism of Australian society. Established in the early days of the colony to ensure, as historian Manning Clark put it in his *History of Australia*, 'that bright prospect of the day when every locality however remote and every family however humble was supplied with the ameliorating influences of an education', it had developed by the middle of the twentieth century into a selective and secular government public school. Admission was on the basis of merit only and to be determined by examination.

As far as elite schools went, it was usually the case in Australia for them to be fee-paying, private and religious – a replication of the stifling English class system. King's School was a perfect example, with its educational philosophy to foster in the boys 'the best security against an addiction to employment and pursuits which demoralise and degrade'. The school's beginnings were coeval with the reign of its patron, King William IV, and entry was open to the select group, with the right sort of breeding, who could afford the thousands of pounds of tuition and other fees. Defining the 'Establishment' in Australia was often a difficult proposition. Fort Street old boy and Labor Premier of NSW Neville Wran once remarked, 'We always used to refer to the Establishment. But we could never define who or what the Establishment was. It was as if there was some powerful hand out there, that was out to injure us in some way.' A King's old boy would probably be a pretty good definition. Nevertheless, Michael Kirby had now joined an exclusive club, of sorts. Fort Street boasted many famous judges, politicians and other distinguished Australians in its ranks of old boys. The list included a prime minister, a foreign minister, a president of the United Nations and a benchful of High Court judges.

Even in this illustrious company Michael shone. He threw himself into all that a school like Fort Street offered. He worked on the school magazine, *The Fortian*, he joined the debating team, and won plaudits for his oration to the whole school on Speech Day. He climbed to the dizzying heights of prefect, and that brought with it a special maroon blazer. He even dabbled in sport, an activity in which he had never before (or since) shown the slightest interest. Admittedly, it was as a rugby referee rather than a player – such a role allowed his judicial tendencies to come to the fore.

Of all his extracurricular activities, it was as a young thespian that Michael really excelled. He had shown a penchant for dressing up many times before. He famously wrapped a blanket around himself, held up a homemade crucifix and blessed the family dog at about the age of ten. Michael would often carefully dress himself in one of Uncle Jack's old suits and disappear into his room to study. His brother David thought this was somewhat unusual behaviour for a young boy, but not for Michael. 'At Fort Street he was in every school play; we used to troop along to watch him,' David recollects. 'None of the rest of us ever went in a school play that I remember, because there was only really room for one showman. He played a number of villains, and was a shocking ham, and encouraged people to hiss in the audience. He loved it. Lapped it up.' Michael could certainly command an audience and this, combined with his studies, opened up other obvious possibilities. He remembers Fort Street with enormous affection:

> Because of my interest and abilities in plays, debating, English and history, I was sort of preordained to be a lawyer, I suspect. I had a wonderful education, magnificent teachers, and they prepared me. And there were a lot of reminders of how so many people from the school had gone on to be judges and lawyers. We were constantly told about the famous old boys: Barton, the first prime minister and later a judge of the High Court,

> Dr H. V. Evatt, who became a justice of the High Court, Sir Alan Taylor, who was a justice of the High Court in the 1950s, and Sir Garfield Barwick. But also, Sir John Kerr and Neville Wran came along later. There were scientists in the old boys, and there were great scientists – Sir Douglas Mawson went to Fort Street. But I kept the image of these judges and lawyers before me. That was encouraged by the school.

Michael finished at Fort Street with a maximum pass in the leaving certificate in 1955. He came first in the state in modern history, twenty-fourth in the state overall, and second overall of his Fort Street year. To say this was an outstanding achievement is surely an understatement. It was a result that gained him a Commonwealth scholarship to Sydney University and a bursary. Without either of these, Don and Jean certainly would not have been able to afford his further studies. He was only sixteen years old.

The family was ecstatic. No one in the Kirby clan in Australia had ever gone on to tertiary education, and to do so in such spectacular style was an affirmation of all Don and Jean had done for their children. Michael was only the first; now they could realistically expect Donald, David and Diana to follow in Michael's footsteps, no matter how daunting that task might have seemed to the siblings at the time.

Fort Street was a unique time in Michael Kirby's life. There were great teachers, excellent resources and a work ethic second to none. The school motto, *Faber est suae quisque fortunae*, 'Every man is the maker of his own fortune', was exactly right for this boy from humble means who had worked so hard to get himself the best education the NSW state system had to offer. He had enjoyed and savoured every moment at Fort Street – the academic success, the fellow students, among whom he made many lifelong friends, and even the extracurricular activity. This might well have been the happiest time in his life.

In early 1956 Michael made the bus trip down Parramatta Road to Sydney University for his first day. What could be more appropriate after all his accomplishments at Fort Street than to turn up at university in his school prefect's blazer, thus proudly wearing, literally on his sleeve, all he had achieved in his public school education?

3

I Was a Non-Sexual Being

It's awful not to be loved. It's the worst thing in the world. Don't ask me how I know that. I just know it. It makes you mean and violent and cruel.

Julie Harris as Abra from
Elia Kazan's film, East of Eden

Cal was only sixteen. He didn't sleep much, never needed it, and he was always an outsider. A keen observer of all that went on around him, but never really a part of it. Sitting on the steps outside the local bank he watched furtively as people wandered by. His sandy, ruffled hair matched the grey of his drill shirt and pants, and his faun jumper sported a tight V-collar and sleeves turned over neatly a couple of inches at the wrists. He was a handsome young man. His skin smooth, his nose slightly up-turned and his lips full and red. His brow and jaw were strong and well defined.

As the woman in green, statuesque and covered head to toe and with a hat and dark veil, strode towards the bank, he did not turn his head, but he felt her presence every step of the way. She walked so close to him that the folds of her skirt brushed by his back…

Michael Kirby absorbed this scene over and over again, until it – and the whole movie – became etched in his mind. Most people would never keep stock but Michael, of course, was meticulous, and he noted that he had been to see Elia Kazan's *East of Eden* twenty-eight times at different cinemas in Sydney, including as far afield as Gymea, nearly 30 kilometres south of his home in Concord. He allowed himself to relax for a moment in the summer of 1956, and from the instant he saw the young actor up on the big screen, in CinemaScope, Michael simply fell headlong in love with James Dean.

It was the story of two brothers, Caleb (James Dean) and Aron (Richard Davalos), one good and one bad. Kazan's Oscar-winner was an adaptation of the bestselling novel by John Steinbeck, an epic of biblical proportions that directly referenced the Genesis story of Cain and Abel. One brother kills the other and is then banished by God. 'And Cain went out from the presence of the Lord, and dwelt in the land of Nod, on the east of Eden.'

The Kirby family would occasionally go to the Embassy Theatre in George Street in the city to see British films. No doubt the large bas-relief of classical Rome above the open foyer of the building would have intrigued Michael, passionate as he was about history. The screwball British comedy *Mad About Men*, a Betty E. Box production starring Glynis Johns, showed there for a long run in 1955 but *East of Eden* premiered at the sister cinema, the Century Theatre, a couple of blocks away on George Street.

> I think I probably just saw *East of Eden* as a one-off and then I became hooked. I liked James Dean's jumper and, in fact, I asked my mother to make a faun jumper similar to the one he wore in the movie, which she did. They were ages before I became tubby and I suppose, putting it on, I could think that I was a kind of living James Dean.

James Dean's first and most accomplished movie was released in Australia three months after the actor's death in a sports car accident on 30 September 1955 and this fact alone gave a special poignancy to Michael's impossible love affair. To call Australia a backwater in regard to cinema releases in the 1950s, and even right up to the 1970s, would be a gross understatement. There was rampant censorship. None of Jean-Luc Godard's films of the 1950s or '60s, for example, were cleared to be shown until at least a decade after their European release, and by and large the Australian market was just not important enough as far as Hollywood was concerned. *East of Eden* didn't arrive in Australia until nearly a year after its US launch. Sydney's *Sun-Herald* announced the opening with a review on 8 January 1956: 'Dead man makes a drama live.' The review sang the praises of the film and Dean's work in particular, and was accompanied by a large image of the actor's head, photographically dismembered from the rest of his body.

Michael was unaware of James Dean's sexuality and he hadn't read the Steinbeck novel before he saw the film. There was something deeply attractive to him about Dean's performance as the sixteen-year-old Caleb, something no doubt that reminded Michael of himself and his own family, brothers and religion, his stern but devoted father. But at the same time, Dean was nothing at all like them. New Wave director François Truffaut writing presciently in Paris's *Arts* magazine in 1956 offered the greatest insight:

> In James Dean, today's youth discovers itself. Less for the reasons usually advanced: violence, sadism, hysteria, pessimism, cruelty and filth than for others, more simple and commonplace: modesty of feeling, continual fantasy life, moral purity without relation to everyday morality (but all the more rigorous), the eternal adolescent love of tests and trials, intoxication, pride and regret at feeling oneself outside of society, refusal and desire to become integrated and finally, acceptance or refusal of the world as it is.

It was not just James Dean's performance; there was something deeper about Kazan's film that Michael responded to. Perhaps it was the biblical references. Perhaps it was the fact that Cal spent most of the film watching from a distance as his brother fell in love with Abra (Julie Harris). That most profound of human emotions was something that Michael felt he must be denied. The film ran for months at the city cinema but Michael chose to travel miles out to the suburban theatres to see his secret paramour on the screen, avoiding any raised eyebrows had anyone seen him returning again and again to the same film. Mostly, though, it was in order to keep the obsession a secret – part of the excitement was that no one else knew. Michael even got hold of the long-playing album *Tribute to James Dean* by Art Mooney and His Orchestra, on the cover a black and white photo of Dean. Every time he listened to 'Theme from East of Eden' the images came flooding back to him: the grand panorama of the opening scenes, the windswept coastline of southern California.

> I wasn't really lonely, but like any other human being I had a yearning for something that was external to myself and external to my family, but there wasn't all that much that I felt I could do about it. So I threw myself with energy into my studies and then with ferocious energy into university committee meetings, and I even ended up enjoying the university committee meetings, and I had good friends amongst the participants – all non-sexual. I was a non-sexual being at the time of my peak hormonal development. That was just what you were expected to do, and in most countries in the world, certainly most countries of the Commonwealth of Nations, that is what young people are still expected to do.

As far back as 1951, at about the time Michael started at Fort Street Boys' High School, he realised he was gay. 'When I came to puberty, I knew that at the time, that was not a good look, and it was one that I was supposed to keep a big, dark secret.' It seemed to the young Michael Kirby that almost every week Sydney's *Daily Mirror* or the other tabloid newspapers would carry a story of shame and humiliation. Often quite well-known and respected men had their lives destroyed; even judges fell victim to exposure. Homosexual acts were illegal, and the NSW Police went on the offensive in 1951. Chief Inspector Colin Delaney gained rapid advancement all the way to Chief Commissioner on the back of an obsession to stamp out homosexuality, which he described as 'Australia's greatest menace'. The statistics in New South Wales reveal fifty or so convictions in 1938 rising to about 350 by 1958. These figures reflect the increased police activity, with the practice of using young, good-looking officers to entrap homosexual men becoming commonplace.

There is no doubt that what became a worldwide crackdown on homosexuality was driven by cold-war certainties. The Americans, in the grip of McCarthyite persecutions of communists, were at the forefront. And in late 1953, journalist Donald Horne wrote in the *Sydney Morning Herald* of a plan by Scotland Yard to 'smash homosexuality in London'. Horne claimed the plan had its origins in advice from the FBI to Britain to remove homosexuals from key government positions because they were subject to blackmail and were therefore security risks: 'The Special Branch began compiling a "Black Book" of known perverts in influential government jobs after the disappearance of the diplomats Donald Maclean and Guy Burgess, who were known to have pervert associates.' Guy Burgess was indeed a homosexual; Maclean was not. Both defected to the Soviet Union in 1951. There never was any convincing link established between Burgess's homosexuality and his defection, which apparently derived from an ideological commitment. Indeed, had his homosexuality become widely known in the Soviet Union, he would have suffered extreme discrimination and hardship.

In the UK a major scandal broke in 1954. A member of the House of Lords, Edward Montagu of Beaulieu, was charged, along with two friends, Michael Pitt-Rivers and Peter Wildeblood, with commission of 'certain acts' and conspiracy to commit 'certain acts'.

This oblique Victorian language alluded to activity that could not be openly spoken about: private consensual sex between two males over the age of twenty-one. The case dragged on for weeks and Michael was confronted with it as the tabloids in Australia covered every prurient detail. The men denied the charges, and only Peter Wildeblood bravely stated in open court that he was indeed a homosexual. All three were found guilty of homosexual offences on the evidence of their alleged boyfriends – two Royal Air Force servicemen who, although given immunity from prosecution, were described by counsel in the most offensive terms.

The Montagu trial was only one of thousands prosecuted in the UK and Australia every year. A member of the aristocracy was involved in this case, so it gained special attention from the newspapers. It quickly became as notorious as the Oscar Wilde trial of fifty years before. All the men caught up in it, both the accused and the accusers, stood to be damaged badly. Nobody had further to fall than Lord Montagu, and the Home Office had apparently targeted him to set some sort of example.

In the end, whatever they thought might be achieved, the whole thing backfired on the authorities and the resulting outcry pushed homosexual law reform firmly onto the agenda. After the verdicts were handed down, the police held the three convicted men in the court cells for several hours in order to avoid the crowd that had gathered outside Winchester Castle Court. But as it turned out, all parties were surprised to find the crowd was there to support the convicted men. People who had sat through the whole tragic and sordid proceedings, and who had previously spat on the accused as they entered the court, now patted each of the convicts on the back and shouted 'Keep smiling!', giving the thumbs-up as they were hustled away. Public opinion was gradually changing as people saw the harm caused by these laws. Three years later, the landmark Wolfenden Report recommended the decriminalisation of homosexuality in the UK. Unfortunately, Australia still had a long way to go and this fact had not escaped Michael's attention.

> About once a week the front page of the *Daily Mirror* or the *Daily Sun* was filled with stories of people, often distinguished people, who were being humiliated and shamed because of their arrest on the basis of their sexuality. So I knew this was a very dangerous and shameful thing, that I should be thoroughly ashamed of myself – and I didn't really feel that ashamed of myself. But I knew that that was how I was expected to react to it and therefore to keep it quiet, including from those who were closest to me – my family.
>
> This is the real mischief that is done by such laws and attitudes and teaching – that at a critical moment in a young person's life they have to hide their reality from those who are their greatest source of love and strength. But that was what you were supposed to do and 'Don't ask, don't tell' lasted a long while in Australia, and I just went along with it. That was just part of the reality of those days.

In the mid 1950s, an open admission of homosexuality would almost certainly be career-ending and could easily lead to a term in jail. Men went to enormous lengths to hide their relationships. No love letters were ever kept and false names were usually exchanged. A man could not bring another man home without eyebrows being raised, so sexual liaisons had to be undertaken at third party locations; sadly, this often meant public toilets or other gay beats in secluded areas of public parks and the like. Under these conditions, of course, developing a long-term or loving relationship with another person of the same sex was virtually impossible.

Michael discovered through his own research that these punitive laws were restricted, in the main, to common-law countries – a nasty legacy of the British. While other types of oppression against homosexuals existed in France, mainly from the Church, it had abolished 'the crime of sodomy' as far back as the revolutionary government of 1791. Lesbian relationships were simply presumed by the patriarchal society and the law of the time to be either non-existent or irrelevant.

While Michael's brothers, Donald and David, were going off to the local dance to meet girls, Michael stayed holed up in his room, studying, perhaps flicking the curtain back to watch them disappear up the street. David never saw Michael conform to the gay stereotype:

> Therefore, it did not particularly occur to us that he was homosexual. We recognised that, unlike the rest of us as children, he appeared to be more isolated. We put that down really to two things. First, his singular devotion to his work, and secondly to the fact that he developed very bad acne. And we thought that that was something which was clearly an embarrassment to him and served to isolate him from socialising in the way that we were. On many occasions during my childhood, comments

> would be made about, you know, the sort of girl he might end up marrying. Because we all recognised that he was unusual, and she would have to be very unusual, and we didn't realise quite how unusual.

In a way, Michael used his application to his academic study as a cover for his sexuality. He buried himself in his work and therefore didn't have to think about, let alone act on, his natural feelings. Comfort also came from an unexpected source – his religion. Michael's religiosity was a bit of a mystery to the rest of the family. Some children are given no option but to follow their parents headlong into the family religion; no other course is countenanced. In Michael's case, as with everything in his life, his religion was a matter for him and him alone. Don Kirby's forebears were lapsed Catholics, while he and Jean were both Church of England. Unlike the rest of the family, Michael chose, for a time, to be a regular churchgoer. He attended the local Methodist Sunday School and joined the choir at St Andrew's.

> At that time about 40 per cent of Australians were Anglicans; it was the biggest church. And we thought it was just sort of natural – the British Empire was the biggest empire and the Anglican Church was the biggest church. So I used to go down to the local church, St Andrew's Church at Strathfield, which is still there on the corner of Parramatta Road and Concord Road. And on both sides of the altar were flags, the Australian flag and the Union Jack, and it just seemed to meld in my mind with the King and the Queen and the princesses. Plant ideas

> in the mind of a child under the age of seven and these things stay with them all their lifetime!

The fact that he was gay, the fact that he knew he was gay from about the age of twelve, did not affect Michael's Anglicanism in any way. He does not remember the local minister ever referring to Leviticus 18:22: 'Thou shalt not lie with mankind, as with womankind: it is abomination', or preaching against homosexuality from the pulpit. For Michael, his religion was and always would be a refuge. It supported him and gave him strength. When there were conflicts in his life they did not stem from his religious conviction.

> The Anglican Church, because it arose out of the reformation and the need to respect the Catholic members of the English community, was always a big compromise. It was always a space for different people and that I think goes very deeply into the roots of Anglicanism – of a place of many mansions, and of mutual respect and willingness to live and let live, and to dialogue. So I can't blame my church at the time for giving me a hard time. I never was conflicted in thinking: Well, your feelings which are entirely natural to you are somehow wicked or hated by God. I just couldn't go along with that. So in my soul I was at peace, but in my daily activities I was postponing reality.

In 1956, Sydney University was full of young men dressed in suits and ties, or sports jackets and neat slacks and ties (only 16 per cent of all graduates and 8 per cent of law graduates that year were women). Michael arrived in his Fort Street High School blazer with its prefect's insignia. He was proud of that blazer and he thought it was rather attractive. But it was not done to wear a *public school* blazer, indeed there were hardly any *public school* students at Sydney University in 1956. Bob Ellis was on to something when, years later, he put to Michael, not entirely facetiously, 'We both yearn to have been in private schools, don't we? And you have adopted the guise more successfully than I.' Michael did not wear the blazer on his second day.

> I arrived at Sydney University in March 1956 and the day is very well described in Clive James's book *Unreliable Memoirs*, because he arrived on the same day, and Robert Hughes, the considerable Australian art critic and commentator, arrived on the same day. Clive James went off to the Student Christian Movement and wore his Student Christian badge. And Robert Hughes decided that he would become a sort of dramatic figure around the campus, and he was wandering around in a heavy, thick jumper and a long Oxford scarf – which did look a bit eccentric given that it was in the middle of a heat wave.

The freshers streamed across the lawns in front of the rather stern neo-Gothic architecture that is Sydney University. Monday, 5 March 1956 was the first day of a packed and somewhat bewildering orientation program: the 'Official Welcome' was in the Great Hall at 10 a.m., then a 'How to Study' lecture, a 'How to Use the Library' talk, the 'Ceremonial Procession and Official Welcome by the

Chancellor' and the 'Combined Church Service'. Michael took it all in. There was even another outing for Glynis Johns in *Mad About Men* with free screenings on high rotation in the Union Hall. By the end of the week, most were glad that no functions were scheduled for the Friday – 'Freshers are to use the day as they will.'

> But it was all a somewhat alien place. And it seemed to me, and I can't put my finger on this, that it seemed to be like a sort of continuation of private school traditions, and a bit posh and not really the same democratic ethos of the public school system that I was used to – where nobody was allowed to get too big for their boots.

Clive James quickly left his high-school blazer behind and dumped his rapidly shrinking boots for a pair of long-toed brothel creepers. Robert Hughes doesn't describe the thick scarf and jumper outfit, preferring memories of himself as 'Jean-Paul' Hughes, with black duffle coat and beret and never without a (foul-smelling but utterly de rigueur) Sobranie, also black, effetely balanced between fore- and middle finger. Michael never smoked; he was one of those, as James put it, 'out and out exam passers'. Before long they would all be in rather conservative gear, slacks and sports coats, although Hughes adopted the rakish bow tie and 'checkboard double-breasted weskit' look.

Sydney University in the mid '50s didn't have much time for minorities. No Aboriginal person had ever attended and the White Australia policy was firmly in place, with occasional debates about the very idea of allowing Africans or 'Negroes' into the country.

Honi Soit, the student newspaper, published a full-page article by the Liberal minister for immigration, Alexander Downer (senior), headed 'A case for restricted immigration', which was the Menzies Government's argument supporting a white Australia. Even the thought of popular singers Harold Blair or Jimmy Little arriving to give lunchtime concerts (30p entry) along with a muted discussion of Aboriginal rights caused some to heckle 'No Abos on campus.'

Women were also largely absent from the classrooms and the debates. *Honi Soit* did its bit to redress the balance by frequently carrying prominent photographs of young women students, invariably captioned in page-three mode: 'Miss Science, Edwina Robertson. She included her phone number, but listed no hobbies. Is this significant?' Even dashing (small 'l') liberal Robert Hughes, recently retired from the *Honi Soit* team, thought it was proper to turn his excoriating wit on the new editors of the paper for daring to publish a poem, on the subject of spring, by a woman!

Sir,

I congratulate you.

Last year, in 'Honi,' we got seven poems on spring, all of which were written by women in Arts I . . . We printed none of these poems . . . Courage, sir, courage is needed, to trot out the occasional cliché. You have courage, I've no doubt,

Yours with interest,

Robert Hughes

As for homosexuality, well, that didn't really rate a mention. Clive James thought it was 'some kind of rare disease' and the prevailing culture on campus was homophobic. If Michael had known about the venues not that far from the university – the Royal George Hotel, for example, with its strange collection of patrons who James described as 'traditional jazz fans and the homosexual radio repairmen who had science fiction as a religion', and with its reputation as the headquarters of the Sydney Push – he wasn't interested. That was all too bohemian for the rather conservative and inward-looking Fort Street boy.

Studies began in 1956 with the first year of a Bachelor of Arts degree. Michael poured himself into his courses with great results, coming in the top 2 per cent of his first English year and the top 10 per cent in philosophy. The law degree began in 1958 and again his results were outstanding. Professor Julius Stone, the doyen of the Sydney University law faculty, marked Kirby as one to watch. He gave him a score of 14/15 for his public international law exam and 19/20 for jurisprudence, a score Stone described as 'superb'.

In 1959 Michael managed to secure an articled clerkship at a small firm of solicitors in the city. Articles (replaced in NSW by the College of Law in 1973) were a kind of formal work-experience placement at a law firm and were an essential requirement for a law student in order to qualify to practise. Not everyone found it easy to get their articles, but without them your options as a law graduate were severely diminished: academia or commerce might be the only recourse. Law students usually fell back on connections from their fathers or relatives, the old school tie, in order to get a position. Fort Street only went so far in that regard. It was not an easy path for the public-school educated boy. Michael sent out many letters, typed by his aunt Lillian, applying to the big law firms for a position, and all came to nothing. None of the establishment firms even bothered to interview this young man who carried such an outstanding academic record.

In the summer of 1960 he obtained a job at a local pickle factory. All the Kirby children were encouraged to work in the summer holidays; Michael was still living at home, and even though he was well into his law degree Don and Jean did not treat him any differently.

It was in the pickle factory that a young co-worker developed a crush. Michael was never rude, dismissive or harsh when this happened, but he also never led any of these girls on. When he was about to leave the factory and return to his studies, the co-worker, a girl called Rick, gave him a poem.

To: Michael
No more will I tease you
By calling you 'Mick'
The thought of you leaving
Has me feeling sick.
I've enjoyed working with you
I'll miss you a lot
And I wish you success
In the new job you've got.
Do let me know
How you're getting along
Maybe I can help
If something goes wrong
Many thanks, Mike, for all that
You've done,

All the orders you've taken on No.1.
Whether the calls been on 1, 2 or 3
Or, if it's someone in person.
You've always worked willingly,
And with a smile
Where others would do it while cursin'.
This is my last little tribute to you
Think of it as you will
But I know that as long as ever
I'm here
I will remember you still.
Toodle-Pip.
Rick.

While brother David would have been over the moon with such an advance by a young lady, Michael remained uninterested. He diligently returned to his regimen of work and more hard work, but it was a kind of monastic existence and it was taking a toll. He could not have continued like that for much longer, something had to give, and it was his devotion to student politics that finally saved him.

Michael Kirby hung out at Sydney University well beyond a suitable period as might be determined by one's bridge club. It would be well into 1969, thirteen years after he'd first arrived at the university, before he completely severed the student ties. Initially there was a certain insecurity in the young man, not just about his sexuality but about his studies, perhaps even his very place in an institution that was almost entirely populated by private school graduates, the wealthy and the elite.

As he approached the end of his legal studies, Michael was determined that he must graduate with first-class honours. He prepared a list – Michael was always fond of preparing lists. Twenty-three consolations if he was not to achieve his aim. Number one, 'My own life', suggested that he didn't have to slavishly follow what was expected of him by others. Number two on the list was a reference to his mother with five big ticks against her name: he would always have her love and support no matter how he went. At number five he listed his past successes – presumably his outstanding results in high school and the arts degree – and at number eight was his job as Professor Julius Stone's research assistant. Number sixteen on the list read: 'Too tired. OK for AMG [Murray Gleeson] not for MDK.' Here he admitted to himself that the demanding schedule he had set out might not be possible to achieve. It was recognition that his closest competitor, fellow law student and stellar performer Murray Gleeson from the elite St Joseph's College, would probably be able to achieve first-class honours, but that Michael might not have the same stamina. Near the end of the list, at number twenty-one, was a rather philosophical point: the 'transience of life'. If he didn't get the first-class honours it wouldn't be the end of the world.

As the years passed, Michael found a natural place for himself in the university community and it became increasingly difficult for him to dislodge himself from it. When he'd arrived at Sydney University he was just sixteen years old – too young to enrol in a law degree (at that time a law student had to be over the age of seventeen). By the time he finally finished his second term as the undergraduate student representative on the University Senate he was twenty-nine. He completed four degrees: a Bachelor of Arts (1959), a Bachelor of Laws (1962), a Bachelor of Economics (1965) and a Master of Laws with, needless to say, first-class honours (1967). Having finished the arts and law degrees, it seemed an odd proposition to enrol in another degree from a new faculty, and undertake it at night while working full-time as a solicitor during the day, but Michael had his reasons. 'Why did I do economics? The public relations answer is that the University of Sydney has a very fine economics department. The real answer is that by then I was in student politics and I was the president of the Sydney SRC, and in order to be legit, to stay in student politics, I had to be doing a degree.' Another student might have enrolled in a course with no intention of really doing it, just to keep in the student political scene. That was not in Michael Kirby's thinking.

Michael's rise as a student politician was meteoric. He nominated for and won every position worthy of his great talents. He was nominated to the Law Society Committee in 1960 by classmate and friend Murray Gleeson, and it was there that he first came up against Mary Gaudron, a few years his junior. Gaudron was a highly intelligent girl from Moree in outback New South Wales. She smoked, drank and swore, priding herself on having the minimum of social airs and graces. She was also far more radical in her political thinking than Michael. When the Law Society came to deal with the question of the very low pay rates of articled clerks, Michael and Mary were on the same side of the debate, but there was an enormous gulf between them. Michael successfully called for the issue to be taken up with the NSW Law Society, with the students voting seventy-five to thirty-five in support. Most of the minority advocated Mary Gaudron's more militant position to refer the matter to the Federated Clerks' Union. In the end, the pay rates were substantially increased.

This rather insignificant post on the Law Society soon led to much bigger things. Indeed, by 1964 Michael had served on twenty bodies within the Students' Representative Council (SRC), four within the University Union, eight within the National Union of Australian University Students (NUAUS), six within the Law Society and four other miscellaneous positions within the university. All in all, thirty-six different roles in student politics. These were his glory days. He served two terms as SRC president from 1962 to '63, and then again in 1963 after his successor was bumped up to head NUAUS in Melbourne. No one had ever served two non-consecutive terms like this before. At the same time he was also studying full-time, working for M.A. Simon & Co. as an articled clerk and then as a full-time solicitor for Hickson, Lakeman and Holcombe, a research assistant for Professor Julius Stone, and in the honorary position of student solicitor – a role he had invented himself.

It was a gruelling schedule but one that Michael loved. He'd be up at 4.30 a.m., head off to the office to do a day of workers' compensation cases, and then race down to the university to chair SRC meetings and meet student clients who had fare evasion charges pending or other matters that required free legal advice. In the evenings he was studying for his economics degree and on top of all that he joined the Sydney delegation to NUAUS; and with senior lecturer in economic history Ken Buckley, he was one of the first to join the state's new Council for Civil Liberties.

Michael had developed from a rather stentorian but nevertheless attractive orator at Fort Street speech nights to a very successful and engaging politician at Sydney University. In 1961 his mother Jean made her own assessment of her 22-year-old son. Like Michael, she was given to preparing lists and on a small piece of notepaper she scribbled down the following appraisal.

> MDK. Born under 7. (Relig. Superstitious. Highly Strung. Very important changed his life) 22 years old. 1961. Lucky person, flamboyant, interested in music art theatre. Too many interests, not enough application to any one thing. If he applies himself to *one* thing much better than spread out. Very liked person. Social Exec. Ability. Bit of a loner. Very authoritarian. Sensitive to the point of weakness. Very lucky person. Ability in the arts. Found life and opportunity coming his way when he needs it. Nevertheless uses opportunities to his advantage. Very thorough in work. Sometimes in life difficulties to cope with but generally he will cope. He puts importance on sensuality [but is] not fond of children of his [own]. Religious and perhaps [illegible] He expects anything or nothing from enterprises. Highly spiritual. Highly developed person. Nervous tension, up and down personality & very fair in dealings.

As he began to feel more comfortable in his student political persona, Michael would gradually dispense with some of these old insecurities. For a time, he would even change his name to *Mike* Kirby, as a symbol of this new-found confidence, although it did not last long. Mike was a rather handsome boy, always immaculately dressed in three-piece suit and tie, his short-back-and-sides haircut allowing for a slightly tousled forelock (James Dean style), and his debating and oratory skills were significant. His voice was deep, comforting and resonant. The voting public couldn't get enough. Inventing the 'honorary student solicitor' role was a masterstroke; it secured his core constituency of law students.

In his first SRC election Mike Kirby achieved a vote of 187 out of a total 370 – sixty-eight votes over the quota and 131 votes ahead of his nearest rival. It was a stunning result, especially for a first-timer. Despite his six years at university, he was still only twenty-two years old.

> It was an exciting time at Sydney University. Germaine Greer was there shortly after [my arrival], and Bob Ellis shortly after that, and as I moved into student politics and into the Students' Representative Council I met people interstate who were in student affairs – like Gareth Evans, John Bannon and Daryl Williams, Rob Holmes à Court. All of these people were big figures in my life. And the university was not just the lecture hall, it was also the student activities. Strangely enough, my grades got better as I got deeper into those activities.

And there was never the slightest possibility of romance. He just locked that part of his life away from public view. Michael's good friend Bob Ellis would happily make the occasional lazy put-down without even realising that was what he was doing, much less that his friend might actually be gay. In his *Honi Soit* film review of *Mutiny on the Bounty* in 1963, Ellis assessed Marlon Brando's performance unfavourably: an actor 'who doesn't yet know the difference between Englishmen and homosexuals'. Some things die hard; Michael was still upbraiding Ellis for his attitude to homosexuality forty years later. In any case, the environment was clearly not conducive to Michael's coming out. By the time he got to criminal law lectures, the true horror of it all was drawn starkly. His law lecturer outlined the section of the *Crimes Act* pertaining to the 'abominable crime of buggery': fourteen years' jail and your photo on the front page of the *Daily Mirror*. The thought of such public disgrace and humiliation was too much for Michael. 'I would rather die.'

But did anyone at Sydney University put two and two together and realise Michael was gay? A friend did comment, when Michael admitted to his twenty-eight viewings of *East of Eden*, that the only logical conclusion was a big crush on James Dean. And *Honi Soit* carried this small verse on the front page under the quote of the week in July 1963:

> TRIALOGUE OF THE WEEK
> McDonald: There is a specific reason for having four people on this trip.
> Harris: So there'll be no odd man out!
> Kirby: If I understand that remark, I'd ask you to withdraw it.

Some of these small gossipy remarks hurt Michael but he never allowed them to derail him. The great thing about student politics was its infinite ability to distract and entertain, and the myriad of different issues that could come to the fore at any one time. While Mike Kirby was fighting valiantly through the Law Society for better wages and conditions for articled clerks, there were also the questions of the English department's overly rigid controls on student essays and the harmful effects of university fee rises.

Battles against censorship in its various incarnations were never far away either. Richard Walsh and Peter Grose, former editors of *Honi Soit*, and Richard Neville, former editor of University of NSW student paper *Tharunka*, were fined £20 each after they published the first edition of *Oz* magazine. Deemed obscene by the police and finally by a magistrate were an article about the history of the chastity belt, as compiled from material in the State Library of New South Wales, and a reprint from Queensland *Hansard* of parliamentary debates over an article from a Queensland University journal entitled 'Are Morals Outdated?' To some extent these censorship battles of the early 1960s were coeval with Michael's own political trajectory. He began on one side, as SRC president, condemning the excesses of *Honi Soit* editors or students' obscene O-Week activities, and ended the decade on the other side, representing, through the courts, those charged with obscenity.

Germaine Greer, then an English masters student, along with actors like John Bell and Germaine's then boyfriend Arthur Dignam, were appearing in student theatre productions that were often on the edge. Greer was to perform in one such Sydney University revue, including a film screening from director Albie Thom, but the whole thing was shut down before it could begin. Police came onto the campus on the orders of the NSW chief secretary because obscenities like the word 'shit' were to be uttered. As Lionel Murphy – who advocated a change to the laws so that 'adults would be entitled to read, hear and view what they wished in private or public, but with the important reservation that they and the persons in their care should not be exposed to unsolicited material offensive to them' – was later to famously remark, in his trademark laconic and understated way, there was far too much censorship in Australia.

On Thursday, 6 September 1962, President Michael Kirby chaired a stormy meeting of the SRC. The debate that followed revealed the essentially conservative nature of student politics at the time. Kirby was certainly no radical; he thought of himself then as a kind of young version of Bob Menzies, in double-breasted pinstriped suits. Even so, his developing interest in human rights and civil liberties pushed him further than half the SRC were prepared to go.

The motion before them was that the SRC support its Melbourne University counterparts in calling for the commuting of the death sentence imposed on convicted murderer Robert Peter Tait. Victorian Liberal Premier Henry Bolte was determined that Tait be hanged. Each member of the Sydney University SRC individually rejected the notion of capital punishment, which had by then been abolished in every state except Victoria, but as a group they were evenly split on the motion. Richard Walsh argued that the SRC should be guided by the wishes of the greater student body before acting. *Honi Soit* howled him down: 'This view is blatantly stupid. It is impossible for the SRC to know for certain how the students feel on any issue. Yet they must vote on many. The SRC was elected not only to represent students, but also to lead them.' Michael spoke in favour of the motion. He justified his position in *Honi Soit*: 'By supporting the NUAUS making statements on human rights issues, the SRC had already shown that it supported the current trend among student bodies to express themselves on such matters.' He went on to condemn 'the essential barbarity of this form of punishment'. Nevertheless, the SRC remained evenly split at eleven–all, and the vote was thereby decided in the negative.

The Tait case was one of the first that showed Michael the immense power of the High Court of Australia. As the ultimate appeal court in the country, criminal matters from the states could end up before the High Court judges. Tait's hanging was to be rushed through less than two months after Michael chaired the SRC meeting. Premier Bolte had scheduled it for 8 a.m. on 1 November. The chief justice of the High Court, Sir Owen Dixon, was forced to convene a special leave hearing in Melbourne as a matter of urgency on 31 October. Counsel pleading the case didn't pull his punches: 'We have been bundled through this court,' he told their Honours, 'to keep an appointment with the hangman at eight o'clock tomorrow morning.' Sir Owen was not amused. He was not to be hurried, and was even less impressed when counsel for the Victorian Government indicated that an adjournment and instructions from the Court to stay the execution might not stop Bolte, since he had already sought advice from cabinet on that possible outcome and had decided, should the High Court adjourn, that he would go ahead with the hanging anyway. At that point Dixon became visibly angry and specifically ordered that the

Victorian Chief Secretary and his deputies be restrained from carrying out the execution.

Even Bolte couldn't ignore such an order from the High Court of Australia. His standover tactics had backfired and Tait spent the next twenty-three years behind bars until his death from natural causes. It was a fascinating example for Michael of how the highest court in the land could actually kerb the populist 'law and order' agenda of a state politician.

Michael formed a close relationship with another student politician, final-year medico Peter Wilenski. They were political rivals, Wilenski far more radical on issues like Vietnam and apartheid than Michael, who was still vacillating on the political spectrum somewhere between the centre and the right wing of the Labor Party. He looked to Wilenski for guidance and Wilenski took Michael under his wing.

Although they were the same age, Wilenski had started his run in politics much earlier than Michael and was already a consummate and accomplished operator. As the years went by, a chart of *Wilenski v. Kirby* began to look like a kind of checkerboard. First Wilenski would be SRC president and Kirby a member, then Wilenski a member and Kirby president. Then Wilenski was an NUAUS delegate, next Kirby; Wilenski was Union president, then Kirby, and so it went. Articles they wrote regularly appeared in *Honi Soit* side by side, and the two young men were often featured in adjacent photographs. Occasionally they even ran against one other, like when Michael tried to achieve his aim of sitting as both SRC president and student representative on the University Senate at the same time. Again *Honi Soit* ran an appropriately distinguished photo of each candidate in suit and tie in an article headed 'The Student Senator'. The wily Wilenski won the day, turning the fact that he was no longer on the SRC (as opposed to Michael, the current president) to his advantage by claiming the two bodies should be separate and therefore without bias. Kirby and Wilenski remained a great double act for two more years until the latter took up further studies at Oxford.

Wilenski had been SRC president in 1961 and the year before that travelled to Ghana as the leader and NUAUS representative of the Australian delegation to the World Assembly of Youth. He suggested Michael lead an upcoming NUAUS delegation to Nigeria. It was another example of Peter Wilenski's prescience: he was always a few steps ahead of Michael, who would never have conceived of such an idea at that time. Once it was put in front of him, though, he became immediately excited by the notion. The trip was an extraordinary experience for the young Michael, who had never been out of the country before. What he saw and the people he met in Africa, and in Asia on the return leg, stimulated a lifelong interest in travel and world affairs.

Writing his president's message to new students in early 1963 from Ibadan, Nigeria, Michael lauded the fact that NUAUS had abandoned its 'rigid apolitical stand of the past. This serves to show, I think, that there is a growing concern among students, nationally and internationally with their role as a vanguard of liberal opinion in the community.' Michael went on to claim that 'it was largely student opinion and action that led to the last-minute action of the

Victorian Government last year on the issue of capital punishment.' This was something of an overstatement, but there was no doubt that the concerted national campaign to abolish capital punishment had been effective. Bolte was a rather bullish and visceral politician and enormously stubborn; the thought that some ratbag students were trying to stop him from breaking Peter Tait's neck might have been enough to push him one step too far in his unsubtle pressuring of the judiciary. Whatever the case, he lost that battle and eventually lost the war as well.

The Nigeria trip took Michael to twenty-five countries, and everywhere he went in Africa the same questions were asked: 'Why do you have the White Australia policy and why do you treat your Aboriginal people so badly?' At the time, no Aboriginal person had ever attended Sydney University and Michael was embarrassed to admit it. The first to do so, Charlie Perkins and Gary Williams, were to enrol the following March. Michael promised the Nigerians that he would work to ensure a delegation of African students could come to Australia later in 1963.

His next stop was the University of Ghana. Like so many African nations at that time, Ghana's democracy was fragile. The university offered one of the few points of opposition to the authoritarian rule of its then president, Dr Kwame Nkrumah, who had survived a bombing only five months before. African politics stood in stark contrast to Michael's experience of Australia's democratic processes, as he noted in his communiqué to *Honi Soit*: 'The learned doctor hides himself behind three high walls from which he seldom emerges – and little wonder in view of the ephemeral existence of West African leaders and the many attempts upon his own life . . .'

At the border, Michael's burgeoning interest in photography got him into trouble. 'I nearly managed to get arrested. When I focused for a photograph of the border scene, native policemen, dressed in red caps and waving their batons, descended upon me from all directions, until I abandoned my objective.

On 21 February he flew out to Cairo and then on to Singapore and Malaysia. In these South-East Asian countries, Michael was treated as an honoured guest by a group representing Asian students who had studied in Australia. Once back in Sydney he told *Honi Soit*, 'I just did not realise how valuable it is for Australia to educate the Asian students here. It is a tragedy that the University of Sydney aims to halve the overseas student rate from 10 to 5 per cent.'

If there was one consistent issue that had slowly but ineluctably seeped into student politics at Sydney University by the early 1960s, it was race. From the polite debates about the White Australia policy in the late '50s, more emphatic statements were now being ventilated, eventually taking a peculiarly Australian form in sport. In July 1963, South Africa's white-only Rugby League team was in Australia and Dr Peter Wilenski, then president of NUAUS, spoke out against the country's policy of apartheid: 'Oppression is aided by any country or people who disagree with it but do not act against it. Therefore, we must act.' He said NUAUS was violently opposed to South Africa's racial policies and that the Canberra boycott 'is the sort of action that is required'. Michael Kirby, meanwhile, entertained his promised delegation of Nigerian students, who spoke about the disadvantage and hardship they faced in their own country. The National Union of Nigerian Students had also passed resolutions against apartheid. The leader of the delegation,

Mr David Obi, who had welcomed Michael to Nigeria, was dressed in the traditional flowing robes of the Babariga. He told the Sydney group that 'the conditions existent in South Africa are a horrible state of affairs'.

This was the sort of activity that Michael found most congenial: diplomatically entertaining foreign guests to the university. The idea of militant student action, as proposed by Peter Wilenski, for example, was nowhere in Michael's thinking and it never would be. Nor did it mesh well with Michael's concept of his role as student solicitor: somehow above the fray and able to deal impartially with issues as they arose.

Three days later, in the Old Geology Theatre No. 1, a large audience of students, which did not include the SRC president Michael Kirby, passed a resolution to be delivered to the South African Government: 'This meeting of students of Sydney University unanimously declares to the Government of The Union of South Africa its abhorrence of the inhuman and brutal racist policy, apartheid. We call on you to abandon this in the interests of humanity.' The lunchtime meeting had heard from a South African businessman now living in Australia who wished to be identified as Mr X, fearful of reprisals should he return to South Africa. The businessman detailed sections of the new *General Law Amendment* that had passed through the South African parliament a few months before, with only one MP in dissent.

> *The General Law Amendment* gives the government sweeping powers over the community. It provides for detention of a person, incommunicado, for a possible recurrent period of

> ninety days, until satisfactory answers have been given to any interrogation, or until such time as the police see fit to release him or her. It also gives the government the right to search all mail and delay it, and provides for a penalty of death, or at least five years, for treason, which is defined as any offence against the State. This includes advocating any form of political, industrial, economic or social change. The Bill also places the onus of proof on the accused. 'Guilty' until proved 'innocent'.

Mr X lamented the fact that the recent New Zealand Rugby League tour of South Africa had gone ahead with the removal of all Maoris from the national team. He suggested that the South African Government would have received a 'tremendous shock' if the New Zealanders had refused to tour without their Maori teammates.

Student politics seems to inevitably follow a set course. The leaders rouse strong emotions over an issue, meetings are called, speakers are booked, resolutions are carried. These are duly conveyed to the government offices, consulates, police and so forth. Finally, a demonstration is planned. This was the trajectory the protests against the Tait hanging took, and also the protests against apartheid. The latter went on for some time (Nelson Mandela wasn't released from jail until 1990).

At the end of April 1964 *Honi Soit* ran an article about the Civil Rights Bill then proceeding through the United States Congress. It described how the southern senators were trying to disrupt the passage of the Bill by filibustering (that is, simply speaking for so long on the floor of the chamber that the Bill would be delayed, possibly permanently). The Bill, among other things, provided for equal health, employment and educational opportunities for African Americans. *Honi Soit* described the imposition of 'poll taxes', where unscrupulous state governments in the South would discourage African Americans from voting by charging them a fee at the polling booth. At the end of the article a paragraph in bold detailed a planned 'demo'. This was radical stuff. Even students in the US itself were yet to come out so strongly. In contrast to this subversive political agitation, Michael was quoted in a separate article on the same page: 'A motion was . . . moved by the President of the SRC, Mr M. D. Kirby, congratulating the Chancellor of the University, Sir Charles Bickerton Blackburn, on attaining his 90th birthday and wishing him continued good health . . .' Again, Michael Kirby was a long way, in his own political position, from the radicals.

Michael did not attend the rally in Wynyard Street, but as student solicitor all his skills were called upon immediately after it. Fifteen hundred students had clashed with a large contingent of police in what *Honi Soit* described as 'one of the most violent demonstrations the students of Sydney University have ever held . . . Mounted police and squad cars knocked girls to the ground. Police making arrests removed their identification numbers.' A photo in *The Sun* showed hundreds of students watching, horrified, as a young woman in jeans was manhandled by a burly cop. It wasn't a good look. In the end, twenty-eight students were arrested and charged by the police.

The week after the rally, Michael convened a meeting in the Wallace Theatre for all students charged, all students who might have film or photographs of the arrests and all students who witnessed the arrests. As SRC president and honorary solicitor, Michael would be conducting the defence himself, with the support of the NSW Council for Civil Liberties.

Two cases came before the magistrate Mr Pocock SM at the Central Court of Petty Sessions on Tuesday, 7 July 1964. Things began badly for the police when they were forced to withdraw the first case before the hearing began. In the second case, the police alleged that the student had said to a policeman, 'You can go and get fucked.' Michael was appearing for the student.

Constable D. Carr (vice squad) claimed that he was addressing a crowd of students when the accused said the words to him. He told the Court that he had identified himself to the student and then arrested him. Constable J. Armstrong (vice squad) was there to corroborate his colleague's account. Both policemen insisted that the incident occurred at 11.10 p.m. Under cross-examination by Kirby they both agreed that if this timing could be shown to be wrong, this would amount to a 'substantial and material difference to their evidence'. Further, Constable Armstrong changed his testimony when pushed by Kirby, first saying there was no reason for him to approach the student and then claiming he had done so 'to hurry the defendant along'. When the student and his witnesses gave evidence, they all swore that the incident took place at 10.10 p.m. and that the plain-clothes policemen had not identified themselves to the defendant.

The final nail in the coffin for the NSW Police was hammered home when Mr Kirby called the traffic manager of the Port Jackson and Manly Steamship Company, Mr G. Marshall. The fact that the students had been arrested as they disembarked from the ferry

South Steyne was not in question. Mr Marshall testified, with some authority, that the ferry had indeed arrived at the wharf, but at 10 p.m., not 11 p.m. as the police claimed. With that, the magistrate told Kirby that he did not need to continue his address, since it was now his intention to dismiss the case. This was simply the first in a long line of stunning acquittals Kirby achieved in these cases. *Honi Soit* sung his praises on the front page, scoring him ten out of eleven victories.

After the civil rights demonstrations at Wynyard, a group of Sydney University students asked themselves why they had been prepared to protest at the treatment of African Americans but not of Australian Aborigines. Thus, the first meeting of the 'Committee for Action on Aboriginal Rights' took place on 7 July 1964. A group of second-year students including Anne Curthoys, Jeannie Lewis and Hal Greenland formed the committee. It was supported by a large number of clubs and societies and the SRC, and the first meeting was addressed by the new NSW Labor senator Lionel Murphy QC. The senator described the Queensland Acts that controlled every aspect of Aboriginal peoples' lives – where they could live, who they could marry and how they could spend their own money. He also spoke of the discrimination written into Section 51 (xxvi) of the Australian Constitution that did not recognise Aboriginal people automatically as Australian citizens and so, like the fauna, they were not even counted in the census.

The first Aboriginal students, Charlie Perkins and Gary Williams, began their studies in March 1963. By late 1964 a new organisation had developed, called Student Action for Aborigines (SAFA). Its chair was Charlie Perkins, and two other students, Jim Spigelman and Beth Hansen, were the co-secretaries. SAFA determined that it would organise a Freedom Ride, like the ones in the United States that protested against segregation in the South.

In January 1965 a bus left Sydney University and headed to country towns like Moree and Walgett in outback New South Wales. The first bus carried twenty-nine young students including Perkins, Spigelman, Hansen and Anne Curthoys, plus a handful of non-students, including Aboriginal lay-preacher Gerry Mason. Gary Williams joined them later. The idea was that the group would head for destinations where racism towards Aboriginal people was a daily, accepted activity. Led by Perkins, they would then attempt to overcome these practices by going directly to the pubs, swimming pools and picture theatres where Aboriginal people were excluded or treated as second-class citizens.

Several Freedom Rides were organised in 1965. The biggest confrontation occurred in Moree, a large township 600 kilometres north-west of Sydney, just south of the Queensland border, where white residents physically assaulted the students. Jim Spigelman was punched to the ground and other students were attacked or threatened. A very nasty outcome was narrowly avoided when the police escorted the students out of the town and then prevented large convoys of angry locals from following. Racism ran deep in Moree, but the specific issue chosen by the students was the segregation of the council-run swimming pool. In the end, the students achieved their aim and the swimming pool was thrown open to all, regardless of the colour of their skin, but it took some time.

The Freedom Ride to Walgett, 200 kilometres west of Moree, highlighted the refusal of the local cinema to allow Aboriginal people to sit in the dress circle with whites. They were relegated to the downstairs seats only. After several student freedom riders were arrested in Walgett, Michael Kirby, as student solicitor, and the Council for Civil Liberties were called in. The *Sydney Morning Herald* carried the story – 'Theatre owner denies Aborigines barred'. The owner of the Walgett Luxury Theatre, James George Conomos, claimed in the Walgett Court of Petty Sessions that there was no bar. 'We might refuse more whites from upstairs than dark people,' he added. Sadly for him, the local police sergeant was more forthcoming: 'I know there is a ban,' he said.

Owen Westcott, a student freedom rider, was charged with one count of obstruction and one count of assaulting police when he allegedly resisted arrest. Michael Kirby prepared the case for counsel.

> The students went with [the Aboriginal people] and tried to force entry and they were then arrested. I was asked, as the pro bono lawyer for the SRC, to get a barrister and to go up there and to defend them. Naturally, I went straight to the top . . . to Gordon Samuels QC, who was a leading barrister. He was later my colleague in the New South Wales Court of Appeal, wonderful lawyer – tremendous aplomb. And he subsequently, of course, became the Governor of New South Wales. So we went up to Walgett, we fought the case. A very wise magistrate sat in the case and he found the offences proved but dismissed the offences on the basis of the good character of the accused.

But not all the students at Sydney University appreciated Michael's hard work, his application and his serious intent, no matter how successful. Some of the younger, more excitable elements thought that as a full-time city solicitor he had no place running their SRC and that he was no more than a professional student. This sentiment was to come to the fore particularly in the relationship between SRC president and the SRC newspaper.

'I may not agree with what you say, but I will defend to the death your right to say it.' It's the favourite line of student politicians and editors of student newspapers, and every couple of years there is an issue to test the famous maxim. At the same time as he was preparing the Wynyard protesters' cases, Michael Kirby was horrified to pick up his copy of *Honi Soit* and see that the editor, Michael McDermott, in his infinite wisdom, had decided to give over a whole page of the newspaper to the National Socialist Party of Australia – i.e., the Nazi Party – replete with prominent swastika, eagle and wreath. Not content with one article, McDermott had allowed for two: the rather predictable denial of the Holocaust, in the form of a long and nasty piece by one Colin Jordan, leader of the British Nazis; followed by McDermott's paraphrasing of an interview with Arthur Smith, leader of the Australian Nazis, advocating the deportation of all Jews and confiscation of their property. It's hard to know which was more offensive, but both certainly were. The deliberately provocative act got the reaction it craved.

The following edition of the paper was full of castigating letters to the editor. Even Julius Stone, the Challis Professor of Jurisprudence and International Law, was not above student politics and he sent in a long piece. He had been in Jerusalem in 1961 for Adolf Eichmann's trial, and it was more than he could stand to see deeply racist ravings given such prominence. Many of the Jewish students at Sydney University felt a sense of shock and betrayal that their newspaper could allow such a vicious attack on them. One student wrote a short but heartfelt letter, asking the tragic question: did his father's death at Mauthausen concentration camp mean nothing at all?

The SRC, under the leadership of its president, Michael Kirby, took a strong position, demanding space for a response from the Jewish Students' Union. When this was interpreted by McDermott as 'Jewish moves to limit editorial freedom' and labelled 'The Jewish Line', the SRC suspended him as the editor of *Honi Soit*. A debate then raged in the pages of the newspaper. Kirby was criticised for saying one thing in February: 'the exodus of the Bohemian set has meant the gradual expansion year by year of a pedestrian outlook and routine diligence that has, let's face it, very nearly robbed the University of the much vaunted spirit of independent inquiry'; and another thing by July: 'Let there be no mistake: *Honi Soit* is the SRC's journal, not the private preserve of the editor.' The same critics thought the president was using the paper for his own personal and political gratification. Supporters of McDermott wrote to the paper deriding the changes after Kirby had become SRC president: '*Honi Soit* became fuller and fuller of SRC material; Kirby's photographs and speeches were everywhere.'

These debates were not new and they were not going to go away. Kirby was involved, in one way or another, in the removal of three sets of editors: Peter Grose and Richard Walsh in 1962, to the advantage of the replacement editor, Bob Ellis; Laurie Oakes's resignation in 1963; and Michael McDermott's departure over the Nazi articles in 1964. As recently as 2009, at a book launch for Ellis, Kirby was still apparently lamenting the fact that he had allowed himself to have been 'manipulated' by Ellis into sacking Walsh and Grose.

> Kirby: So, you were behind that?
> Ellis: Yes, me and Laurie Oakes, yes.
> Kirby: I've always thought that was the most shameful thing I did in student politics. It was an assault on free speech . . .
> Ellis: And human decency.
> Kirby: . . . and I hereby publicly apologise. We're in the mood of apologies in Australia now, and I apologise to Richard Walsh for sacking him. And I now know you were behind it.

Laurie Oakes didn't last that long either. He became unpopular with the SRC and the University Senate and later resigned after *Honi Soit* was censored over an attempt to publish a short story that was deemed 'obscene'. The SRC, with Kirby a member, stopped publication of the piece in which two men kissed. 'A kiss,' the SRC's Director of Student Publications said, 'is a sexual act.' Ellis returned as editor after Oakes's departure. As Kirby commented years later, in the early '60s, homosexual rights were not on anybody's agenda; they just weren't spoken about. This sort of censorship was rife. Kirby wasn't one of the most liberal students but even if he had been, it is unlikely he would have demurred. Laurie Oakes was on his own on this one.

Michael Kirby took his duties as SRC president extremely seriously. He was not in office because of the support of any political group, he had achieved political success out of a personal support base; therefore no one was well placed to keep him in check. Like many young people who go into student politics, he could be overbearing and autocratic. His brothers and sister would attest to the fact that Michael had these qualities at home, where he organised them in all things from homework to chores, and in the student political scene they came to the fore. He was a few years older than most of his contemporaries and also working full-time outside the university as a lawyer. All this combined made him even harder to take. He could be bumptious, dressed in a three-piece suit, demanding everyone follow process and always insisting on the formalities.

It was truly ironic, then, that while Kirby was being attacked by the more radical students for being too controlling, uptight and conservative, at the other end of the political spectrum he was seen as left wing, even subversive. In fact, his political activities up to 1964 had, astoundingly, led to the Australian Security Intelligence Organisation (ASIO) opening a file on him. This was more a reflection of the kind of particularly partisan and inept organisation that ASIO had become under Menzies than it was an accurate assessment of Kirby's radicalism (even later Liberal prime minister John Gorton thought of them as 'stumblebums'). His associations with foreign students, like the Nigerian delegation and his trip to Africa and Asia, his condemnation of the Malayan Government for trying to control the Malayan Students' Association, his support for Aboriginal rights and against apartheid, his membership of the Council for Civil Liberties and especially his joining the Australian Congress for International Cooperation and Disarmament (ACICD, later the AICD) in 1964, all apparently pointed to his subversive tendencies.

The ACICD was formed with the basic aim of trying to reduce the threat of nuclear war by promoting peace and disarmament. It was considered by ASIO at that time to be no more than a communist front.

The ASIO file itself was ridiculous. The most they could come up with regarding Kirby's early life and associations was that his rather radical Aunt Glory had once told a friend (presumably an ASIO agent) that Michael was very smart but also very reactionary. Kirby had never even joined a political party. The absolute degree to which the security police were monitoring legitimate political activity of law-abiding Australians wasn't finally revealed until the mid 1970s, when a series of security scandals and the Hope Royal Commission detailed how files had been kept on every Labor member of parliament, every peace activist, and even church groups. More insidiously, ASIO established a special unit, the sole function of which was to secretly leak these files to sympathetic journalists and media commentators.

Kirby's activities, perhaps not surprisingly, then, had come to the attention of somebody far more influential than ASIO. Eric Baume was an early shock jock, working for radio station 2GB, and very much an Alan Jones or Andrew Bolt of his day. He frequented the university, often accepting invitations to student debates. *Honi Soit* recorded one such encounter: 'Amid boos, cat-calls and cheers, together with a fusillade of rotten fruit and miscellaneous objects, Mr Eric Baume dramatically stalked out of a lunchtime meeting at the university last Tuesday.' Baume was to speak on the topic of 'Germany today – the Nazi legacy'. As things transpired, he only got a few words out – declaring that German university students were 'the foundation of the new Germany' (and by implication, the audience took it, that Sydney University students were no good) – before the meeting degenerated into a fracas. Baume stormed out, telling his audience to 'go back to Redfern', the rather less than respectable adjacent suburb.

Baume was fond of issuing invitations of his own, and demanded on several occasions that the SRC president debate him on various topics. One in particular was the less than edifying and now notorious 'hambone' incident. A student had decided to strip off, revealing his genitals, as a stunt during orientation week. At the following SRC meeting, President Kirby reaffirmed that he believed that discussion of sex, politics and religion were essential to the university, especially in orientation week. He would not discuss, though, the 'hambone' incident, given that it was now the subject of a Proctorial Board investigation, the formal disciplinary body of the university. Kirby accompanied the student in question to a meeting with the vice-chancellor, and before that to an interview with the vice squad. Although unremarkable today – redolent as it was of a Monty Python sketch, and simply a foretaste of what was to come in the swinging sixties and the liberated seventies – in Sydney in 1964, the student's horseplay could have led to expulsion from the university and possibly a jail term.

Eric Baume's imagination had been excited by these events and he issued a demand for Kirby to turn up and justify himself, to the whole of Sydney, on 2GB. In his broadcast, Baume read out a letter he had received from retired stipendiary magistrate F. L. McNamara urging police action against the 'creature' who had performed the act. Kirby told a meeting of the SRC that he had no intention of acceding to Baume's demands. 'I am reliably informed that Mr Baume's popularity and listening audience have greatly diminished over the past year. This is just another case of familiarity breeding a well-earnt contempt. His aim, therefore, must be to engender controversy over small issues. For this reason, I feel disinclined to assist him in his endeavours.' The SRC concurred.

Baume made his views known: 'I think that the vice-chancellor of the University of Sydney, the Students' Representative Council and its chairman or president or whatever the young chap calls himself, have grossly insulted the population and the people of this state by their secrecy over this young [expletive deleted from transcript] who stripped himself naked.' In the end, both the vices – chancellor and squad – stepped back. The university issued a statement saying that the student had been severely reprimanded and heavily fined after apologising to the chancellor.

Kirby's initial attempt to remain somewhat apart from the more radical student political agenda had worked tolerably well up to this point. He rarely involved himself directly in the public protests and the militant actions but he was always there to defend the right of his colleagues to agitate. He was also becoming increasingly aware of the power of the media, first in the immediate effect the student media had in securing his political ambitions on campus, but then, more broadly, following his interchanges with the likes of Eric Baume. These interventions drew the attention of figures in the Labor Party, who immediately liked what they saw.

By the middle of the decade, student politics had begun to

change. Kirby's second term as SRC president had come to an end and he moved away from SRC involvement and into the University Union. The union was a more congenial affair. Although a student organisation, it existed primarily to provide services to the whole university community, including academic and general staff, in the form of clubs and societies, sporting facilities, catering and dining rooms and on-campus entertainment. No hamboning there.

The photo in the *Union Recorder* shows the office bearers of the 1964–65 union. All men (there was then a separate Women's Union), all appropriately attired in suit and tie, three appointed by the University Senate, including a professor and, in pride of place, the president, Mr M. D. Kirby BA LLB. This was another handball from Peter Wilenski. He had been the president of the 1962–63 union and, having completed his medical degree, had now left Australia to study for a BA at Oxford.

As the student population ran headlong towards anti-Vietnam War protests, women's lib, sit-ins against the Proctorial Board ('the jury, judge and executioner' on student disciplinary matters), draft resisting and free love, Kirby maintained an interest but an increasing detachment. Almost overnight, right across the campus the suits and ties disappeared, a lot of beards sprang up (no longer just on science students) and a candidate for the SRC could easily appear wearing a full-length, white lamb's wool jacket and no one would blink an eye. But Kirby was an institutional person and no amount of perfervid debate from the anti-establishment types was going to drag him away from that.

It was around this time that he began to seriously consider whether his future might involve party politics. Kirby attended a single ALP branch meeting but it was a dreary affair. Looking around at the broader Australian political context, there wasn't a great deal to excite the imagination; the conservatives had a clean sweep.

In New South Wales, Liberal Premier Robin Askin had come to power on the catchcry of 'fixing up the Opera House mess'. He certainly did that, forcing the architect out of the country and installing a third-rate program that left the interiors in tatters. Later, it was regular brown paper bags of money from the police chief. In Victoria there was Bolte; in Queensland, Joh Bjelke-Petersen was on the rise to political power and a life of systemic corruption and of course, federally, Sir Robert Menzies was well into his third decade as PM. Kirby had met Gough Whitlam, the new deputy leader of the Labor Party, having arranged for him to speak at the 1964 union dinner, and was impressed, but otherwise the political scene was pretty bleak.

Nevertheless, Kirby was a natural and he considered his options very seriously. His family thought he was heading to greatness – his brother David had no doubts: 'Certainly it was assumed by all of us that Michael would go far. Indeed, we all thought that he ultimately would be prime minister.'

Second-year arts/law student Geoffrey Robertson was one of the orientation week directors in 1965 and later SRC president. He never forgot one NUAUS meeting at Melbourne's Windsor Hotel with Richard Carlton and Robert Holmes à Court:

> We were all tyros in student politics and the two grandees of student politics in Australia were of course Michael Kirby and Gareth Evans. They came along and did a show for us,

> and we took bets on who would become prime minister. I bet with dear old Richard Carlton, who was on *60 Minutes* of course, that Gareth would be foreign minister, but in Michael Kirby's cabinet. Yes indeed, he seemed to be cut out for it. He had all the right connections, the respect for Doc Evatt; he was quite conservative in his religious beliefs, and I guess the monarchy wasn't an issue in those days. Little did we know that he had personal aspects that probably dissuaded him from going that route.

Kirby's work, especially his sparring with Eric Baume, came to the attention of another Sydney legal figure, Neville Wran, a Labor lawyer of some repute who would eventually move into NSW state politics and all the way to the Premier's office. 'He was very encouraging,' Kirby remembers. 'He called me up to his chambers and asked me what I was going to do when I finished my articles. He sounded me out about whether I wanted to go on to be a partner in a law firm for Labor counsel and, effectively, I said no, not really.' It was at this time that Kirby occasionally bumped into Lionel Murphy QC, the newly elected senator for New South Wales, who was in the same chambers as Wran and who specialised in industrial law. It was the beginning of a lasting connection, and both men would go on to play pivotal roles later in Kirby's career.

Having finished his law degree and articles, Kirby was now committed to his job, mainly dealing with workers' compensation cases at Hickson, Lakeman and Holcombe. In the beginning he was excited by the prospect of being a solicitor-advocate, but it soon took a toll.

> It later turned out to be a very exhausting job, to be both a solicitor and a barrister. Very hard to combine the life of an advocate with getting the subpoenas done and organising the witnesses and so on. So Neville was very interested in my career, and rather unselfishly so. I think he may have seen some similarity with some of the values he had had as a student.

Neville Wran was soon to take on at the NSW state level the job that Gough Whitlam was so successfully doing at the federal level: making the ALP a viable and attractive Opposition. Neither he nor his good friend Lionel Murphy shared Kirby's religious beliefs – they were both lifelong atheists – nor his devotion to the monarchy. In fact, even in the 1960s, and especially in student politics, monarchists like Kirby were fairly scarce on the ground. As Kirby moved more into Sydney University Union politics and further away from the SRC, he was able to indulge some of these tendencies. As union president, dressed in dinner suit and bow tie, he was keen to welcome Her Majesty's governor-general, the last of the Imperial viceroys, His Excellency, the Right Honourable William Philip Sidney, First Viscount de L'Isle, VC, KG, GCMG, GCVO, PC, to the union dinner. On another occasion, the Right Honourable Sir Garfield Barwick, GCMG, QC, PC, the chief justice of Australia, attended.

There were also opportunities for humour, not uncommonly at Kirby's own expense. He had certainly loosened up a bit since the SRC days when he'd demanded an official censure for a representative who had referred to 'God Save the Queen' as the 'bloody national anthem' (which at that time it certainly was; 'Advance

Australia Fair' wasn't officially adopted until 1984). At Union Night on 1 March 1967, Kirby delivered a satirical 'Speech from the Throne read on behalf of Her Majesty'. 'Elizabeth II, by the grace of God, Queen of the United Kingdom, Great Britain and Ireland, and of the British Dominions beyond the seas, Empress of India,' he began, 'my husband and I, through our Lord Lieutenant and Student Senator of the University of Sydney, Michael Donald Kirby, desire you to know that we are ever conscious of the honoured and ancient position held, and of the worthy function performed, by this House and its members . . .' He continued at some length but it must have gone down quite well with the audience because he appeared again with a similar routine at another Union Night. It was all in the delivery.

This was Michael Kirby's baroque period in student politics, his twilight years, and he knew that he would soon have to face the inevitable, the thing he had delayed and deferred for so long – to say goodbye to the protection and comfort of Sydney University and step out into the world.

> In a sense, looking back, it was an endeavour on my part to postpone coming to grips with the reality of my life as a human being, as a human being with sexual feelings and a person who needed to explore and discover love.

If his years at Fort Street had been his happiest, then this long period at Sydney University and his high-flying student political career had been the most exhilarating. There were huge highs but there were also lows. When he returned to his room at Sydney Street after a long day in court and then on campus, he closed the door and was alone. It was a loneliness that seemed to eat into his very being. At Fort Street he felt equal to every one of his contemporaries but throughout his entire time at Sydney University he was incomplete, unfulfilled. As the years progressed, everywhere he looked his peers were meeting members of the opposite sex, having fun and even marrying. That, of course, was impossible for Kirby. So as he inevitably withdrew from the student life he simple poured himself into his work at the law and still he refused to contemplate a personal life. It was a sensible interim strategy, or so he thought, but eventually, something had to give.

4

I Couldn't Live a Lie

> Certainly the activities with the students' council led to my being elected unopposed as the honorary solicitor; there weren't too many volunteers who wanted to be the honorary solicitor for the students. That led me into activities defending students, into the Council for Civil Liberties, into representing a lot of people in minority positions. That gave me a perception of the fact that the law that I was practising as a young solicitor was not always just in the way it fell upon those minorities. And that got me interested in law reform.
>
> *Michael Kirby*

Bob Ellis had become infatuated with the daughter of David McNicoll, the prominent Sydney journalist and editor of *The Bulletin*. They had first met when Ellis was a 'prolific features writer' on *Honi Soit* and Penny McNicoll was features editor. There was nothing particularly unusual in this – Ellis was frequently infatuated with his girlfriends, and a lot of other women besides. His obsessions even included a fear of impending apocalypse, a hangover from his ingrained Seventh-day Adventism. In October 1962 he disappeared without a trace from Sydney University, leaving his fellow *Honi Soit* mates to carry on without him – something about the Cuban missile crisis, nuclear disaster and the end of the world.

Penny McNicoll was nineteen and Bob Ellis not much older, and their affair was stormy and short-lived. Sometime after the break-up, Bob made the rather ill-judged decision to break into Penny's Bellevue Hill home, possibly by climbing through her first-floor bedroom window, a stunt he had performed on previous occasions. 'Bob appeared at the house one afternoon when I was alone, and grappled with me,' Penny wrote later. Of course, the inevitable happened and the police showed up. They asked Penny if she wanted to press charges, but she didn't. Her father, the stern figure of David McNicoll, had never thought all that much of Ellis, but Penny says it was her mother who laid the charges. In the end, the full weight of the law was thrown at the 'lovesick' and penniless student. Today this kind of behaviour would probably be described as stalking.

Michael Kirby, as the pro bono Sydney University students' solicitor-advocate, was enlisted to defend Ellis. It was a process he had become very familiar with: he would prepare the case as solicitor and then brief himself, as it were, to appear in the court as a barrister would – all with no fee. Even for Kirby this was a very demanding proposition and he was on his feet all the time. Michael had not yet been admitted as a barrister, and although solicitors could appear in the lower courts, most never did so. Taking on both jobs of preparing the brief and then acting as the advocate is only an option for the most energetic of over-achievers.

In their first consultation in Kirby's office, according to Ellis, he offered the important observation: 'Now, Robert, I'm not suggesting you change your evidence, but if the gate was open when you entered the property there could be a very different outcome to this case.' When Kirby recently heard this mischievous recollection from Ellis, he was a little surprised. 'I'll probably be struck off the rolls for this. My career nipped in the bud, after the bud has been in full bloom!'

They turned up before a magistrate in the Paddington Court. Penny didn't show – the evidence was compelling and the outcome seemed in little doubt. Kirby salvaged the situation by suggesting that the charges could be dropped on the proviso that Ellis observe an undertaking not to go near Penny McNicoll. The magistrate agreed. It's unclear if Ellis ever abided by the undertaking.

Ellis wrote the story as a 'fictional' piece in the Sydney University law students' journal, *Blackacre*, but it wasn't that far from autobiography and Kirby was an important character. Ellis also used the incident in his film *The Nostradamus Kid* (1993), where the character of Kavanagh was a conflation of Michael Kirby and the then *Honi Soit* editor and later well-known publisher Richard Walsh. The very thought of this admixture of different traits was something Kirby found most odd indeed. Perhaps because Walsh was a lot like Kirby and a good friend, thoroughly enmeshed in student politics, boyish, enthusiastic and earnest. The film also featured former judge and Whitlam Government minister the

Honourable Jim McClelland playing the role of the magistrate, and actor Arthur Dignam, Germaine Greer's early Sydney University beau, as one of Ellis's Seventh-day Adventist pastors. It was a crazy, rollicking movie and a rather sentimental one. 'I remember his story, and like a lot of other things that Bob Ellis has written, it is full of historical illusions that are more likely to be referring to King Richard III than to real-life, modern Australian characters,' Kirby observes. 'But I believe I did appear for him. I appeared for an enormous number of students. Many of them on fare evasion charges, and I got a lot of them off. Some of them are very distinguished judges nowadays.' (By the late 1960s Ellis was a regular on ABC TV's *This Day Tonight* as a kind of roving reporter. Affable frontman Bill Peach introduced him to audiences: 'And now our resident cat-burglar, Bob Ellis.' Cut to a shot of Ellis sitting high up on a wall in Darlinghurst Road.)

The names had been changed, Ellis said, to protect the guilty, but the description of the lower courts, of the almost Dickensian attitudes of many of the magistrates and police prosecutors, was florid but all too real. Ellis called his piece in *Blackacre* 'My Life in the Lower Courts'.

> Staunchly beergutted under virtuous checkboard double-breasted weskits, watch-chained and cuff-linked, surmounted at the choker with amethyst tie-pins, undulating dewlaps, burgeoning grog-blossoms and earlobes of bright puce, their fat, suet cheekflesh studded with incidental eyes, lint in their periwigs, dandruff in their nose-hair, with fat mouths crouching foxy under thin, blue, business-like lips, brass tacks on

> their brassy, tacky tongue-bones, airy, adenoidal, Rothman-snooty, breaths filtered, socks suspended, belly buttons crisply perfumed, in elasticized underpants sopping fluoride sweat, the barristers of our town look pincenezzily down on burglars.

As solicitor-advocate, and on top of his paid work at Hickson's in workers' compensation and negligence, Michael Kirby was conducting or instructing in a series of pro bono cases brought by the Council for Civil Liberties and he would regularly come face to face with nasty, entrenched prejudices. One case would stick with Kirby for nearly thirty years because of the manifest injustice of the outcome for his client and the dramatic way in which it unfolded. Ken Buckley, the founder of the CCL, would later write it up in his book as 'a travesty of justice', and that it certainly was.

Glenn Corbishley was a 28-year-old disabled man, an invalid pensioner, who had suffered brain damage after contracting encephalitis when he was twenty-four. As a result he was frequently affected by 'turns', which might cause him to suffer disorientation, double vision, inability to communicate, difficulty in breathing and even physical collapse. He explained that on these occasions he behaved 'very much as if I am drunk'. One night at about eleven-thirty in February 1967, Corbishley was passing a cafe in Bondi that he knew well when he had one of his turns. Thinking that if he could sit down and perhaps drink something he might recover more quickly, he entered the cafe, which appeared to be open. The husband-and-wife owners asked him to leave, explaining that they were about to close. What then transpired was the subject of dispute. The cafe owners told police that Corbishley assaulted the husband and then kicked in a pane of glass on the shopfront. Mr Corbishley insisted that he did not assault the owner but simply grabbed hold of him during a fit. In turn, he claimed, the husband had punched him in the face (indeed, Mr Corbishley did subsequently have to have two teeth removed). He said he had no recollection of breaking the glass but that it may have happened during a convulsion. The Bondi police preferred to believe the evidence of the shopkeepers and charged Corbishley with assault and malicious injury to property.

Unfortunately for Glenn Corbishley, he drew the short straw and had to face stipendiary magistrate Mr G. A. Locke in the Paddington Magistrates Court. Locke was notorious – Geoffrey Robertson later referred to him as 'the mad magistrate'. It was Locke who almost ended the brilliant careers of Richard Walsh and Martin Sharpe by sending them off to jail for publishing *Oz* magazine, a decision later overturned on appeal. The sad reality was that many police magistrates weren't really independent thinkers at all; instead, like Mr Fang in *Oliver Twist*, they simply accepted without question whatever evidence the police presented and treated the accused very harshly as a result.

Throughout the proceedings, Corbishley complained that he had no legal representation and that he wanted an adjournment in order to seek counsel. Locke simply ignored his pleading. Unfortunately many people on minor charges, like this one, would go through the courts without legal representation, and to this day still do, but it has never been the proper role of a magistrate to stand in the way of a defendant seeking to obtain legal advice. Incredibly, Locke decided that, before hearing any defence, he would remand

Corbishley to Long Bay jail to undergo 'medical and/or psychiatric observation'. After two weeks in prison, Corbishley faced Locke once more, but still no defence case was heard and again the defendant had no legal representation. Before deciding the case, Locke examined a highly prejudicial report prepared by a psychiatrist at Long Bay, and a purported list of Corbishley's previous convictions provided by the police. (When questioned by Locke prior to sentencing, Corbishley denied any convictions in Australia, but admitted to one in the United Kingdom as a child.) Locke then promptly found Corbishley guilty and imposed a bond and a substantial fine.

Corbishley left the court indigent, distressed, sick and without any idea of what to do next. Serendipitously, his situation came to the attention of the CCL. With the recognition that a gross denial of natural justice had likely taken place, the CCL lawyers decided to put their weight behind Corbishley's case. An appeal straight from the Magistrates Courts to the Supreme Court, bypassing the District Court, was notoriously difficult to achieve, and if it failed, all further options would be exhausted. The advantage in this course of action was that, if successful (and given the strength of the case, the CCL felt this was likely), it would short-circuit the process and lead to an immediate acquittal. Thus the CCL was faced with a predicament: either appeal from the Magistrates Court to the District Court in the usual way, or take the more difficult and risky path of circumventing the lower courts altogether and going straight to the Supreme Court on a point of law.

In the end, the CCL lawyers decided to do both, assuming that while the Supreme Court appeal continued, the District Court proceedings might be successful and vice versa thus giving Corbishley a double chance. This decision was to have tragic repercussions for Mr Corbishley.

Maurice Byers QC was briefed to argue the case through the Supreme Court of Appeal on the grounds that natural justice had been denied to Mr Corbishley. Indeed, at almost every point the magistrate had prejudiced Corbishley's chance of a fair trial. The list of transgressions was extensive: Locke had sent Corbishley to jail before hearing any defence; repeated requests for adjournment were denied; and prejudicial material in the form of a psychiatrist's report and a police record of convictions were considered before judgement was delivered (these should only have been used for sentencing purposes). Byers, later the Commonwealth solicitor-general, eloquently won all three justices to his cause. Mr Justice J. D. Holmes was scathing of the magistrate.

> The picture is one which shows how the poor, sick and friendless are still oppressed by the machinery of justice in ways which need a Fielding or a Dickens to describe in words or a Hogarth to portray pictorially. What happened that day to the applicant was only the beginning of the terrors which were to confront him before the proceedings before this stipendiary magistrate were completed.

The 'terrors', unfortunately, were to continue unabated. Despite this positive outcome in the Supreme Court of Appeal, the process in the lower courts had already begun, so it was there that the case had to be resolved. Appeals to higher courts always overrule the decisions in the lower courts, but in this instance there had been no decision from the District Court, it was still pending, so Mr Corbishley had almost literally fallen between the cracks. Having made their strong statement on the conduct of the Magistrates Court, the Supreme Court justices were no doubt confident that the lower court would do the right thing. Sitting with his client in the District Court, Michael Kirby was horrified when he realised His Honour Judge K. F. Torrington was not going to deliver the conclusion the justices of the Appeal Court had envisaged, even hinted at.

> Sadly, he came before a judge who felt it to be his duty to actually increase his penalty from a bond and a hefty fine to full-time imprisonment. So Mr Corbishley won his case, but he lost his liberty. It was a terrible blow to me as he was hauled off. The judge did not follow the time-honoured course, observed by virtually all of his colleagues: he did not signal that he was considering an increase in the penalty to give Mr Corbishley the chance to withdraw his appeal.

Corbishley's case had only been revived in order to gain him a better outcome. It never occurred to Kirby or the CCL that he would be jailed again. All lawyers lose cases but here the defendant had been encouraged by the CCL to mount the appeal, so Kirby felt he bore an added responsibility for the harsh result. This turn of events shook the young lawyer. 'That wretched case of injustice stayed in my mind for nearly thirty years.'

No matter how hard Kirby worked at the law he knew full well that some injustices would never be addressed without political changes and changes to the law itself – maybe quite radical changes in some areas. The work of the CCL certainly highlighted the areas in which major overhaul of the state's laws were necessary, but other than strenuously defending in particular cases such as Corbishley's, even a dedicated civil liberties solicitor-advocate such as Kirby was severely hamstrung. Clients like Glenn Corbishley would never get true justice until the law was reformed. Here it seemed that, paradoxically, the intervention of the CCL had led to more harm for the client than good. Even 'the mad magistrate' had only fined Corbishley $20, admittedly after remanding him in jail for two weeks, but Torrington had added a further month's imprisonment.

Several positive developments did ensue from Corbishley's case. It is unlikely that these advances would have occurred had the CCL not taken the action. The unconscionable behaviour of Mr Locke was brought starkly to the attention of the NSW minister of justice, and this was not the first time Locke had behaved badly – the jailing of Walsh and Sharpe in the *Oz* case had already caused enormous controversy. This time Locke was finally removed from his position at Paddington Court and brought under the direct supervision of the chief stipendiary magistrate in the Central Court. There was also the issue of the legal anomaly that led to the absurd situation where Corbishley's victory in the Supreme Court of Appeal had no bearing on the final result in the lower court. A more just outcome should have resulted in Corbishley's conviction being quashed by the Supreme Court. This anomaly was addressed by the minister and as result of Corbishley's case the law was changed. Overall, the educative value of such CCL actions was important. Most citizens were unaware, for example, that a request to any magistrate for an adjournment in order to seek legal representation was routine and normally approved. Thanks to the work of the CCL this issue alone was given some prominence in the media and even in parliament.

Perhaps the most important legacy of all from Corbishley's case was actually the indelible impression it left on the young solicitor Michael Kirby. On top of all that Corbishley had to endure, it was almost too much that Judge Torrington should think it fit to increase his sentence at appeal without warning. In another capacity almost thirty years later, Kirby was finally able to right the wrong. As president of the NSW Court of Appeal, Michael Kirby found in *Parker v. Director of Public Prosecutions & Anor* (1992) that 'a failure of a trial judge to disclose that he or she was contemplating imposing a custodial sentence, in lieu of a non-custodial penalty appealed from, would amount to a denial of procedural fairness.' Kirby observes: 'Interesting, is it not, how, in due course, the wheel comes round full circle and ancient wrongs can sometimes be corrected?'

Ken Buckley's history of the CCL published in 1970 began with the words: 'Australia is not a police state. Nevertheless, certain kinds of incidents recur with such frequency as to raise a question: how safe are our civil liberties in this conformist society?' The book was titled *Offensive and Obscene* and he was pointing the finger squarely at the censorship laws. For two decades from the early 1940s the law in Australia was used in a series of cases against artistic and literary figures. A number of different legal pretexts were used, from obscenity and indecency charges to criminal libel, but the desired and often achieved outcome was always the same: to stop the development and dissemination of what was considered, by a very powerful and conservative political, religious and legal establishment, to be a 'degenerate' modernist aesthetic. There was something particularly confronting about the modernist movement as far as the conservative-minded were concerned. In the 1930s both Nazis and Stalinists abhorred the modernists, responding with severe repression – the Nazis with painting and book burnings and far worse. While Australians at home were spared those horrors, they did have to endure the legal and artistic predilections of Garfield Barwick, who was to be a dominant conservative legal figure in the country for most of the second half of the twentieth century.

Barwick appeared as barrister in 1944 for two disgruntled painters after the nation's most prestigious prize for portraiture, the Archibald Prize, was awarded to William Dobell for his painting of friend and fellow artist Joshua Smith. The claim was made that the work was caricature not portraiture, and therefore ineligible for the prize. Although the first to admit he knew nothing about art, Barwick focused his withering powers of cross-examination on the witnesses, tangling them up in their own language. As well as the belittling of Dobell's artistic vision there was also nasty scuttlebutt put about that Dobell and Smith had been more than just friends. (At that time, as with so many, Dobell did not want to and could not reveal his homosexuality.) Barwick lost the case, but it nevertheless hurt Dobell enormously.

While Robert Menzies' elder brother Frank was Victorian Crown solicitor, two prominent cases were brought against writers. In 1946 Robert Close was sent to jail for two years for obscenity after using the word 'rutting' in his critically acclaimed novel *Love Me Sailor*. The conviction and jailing destroyed his literary career and almost destroyed his life. The legal issues raised in the case set a precedent in Australian law for charges of indecency and obscenity and it was still regularly being referred to right up into the mid 1960s.

The other case taken over by Frank Menzies was in 1951. Author Frank Hardy was charged with criminal libel over his novel *Power Without Glory*, a thinly veiled biography of millionaire businessman John Wren. It was alleged that he had libelled Wren's wife in the passages of the book where the character based on Mrs Wren had an adulterous affair. Libel, of course, is a civil matter that might result in damages if proved; criminal libel was an archaic offence similar to sedition – hardly ever used before in Victoria and by its very nature political (it could only be initiated by the state). Hardy, having ended up with the same judge who sent Robert Close to prison, firmly believed he would die in jail – he was a communist, and in the atmosphere of anti-communist panic of the day, it remains a testament to the extraordinary skill of Hardy's counsel, Donald Campbell KC, that he was acquitted. Again the work itself was a ground-breaker; with its blend of fact and fiction, *Power Without Glory* sold millions of copies worldwide and has never been out of print.

In both these cases, as with Dobell, freedom of artistic expression was being severely constrained. The attacks were not just moralising wowserism: that would be bad enough. There was also a reactionary conservative political thrust to it all. Whereas Frank Hardy had to create his own 'Defend Hardy Committee', by the early 1960s the CCL had stepped into this role and began defending a number of obscenity and indecency cases.

By 1967, the now *Sir* Garfield Barwick had had a relatively short parliamentary career and then been elevated straight from his role as Liberal minister for external affairs to the chief justiceship of Australia by Prime Minister Sir Robert Menzies. It was in this new role that Sir Garfield, along with four of his fellow justices, had to determine the fate of Michael Kirby's latest client. Early in 1967, Kirby, as student senator, had hosted Barwick at the Sydney University Union welcome dinner. Less than six months later he was appearing before him. Kirby's first case in the High Court of Australia was as junior counsel in a CCL matter of a charge of indecency.

Richard Graham was a New Zealander who had published and edited two Sydney magazines, *Obscenity* and *Censor*, each with a very low circulation. The publications were mildly bawdy works, which today, needless to say, would hardly raise an eyebrow. They featured *Playboy*-style cartoons, female nude photographs and extracts from such classics as the Marquis de Sade's *Juliette*, the *Karma Sutra* and Boccaccio's *The Decameron*. Selections from John Cleland's *Fanny Hill* were also reprinted. Cleland had himself been charged with indecency, but it is instructive to remember that that was in 1749. When reading Sir Garfield's judgement, one could be forgiven for thinking some of his language and concepts reflected not Sydney in the swinging sixties but Edwardian or even Victorian England.

Michael Kirby's first appearance in the High Court was unsuccessful. His client, who had won an appeal to the NSW Supreme Court over a magistrate's $20 fine for indecency, was to have the fine and conviction reinstated by the justices of the High Court, led by their chief, Sir Garfield, who wrote:

> The magistrate took that to be indecent which offends the ordinary modesty of the average man . . . Here, for example, sexual matters were referred to in the issues of the magazines in a way which might pass muster in a tap room or smoke concert but which, displayed in print to the reader of the magazine, could, in my opinion, be held to offend the modesty of the ordinary man.

Of course, tap rooms have nothing to do with tap-dancing but what on earth is a smoke concert? Well, the answer to that question says much about Sir Garfield Barwick: a smoke concert is a Victorian-era venue where gentlemen could smoke, drink, listen to live music and discuss politics and other matters, free from the constraining presence of their women. Whatever the esteemed chief justice had in his mind, it did not and never would accurately reflect the changed mores of a new generation of young Australians. The only progress here was that in the twenty years since poor Robert Close had been jailed, the penalty imposed for indecency in this case was only a $20 fine.

Richard Graham's case had gone all the way to the High Court but most of the time Kirby was working in the lower courts, which were, and to some extent still are, ultimately full of trivial matters. His workers' compensation and negligence practice, his 'day job' at Hickson's, was rewarding, but it was really never going to be more than a stepping stone to something else. He was starting to feel like he had achieved as much as he ever could in that role. Kirby determined that he would leave his position at Hickson, Lakeman and Holcombe and go to the Bar. Some of the more senior barristers he had been instructing as a solicitor, people like Neville Wran, had long advised him to do this. They told him he was wasting himself working as a solicitor. Many of his colleagues no doubt thought Kirby rather brash and overly confident, but others could see the great potential of this eager high-achiever.

So, in mid 1967 he was admitted to the NSW Bar to practise as a barrister, his admission moved by the Rumpolesque, monocled Antony Larkins QC. Kirby arranged to move into the eighth floor of Wentworth Chambers in Phillip Street. The fourth floor there was dominated by Labor lawyers, most notably Senator Lionel Murphy QC and Neville Wran. Murphy's career path, in particular, was something of a model for the young Michael Kirby – he had achieved success at the industrial Bar, appearing for a number of trade unions, been active in the CCL and taken some pro bono cases. He had been appointed to the ranks of the senior counsel in New South Wales (often referred to as 'taking silk' in reference to the robes of the Queen's Counsel) and then secured Labor Party pre-selection for the Senate. Murphy was now a senior member of Gough Whitlam's shadow ministry and an important part of the federal government-in-waiting, even though the waiting would go on for another five years.

Although Kirby was a very junior player in the CCL, it gave him the opportunity to rub shoulders with a wide range of prominent and up-and-coming legal figures from both sides of the political spectrum. Many a QC, state or Commonwealth judge, solicitor-general and even a High Court judge or two arrived at their lofty perch by way of the CCL. Kirby particularly liked the collegiate and bipartisan atmosphere.

> One of the best things about the CCL, as I remember it, was that it boasted a good sprinkling of people from differing political philosophies. Peter Baume, a senator for the Liberal Party, warned of the danger of aligning the CCL to any one political party. Correctly, he made the point that within all parties there are champions of civil liberties. Sometimes 'radical Tories' can have a deep commitment to individualism and a healthy suspicion of official autocracy. Thus the CCL has generally boasted of a mixture of political alignments, proving once again that party loyalties can sometimes be an obstacle to the achievement of progress.

A few years after joining the newly founded CCL, Kirby was co-opted onto the subcommittee investigating the law in New South Wales relating to homosexuals. In 1957 the Wolfenden Report in the UK had recommended the decriminalisation of homosexual acts between consenting adults. This had partly been a response to the Kinsey Report, which had provided persuasive scientific evidence that nearly 10 per cent of men in the United States were solely homosexual in orientation. Ten years later, in 1967, with the British Labour Party in government, the UK laws were changed. The then Home Secretary Roy Jenkins neatly encapsulated the existing attitudes on the matter.

> This is the end of a long road. It is almost exactly seven years since my Right Honourable friend the Minister of Health introduced a Motion in support of Wolfenden, which I had

> the honour to wind up, and we were defeated by a vote of more than two to one. Opinion has moved considerably since then in the House and, I believe – though we can all have our own views – in the country, and the position which we have now reached broadly mirrors that movement. It would be a mistake to think . . . that by what we are doing tonight we are giving a vote of confidence or congratulation to homosexuality. Those who suffer from this disability carry a great weight of loneliness, guilt and shame. The crucial question, which we are nearly at the end of answering decisively, is, should we add to those disadvantages the full rigour of the criminal law? By its overwhelming decisions, the House has given a fairly clear answer, and I hope that the Bill will now make rapid progress towards the Statute Book. It will be an important and civilising Measure.

The House of Commons passed the Bill ninety-nine votes to fourteen. In Australia there was no possibility of the same outcome. It had only been in May of the same year that Australians had taken the first step to addressing Indigenous disadvantage by allowing the federal government to make special laws for Aboriginal people and thereby lifting them, to some degree, out of the mire of racism and neglect that they suffered at the hands of the state governments. The Australian people had done this by amending the Constitution in the famous 1967 referendum. Gay rights were still some way off. Even if law reform had been achievable, the climate, even in the UK, as demonstrated by Jenkins' remarks, was far from accepting. Therefore even talking about law reform became a difficult proposition, since those most affected by the laws were least likely to openly protest against them.

Kirby prepared a twenty-page overview of the literature, covering every area with classic Michael Kirby attention to detail. It included these headings: Meaning and Definition; Homosexuality in Various Communities; Historical Times; Animal Behaviour; Incidence Today; Causes and Cure; Clinical Aspects; Treatment and Prevention: Castration, Endocrine Therapy, Self Cure; Designation as Sociopaths. Kirby highlighted one note in particular under recidivism after treatment: 'Police records show only 10 per cent.' Kirby's own personal experience led him to doubt this statistic. Nevertheless, his work on the CCL subcommittee made one thing clear: the law in New South Wales regarding homosexuality needed immediate reform. No other group in the community faced jail for private behaviour, in their bedroom, between partners over the age of twenty-one.

Homosexual law reform wasn't the only area needing attention; this was the case with a range of discriminatory practices and entrenched unfairness in Australian society in the mid 1960s. The White Australia policy was still firmly in place. Although immigrants from Britain and, in the post-war years, increasingly from Europe – Italy, Greece, the Netherlands and Yugoslavia – were encouraged and even given assisted passage, no African or Asian faces were allowed in, while white South Africans or Rhodesians had no trouble at all. Women were discriminated against on a daily basis. Equal pay seemed out of reach and, once married, a woman was required by law to resign from any public service position. Other forms of discrimination were legally sanctioned, with government job advertisements often carrying the rider 'Catholics need not apply'. Divorce law was positively archaic, with the base notion of the apportioning of 'fault' still the only way two adults could legally go their separate ways. Censorship was rife, with characters like Victorian Premier Henry Bolte authorising the vice squad to scour the shops for replicas of Michaelangelo's *David* and confiscate them as obscene. And despite Menzies' rhetoric as a friend to the 'forgotten people', the poor and working classes continued to miss out. Health, education and housing were frequently unaffordable. A university education was, all too often, the preserve of private school graduates.

Law reform seemed to come at a grindingly slow pace and it became increasingly clear to Kirby that direct political action was what was now required. He therefore made up his mind: he would join the Australian Labor Party. As he moved away from student politics, the world of party politics seemed the next natural step. He had seen something of the extreme left fairly close up – from an early age, with the activities of his Uncle Jack, and more recently at university – and he didn't take to it. He had, like his father, always voted Labor, and its socialist philosophy was, up to a point, attractive. An article in the ALP journal in 1961 described socialism as 'anti-war, anti-poverty, anti-greed and anti-race discrimination'. The first leader of Britain's Labour Party, Keir Hardie, put it thus: 'Socialism is at bottom a question of ethics or morals. It has mainly to do with the relationship which should exist between a man and his fellows. Therefore it is the equaliser in the position of the rich man's too much and the poor man's too little.' This was close, philosophically, to Kirby's conception of Christianity.

Accordingly, Kirby wandered along to the Double Bay branch of the ALP. It was, perhaps, rather incongruous to have Labor Party meetings in one of the most affluent of Sydney's leafy establishment suburbs. Nevertheless, Neville Wran and Lionel Murphy were members there, along with Jim McClelland. McClelland, later a minister in the Whitlam Government, at that time ran a firm of solicitors and he acted for Kirby in personal matters. The two were to become friends and McClelland later recalled how he would turn up to those local ALP gatherings: 'I suppose like your ordinary Catholic goes to church on Sunday. [It was a] small branch, and there were the three of us, with a few other wealthy kids from the eastern suburbs who used to roll up in the old man's Mercedes to the branch meetings. It was a really funny little branch.' Kirby didn't like it that much.

> I saw a lot of very nice people, fine people, but I found it excruciatingly boring and trivial, and I knew that this was not only unlikely to lead far in my case, but that it really wasn't what I wanted to spend a lot of time on. A life of barbeques and prawn nights was not for me. That was even worse, it seemed to me, than a life of university committees – and that's saying something.

Federally and in all the states, the Liberal and Country parties ruled supreme. The NSW state election in February 1968 saw a return of the Robin Askin Liberal–Country Party Coalition Government. The victory was due, in part, to an electoral redistribution the year before, which Askin arranged, and which resulted in more voting power to Liberal–Country party electorates in outer urban and regional New South Wales.

Only in South Australia, where the young and flamboyant Labor Premier Don Dunstan had begun what was to be a long political career, did immediate change seem possible. Dunstan had been a barrister, like Kirby, and had taken silk in 1965. His early cases, also like Kirby, had been around issues of civil liberties and anti-discrimination. Don Dunstan was more than a decade older than Kirby and he had attempted to deal with the brutal injustice of the law as it was applied to those on the margins in the 1950s. Kirby could immediately see that as a lawyer Dunstan had faced many of the same issues in the law as he himself had, but as Premier he had a real opportunity to address them.

Dunstan was one of the new breed of ALP leader. Like Murphy, Wran and Whitlam, his was a socially progressive stance and he championed Aboriginal land rights, abolition of the White Australia policy, consumer law reform and loosening censorship and liquor laws. South Australia truly was moving into the twentieth century under his leadership. Don Dunstan himself was a very unusual Australian politician, and was a particularly rare example of a Labor leader. Neville Wran and Gough Whitlam were frequently criticised by the conservative side for being 'toffs', and in Gough's case even a class traitor, yet neither man came from upper-class backgrounds and both attended state high schools (although Gough also attended grammar schools). Don Dunstan, on the other hand, went to a rather exclusive private boys' school in Adelaide and his father was a prominent Liberal businessman and manager of the Adelaide Steamship Company. He married at the early age of twenty-three and had three children. He may well have been bisexual (he spent the last decade of his life living with his male partner), but if so, that part of his life remained private, certainly up to 1968, as was the requirement for all gay men then in public life.

Politics in Australia in the 1960s, as today, was a hard game and for a young gay man there were few options. It was possible to completely sublimate any desires and live a monastic life of a bachelor, as some claim the British prime minister Edward Heath did. Even that, of course, demands living a lie: that 'Miss Right' just never came along. The other, more common course of action was to marry and have children. Even today this is the option taken by many gay men. There is, of course, the constant fear of being outed. In 1967 this would have meant the end of any career, possibly the end of any marriage and finally – the ultimate disaster – criminal charges and jail. Kirby's successor in the Sydney University SRC, Geoffrey Robertson, had no idea Kirby was gay, but he understood very well the culture of the time:

> Everyone spoke of poofters, and poofter-bashing and so forth. There was a lot of dislike, there was a lot of prejudice, an incredible degree of ignorance. You have got to remember this was Sydney just out of the Menzies era, where there was a great deal of wowserism, and there was almost a fanatical and stupid hatred of anyone who was different.

But a lifelong interest in ideas and debates and a strong desire to get in there and do something, to see positive changes made where they were needed, wasn't going to disappear overnight. Kirby was a joiner and an institutional person and he always would be, but he was going to have to think more carefully, and strategically, about his next step. The real world of party politics was a very different thing to the rather cosy, almost literally cloistered environment of student politics he was used to. If he was to take that step into party politics, it wasn't going to be now, and it certainly wasn't going to be through the Double Bay branch of the ALP. It was one thing to be discreet about your private life, but quite another to be forced to behave like most gay politicians and end up weaving a web of deceit.

> Most of them married and I wasn't of the view that that was a very moral or attractive thing to do. In fact I think it's just horrible. Depending on your sexuality; some people are genuinely bisexual and they can do that, but I couldn't, so it would have been cruel to me and cruel to another human being. And I just wasn't brought up to have a life of deception. It's one thing not to be truthful, fully truthful and ram your truth down everybody's neck – which no one did at that time, because the rule was 'Don't ask, don't tell'. So I didn't do that, but I wasn't being a hypocrite and a liar and therefore I just thought that politics was not going to be for me.

Michael Kirby's family were so confident of his capabilities and his destiny that they had assumed he would one day be prime minister. But they were unaware of his private reservations. Michael's brother David was the closest to him, working at that time at Hickson's as his clerk, and even he had no inkling that Michael was gay.

> Had he set his mind to it, I think he would have, at least, been well and truly in the running. Obviously, to become prime minister involves a certain amount of luck. But I think he had the capacity and the charisma to ultimately attain that objective, had he devoted his life to it.
>
> What was different about Michael was that at a certain point, he recognised that although that was an objective that he might obtain, he was not prepared to sacrifice the rest of his life to its achievement. And he therefore, very deliberately decided to put that ambition to one side, and to focus on something else, and ultimately the law, and instead to embrace his sexuality and seek love in his life. And it was only just that he should do so – and he would be a much diminished person had he not done so, I think.

Kirby's legal career was pretty much on track: politics was off the agenda for the foreseeable future; he had chambers, was building a practice and the briefs were coming in, initially from his former employers at Hickson, Lakeman and Holcombe. David Kirby, among others at Hickson's, sent work across to his brother. But his personal life was non-existent. He was working pretty much seven days a week, and on the odd occasion he wasn't working would sit at home by himself, listen to Bach or maybe, very infrequently, watch TV. But Graham Kennedy's *In Melbourne Tonight*, via co-axial cable from south of the border, or even a live performance of 'All You Need Is Love', from Abbey Road by satellite, was not enough. It had taken him a long time but Kirby finally made two of the most important decisions of his life. First, he was going to move out of the family home. Second, he was going to pursue love.

The move out of the house in Concord was a difficult one, precipitated largely by Michael's parents. Don and Jean did not think it was any longer appropriate for their 28-year-old son to be still at home. He needed a hefty push, but in the end Michael knew it was the right thing to do. Again David came to the rescue. He and his girlfriend, Susan Martin, helped Michael move, and David even lived with him for a time in the new digs. Michael's home now was Clifton Apartments – then a brand-new block of flats a short walk from the railway station and situated even closer to the Kirribilli ferry terminal. Michael's unit had a stunning view across the harbour to the still-untiled concrete shells of the Opera House at Bennelong Point.

Once Michael made up his mind to find love, he made it his business to find the 'respectable' gay haunts and to attend on a semi-regular basis. In July 1968, Kings Cross was alive with US military personnel on rest and recreation leave from Vietnam. Soldiers, marines, airmen and sailors were bussed in to make the most of the Whisky A-Go-Go, the Pink Panther, the Savoy Hotel, Stripperdelic or Les Girls! They had a week to spend their money and then it was back to the American war in Da Nang, Khe Sanh and Saigon. The manager of the Whisky A-Go-Go, one Mr Ivor Balmain, a rather frightening character straight out of Scorsese's *Casino*, had the job of vetting the girls that turned up to his club. He told ABC-TV:

'We like to see a girl that's pretty wide open, feminine type, nice hair, hasn't got that vindictive look on her face . . . I like to see a nice way-out girl, a good little swinger.'

There was plenty of interest in the American boys, and not just from girls. In fact, there were places that only boys attended – not necessarily the boys from Sir Garfield's smoke concerts. Venues like the Rex Hotel in Kings Cross and, further out, the monthly Saturday night dance at the Petersham Hall. These were places Michael Kirby would normally avoid at all costs – the Kings Cross nightclubs because they were tacky heterosexual pick-up joints; and the gay bars because he had deliberately kept himself ignorant of their very existence.

Cruising the beats was an activity Michael was never going to adopt. The thought of meeting men for hot, sweaty, casual sex, in the dark, in the middle of the night, in a toilet block in Bondi or the bushes in Centennial Park, horrified him. Policemen regularly entrapped men at such places. Sometimes, just for fun, they would take a break from their squad car duties to sneak up on a seemingly deserted and dimly lit convenience, usually in the middle of a park, and bang loudly on the door: 'Police, police!' As one senior constable laughingly related, 'They would come running out, you should have seen the look on their faces! Falling all over each other to get out. They were shitting themselves. Geez, it was funny.'

One fresh July Saturday evening in 1968, Michael headed out to the dance at the Petersham Hall. There were only really three well-known gay venues in Sydney in the late 1960s: the Bottoms Up Bar at the Carlton Rex Hotel, originally in the city, but now moved to Kings Cross; Ivy's Birdcage nightclub in Bondi Junction, a winebar (and with the strict licensing laws in those days, that meant only wine); and the Petersham Dispensary Hall on Parramatta Road – a private function run once a month with a dance band. There were also a couple of drag clubs, including the Purple Onion, a BYO place on Anzac Parade in Kensington.

The Petersham Hall was a quaint, old-fashioned sort of arrangement. The music was a fifty-fifty mix of foxtrots and barn dances or jive and jitterbugging. The trestle tables were covered in white butchers' paper, and clientele would bring their own alcohol and food. There was a small cover charge. No one went solo; instead, there were organised line dances and if eyes met, then pairs would break off to dance alone. All sorts of men showed up: students, travellers, cross-dressing truck drivers and even barristers. On this particular night, Michael was attracted to a young and very fetching dark-eyed Spanish traveller, Demofilo Solera. Michael was instantly struck by Demo's deep brown eyes and his long, long eyelashes. At the end of a night of dancing close together, the two returned to Michael's Kirribilli flat. Michael gazed adoringly at his new-found companion, his first. Michael Kirby was somewhat amazed that this 24-year-old beauty was asleep in a warm alcoholic stupor in *his* bed. Perhaps Demo had had a little too much of Michael's Cinzano; Michael, as ever, was abstemious.

In the morning the two shared breakfast and Michael gave Demo his phone number. As his new friend left the apartment Michael watched the door close and wondered if he would ever see him again. But Demo did ring and as the days went by the two began what was to be a passionate love affair. All those dreams of years before, the James Dean imaginings, had come true and the reality of it was so much more powerful and intoxicating than the fantasy could ever have been. Finally Michael had found happiness and love, and he was determined to make the most of it.

But this was still a Sydney that was firmly in the closet as far as gay men were concerned. Because the stakes were so high, people went to enormous lengths to keep secrets. Once, at the Rex Hotel, Michael had even seen a judge across the room. This could have been difficult, but as it turned out they kept their distance and maintained the anonymity. (As with that last bastion of homophobia, the football world, what happens on the field stays on the field.)

It was no coincidence, then, that Michael took Demo out of town for their holidays. They travelled to New Zealand – the first real holiday Michael had taken since he was a child. 'Back in 1968 it was more a country town,' he says. 'A place to get away from books and courts and wigs. Just for a weekend, to be oneself.' Surely here they could enjoy each other's company as a heterosexual couple could do routinely. Michael and Demo simply felt like any two people in love, confident and happy, safe in each other's arms, just content to take pleasure in the moment. Unfortunately, even in the land of the long white cloud, Michael was not safe from prying eyes.

> It happened in a secluded restaurant. The world of law seemed far away. But, as it proved, not far enough. Into the restaurant came a group of colleagues – Sydney barristers. Wives and girlfriends on their arms. Little did they expect to see, sitting quietly in a corner, their rather pushy, ambitious colleague with a handsome young Spaniard. Today, most people in such

> a situation couldn't care less. But in the era of 'Don't ask, don't tell' I could have fallen through the floor. Everyone insisted on introductions. Nothing unpleasant. But on return to Sydney, the halls of gossip were not only filled with the tale of Mr Brown Eyes, but also the white trousers – code language for the gays. Well and truly sprung. The Spaniard had come to Australia to escape his conservative parents who never wanted to hear about his real life. Today, forty years later, we exchange thoughts about gay marriage [now legal] in Spain. Who ever would have thought that religious Spain would overtake Australia in so short a time?

It was not the first nor the last time that gossip was circulated about Michael's sexuality. But the 'Don't ask, don't tell' rule meant that as long as he continued to be discreet, people might whisper behind his back and if he was lucky they would do no more. Michael's first love affair lasted only six months. At twenty-four, Demo wasn't looking for a long-term relationship and he announced that he intended to continue his travels and he would be moving on to Melbourne. Michael was devastated and pleaded with him to stay but it was no good. Demo had made up his mind.

After moving out of Sydney Street, Michael had made the active decision to find love, and during this time he had also, rather reluctantly, put a distance between himself and his family in case there might be some awkward questions. He thought he had kept his relationship with Demo entirely private, but his father had somehow put two and two together, as only parents can, and rang Michael to ask those awkward questions. Some things, it seems, are easier to write down than to say. On 23 December 1968 Michael wrote to his father:

I find it pretty hard to say face to face but I am very grateful that you had the courage to phone me. I knew before you phoned of your tolerance and generosity to me. It is a constant standard for me to live up to. In many ways I am like you. I sometimes do or say a certain thing and I know what you would have done. Like you I am, I fear, gentle and a bit too sensitive. I want desperately to love and be loved. Unfortunately this seems to be eluding me. But at this point I remind myself that I must not fall back into the usual trap of feeling sorry for myself. How easy that would be in my predicament. I try to remain optimistic.

I hope you understand why I have cut myself off somewhat from the rest of the family. How I wish it did not have to be so.

About a month later Michael received a reply from his father.

I'm glad you're fully aware of the family failing i.e. self-pity – that's good. But you've overlooked as usual an even more dangerous trait – being an ostrich. That's bad.

Being born with brains and ability is a mixed blessing as you've found out by now. Its price is greater responsibilities and heavier burdens and of course as with everyone, but especially with you, there are those around you who will do harm if they can. Therefore, Michael, I am coming straight to the point because you are my son and it's my duty to do so. I'm telling you bluntly to watch your reputation and do NOT commit professional and social Hari Kari. You won't get way with it. It soon gets around and you become a figure of ridicule and those unworthy of your friendship will snigger behind your back. This is the truth.

This is a rather ungenerous letter for such a generous person as you are to get, but I've been wanting to talk to you for some time now.

This is confidential and further post-mortems are unnecessary unless you ever wish it.

Always, your friend,

Dad.

Don Kirby had included in the letter a torn-out page from a daily calendar with a quote at the bottom: *'Associate yourself with men of good quality if you esteem your own reputation; for 'tis better to be alone than in bad company.' George Washington*. Like so many people at the time, Michael's father understood that some men had 'unnatural' urges, but he believed that they had a choice not to give into them. He hoped and prayed that his son would eventually be 'cured'.

Michael was not shocked or even surprised by his father's view. It was all too common. He was not going to be deterred by it. The course Michael had set for himself now was not to seek a cure, but instead to carefully, gradually change his father's attitude. He wasn't totally convinced it was going to be possible, and that worried him, but perhaps, with luck, one day it would happen. In the meantime it would be a process of mitigation.

Michael knew that the love that he had felt so strongly for Demo and the love that was returned to him was nourishing and good. It did not matter how fleeting it was, he would never turn back from that now. But in January 1969 he farewelled the young Spaniard at Sydney's Central Station. Demo climbed aboard the *Spirit of Progress*, heading to more adventures in Melbourne. He stood in the open doorway of the train carriage as it heaved out of the station, slowly disappearing into the haze. Michael burst into tears. They would probably never see each other again; his first and only lover had gone.

David Kirby had only spent a short time living in his brother's flat and had now found his own apartment with his girlfriend. He had never met Demo and was shocked when he saw Michael in his chambers that January. 'He said to me, "I've just finished an affair of the heart."' Michael didn't want to go any further into his sadness – he didn't explain to his brother that he had fallen in love with a man. David was close to Michael but he had no idea that Michael had been seeing Demo, nor really anything about Michael's love-life. He was entirely unaware of the correspondence that had been exchanged between Michael and his father.

> I immediately wondered whether it was a woman. The question certainly had by that stage arisen in my own mind as to whether it could be a man because he was still single, even though he was about twenty-eight, and hadn't pursued what the rest of us were pursuing with great vigour. But he didn't let on, and I think my instinctive reaction was that it was a woman. There is a difference between knowing and *knowing*. It's a huge difference. You can know almost to the point of certainty, but still wonder whether you've got it right, whether you're drawing the right inference.
>
> I can't actually remember precisely where I was or when it was, but I do remember the moment of knowing, in the sense of 'knowing' – and that that was a jolt. Only fleeting, because

> he was no different, and he remained no different. But a recognition in an instant, which every parent must have in the same instant, that we'll never know what Michael's children are like, and so on. So that that's closed off and this is the new reality. It's not hard to adjust to, and you adjust to it in micro-seconds, but there is an adjustment.

So much had changed in Michael's life. In some ways he felt more alone than he ever had before. There was a distance now between him and his family that he had never imagined was possible. He was alone in the Clifton apartment and he had lost his first and only love. He was heartbroken and there was not even a shoulder he could cry on. Where once he would have talked the whole thing through with David and then probably the rest of the family as well, this time he could only bring himself to reveal the sketchiest of details to his brother; it was far too painful to do anything more. Only a few days had passed since Demo had left him and each hour had been agonising. He wondered how he was going to get through it. Somehow he managed to get through his daily work in court.

Then Michael Kirby remembered the sage words of his father: to avoid at all costs the 'family failing' of self-pity. This thought lifted him out of his depression and shook him into action. Michael went to his bedroom and began dressing to go out.

5

The Right Place at the Right Time

> I had gone to what I had by then discovered was one of the two or three gay bars in Sydney. This was before I was appointed a judge, because judges in those days, and possibly still today, were not expected to go to bars. Bars were where common people went. Judges would go to clubs where the wealthy and the big end of town would go. In common people you might meet a few criminals (of course, now we know in clubs you sometimes meet a few criminals as well). However, I went to the bar and there was this very handsome young man.
>
> *Michael Kirby*

Michael headed, once more, to the bar of the Rex Hotel. This time he was alone, staring through the smoky haze into an untouched glass of beer. It was a Tuesday night, 11 February 1969. The regulars were drinking schooners. They mostly seemed ancient to Michael, probably in their forties. The music, as usual, wasn't particularly to his taste, pop belting out – top-forty selections, The Beatles, The Delphonics – and, as it got nearer to closing time, slower tracks like Herb Alpert's 'This Guy's in Love with You'. There was every chance that it would all end in predictably maudlin fashion and Michael would mooch off once more to Kirribilli alone.

But that night was going to be different. As Michael surveyed the room once more he realised there *was* a good-looking young man at the bar, drinking by himself. Michael summoned up his courage and moved next to him. He was in his twenties, and Michael had never seen him in the Rex before. He was every bit as handsome as Demo but in a different way. Dark hair with a pale complexion, and when he turned to look at Michael it was with the most beautiful blue eyes. He spoke excellent English with a European accent. 'I thought he was a German,' Michael says, 'and I'd learnt German at school, so I thought that I would ask him what he thought about von Ribbentrop.' To Michael this seemed a perfectly sensible approach; if he were German he might very well be interested in von Ribbentrop – after all, several recent scholarly books had raised fascinating questions about the fascist diplomat's role in Hitler's regime. On the other hand, Michael had not quite thought through the ramifications if his new acquaintance was not German.

The young man was Johan van Vloten, a Dutchman, who had migrated to Australia in the middle of 1963 for the warmer climate. Johan recalls: 'I left Amsterdam in the midst of their summer at 15 degrees, arrived here in the winter – a few degrees warmer, so I thought that part is all right.' He had been a merchant seaman and, having retired from the service, he could not settle down back in the Netherlands. It was the dreary weather, cold, wet and claustrophobic, but it was also Dutch society that he could no longer tolerate. 'I found the Netherlands repressive at the time because I left in '63 and nothing had happened in my town since 1619. So it was not just the climate but also the feeling of isolation.'

His first night in Sydney as a new Australian was a little confronting. Stepping off a KLM flight from Amsterdam, he was faced with directions from the Australian Department of Immigration to proceed to a bus, which would take the assisted-passage migrants to a camp in Wollongong, and from there by train to Bonegilla. Eighteen kilometres from Albury, Bonegilla was really an isolated military barracks, which had first taken refugees after World War II and now took European immigrants. A couple of years before, during the 1961 economic downturn, there had been riots at Bonegilla, as migrants vented their rage at being left to languish for long periods while waiting for jobs or homes that never eventuated. Johan simply picked up his suitcase and walked in the opposite direction, to a taxi rank and a quick ride to the centre of Sydney. The Australia he found himself in was a very different place from the sophisticated European cities he knew.

> It was a little bit backward, or different, especially the first night. It hit me because I went into the city. I stayed in the YMCA the first night and it was a very quiet town – Sydney after 8 p.m. In those days you could shoot in any direction and hit no one and I thought, 'Gee, this is not a fun town. What's happening here?' But then I started to get more understanding that it was towards the suburbs you had to go to find life and people.

Johan had found a job and somewhere to live pretty quickly, and organised for his parents to join him from the Netherlands. At the age of twenty-nine, just one month younger than Michael, he too had led a quite monastic existence up to this point. He was not a partygoer like Demo. He preferred books, and his trip out to Kings Cross that night was unusual for him.

Michael had arrived at the Bottoms Up Bar at the Rex Hotel dressed in an outfit that he thought appropriate, neat but casual: a pair of trousers and a pullover in bright contrasting colours. When Johan was confronted with this walking inconcinnity asking questions about the Nazi foreign minister, in German, he was startled.

> He was dressed in a very odd combination of clothes. It was February and it was hot, and he wore an orange jumper, a very heavy type, and yellow corduroy trousers. The colours appealed to me because they were like the House of Orange, which we only wear on the Queen's Birthday in the Netherlands. But his voice was interesting. Well, the first question was a bit odd. First he said, 'Who do you like in this motley crew?' and I didn't quite know the word 'motley' but I knew 'crew' and haughtily said, 'No one in particular.' And so then he heard my accent and the next question was, 'What do you think of von Ribbentrop?', which confirmed my first impression, after the clothes, that this was a mad guy – my luck.
>
> But after I gave the answers, the next question was more interesting and from that moment on we clicked. It was ten o'clock, closing time, and so we went for a cup of coffee. The coffee shop, which I had spotted a few years earlier, didn't exist

> any longer, and so he suggested we have it at his place, across the harbour in Kirribilli. And from that moment it was a connection relationship – without the coffee.

Johan van Vloten and Michael Kirby formed an immediate and lasting bond. A thinker and widely read, Johan understood Michael, and with a very funny, deadpan sense of humour, in many ways he also complemented him. Michael's tendency was to be less concerned about the practicalities of life. He couldn't drive, didn't worry much about clothes, wasn't at all concerned about where he lived (had only just moved out of the family home, after all), and was nearly solely focused on work. Michael was almost over-educated with arts, law and now economics degrees, while Johan had left school at fifteen. Michael was the supreme diplomat; Johan was straightforward in manner and action. He was organised and opinionated about all things, particularly how and where he lived.

Johan loved Michael's brand-new apartment with its views across the harbour to Jørn Utzon's Opera House, certainly more salubrious than the single room at his father's city office where he currently lodged. The following day Johan moved into the Kirribilli flat. Michael was delighted. 'He took one look at the apartment and out the window and thought, "This is a person with a future bank balance",' Michael joked.

> And so from that moment on, we've been together. Strange, isn't it? Just a matter of luck, but most heterosexual, bisexual people tell similar stories – it's just being in a place and your life changes instantly. What if I had had a long case that day?

> What if I'd been too tired? What if I had been working back? What if I had not gone? My life would have been so different. I'm really a very lucky person.

All relationships are tested, especially in the early stages, and when Demo phoned a few weeks later, Michael was conflicted. His first love was an important part of his life and he did not want to lose him. He felt he had to see the Spaniard again. Johan was not happy when Michael decided he would go to Melbourne and spend the weekend with Demo, but he also would never stand in his way. Michael went south and saw Demo and afterwards they stayed in touch, exchanging postcards. In the end the lure of music and dancing, cruising the gay scene with the beautiful Demo Solera was not enough to satisfy Michael – he needed something more. The two parted as friends, but it was to be Johan that Michael remained with. Demo was a little hurt that Michael had found Johan so quickly. 'Just two weeks of mourning,' he said later. 'It's not enough!'

Michael's father, Don, was surprised to see his son appear with a young, lithe, dark-haired man at the family home in Concord. Michael introduced his companion to his parents: 'This is Johan.'

> Well, he brought him home one Saturday afternoon. I remember him walking in, and we didn't know, at the time, the relationship. We thought they were friends, you know, mates, or whatever they call them. And anyway, we accepted him – he was very nice, very Dutch, and very courteous, one of those people that dot their i's, and very polite. Jean got on very well with him, and I did too, we both liked him. And eventually

> they lived together and we thought, 'Oh well, that's all right, I suppose, that can happen.'

Michael hadn't discussed his sexuality with any of the family besides his father but they all obviously had their suspicions. Although Johan never felt uncomfortable with the Kirbys, he got on better with Michael's mother Jean than with Don Kirby.

> There were some reservations on Michael's father's side, but never on the mother's side, and the brothers and the sister – definitely not. They liked me straightaway. We never lied about it or tried to avoid it. In a very short time I was introduced to his parents. Let's say within two or three weeks. I told my parents straightaway that I think I've met somebody that I'd like to share my life with, or a part of it anyway, and they took it. They suspected, like any parent would suspect that already. His parents put him out at the age of twenty-nine, so . . .

At twenty-eight Michael's parents had told him he had to go. He took his time, and a year later was in the flat at Kirribilli. There had never been any girlfriends, and only rarely would a girl accompany him to a university function. Indeed at any particular time, to David's lasting chagrin, there was no shortage of women interested in Michael – he just showed absolutely no interest in them. All these things put together certainly set his parents to thinking and had eventually led to Michael and Don Kirby's correspondence in late 1968. Jean had been unaware of their discussions, but when Johan arrived on the scene it was the final piece in the puzzle. Jean and

Don never discussed their son's sexuality with each other. Don then kept on thinking that only he knew what was going on and that sooner or later, he hoped, Michael would see the error of his ways.

Michael and Johan had been together for less than a year when Don Kirby, unable to contain himself any longer, decided he had to press Michael on their relationship. The two young men had been travelling overseas together in a VW kombi van and, as Michael's friend Geoffrey Robertson observed 'from his sleeping arrangements' in the kombi, Don already knew he and Johan were more than just good friends. Don wrote to Michael in Kuala Lumpur when they had been gone less than a month. He had previously made it clear that he felt Michael was risking all in his affair with Demo; things now appeared to be going one step further, into a serious, long-term commitment, and Don could not accept it. The letter shook Michael and he initially didn't know what to do.

Michael never had the slightest doubt that his mother, Jean, would always be there for him no matter what. According to Don, she was apparently blissfully unaware of his sexuality, but either way she would never turn against him, Michael was certain of that. Don Kirby was an entirely different proposition. He had been deeply wounded by his own father's desertion of his mother and of Don himself. Don never forgave his father and went to the extreme of cutting him off completely. From the late 1930s until his father's death in 1989, Don never spoke to him or of him again and the entire family were expected to do the same. Michael was very concerned about how Don would respond now to the news that he and Johan were more than just a passing phase. Don believed that homosexuality was a condition that could be cured and that should not simply be accepted, and Michael didn't want that to affect their close relationship.

Eventually Don received a reply, addressed to him at his place of work, BP House in Milsons Point. In this way they both believed the ongoing correspondence between the two would be kept entirely secret from Jean.

> They went overseas and he wrote me a letter and gave all the details. And of course I never said anything to Jean about receiving it, which I should have, I know now. It was a great shock. I just thought, oh, maybe if he has an operation? You know, in those days you thought something happened and you could get it fixed. But as time went on I realised, no, it's just how you're born, and accepted it. But I never said anything to Jean about that letter, and it did upset me. And in my lunch hour I used to go up to St Thomas' Church at North Sydney, and just kind of try to get comfort, and pray, and all that. And I was quite disturbed about it, for both of them, because I liked them both. But particularly for Michael.

Nearly two months went by and Michael did not receive any response from his father. He was becoming distressed at this gulf of silence. In late March 1970 he wrote again, from Udhampur, India, to the BP House address.

28.3.1970
Dearest Dad,
I have wanted to write to you since receiving Mum's letter in Delhi but

somehow I find writing painful. I have received no letter from you at all since the one I got in Kuala Lumpur. To this I wrote a very long letter in Thailand. But I don't know whether you received it. I suppose you did.

I have mixed feelings as to whether I want you to have got it. On the one hand, I would want you to know what I wrote there. On the other hand I am sorry now to have written such a solid tome [. . .] In a way I can see that I was responding like a pent-up coil to the letter I got in Kuala Lumpur: so full, I thought, of harsh and ill-considered contempt and distaste for me. In other words, I was thinking mainly of my own reaction and not yours in reading such a solid piece. But if this was selfishness in one way it was also a desire that you should know and love me as I am, as Cromwell said, 'warts and all'.

Freed of the necessity of rushing off to exams, meetings or court, I have had time lately to indulge in memory. They say that in old age people remember vividly their childhood. But I think this is only because it is in old age that you get the time to indulge the memory.

I have remembered you working in the shed; mowing the lawn without your singlet (how sensible I can now see this outrageous behaviour to have been!); typing in the lounge room (I remember complaining I couldn't sleep and properly being shut up for the selfish brat I was); presiding at Christmas dinners; reading us Grimms' fairytales; searching for us through the house (with me unimaginatively hiding always in the same spot on top of the old wardrobe in the bedroom); cooking for us when Mum was in hospital (you claimed to be a 'tasty cook': a claim I now make); I remember you and Mum sitting up in bed listening to the tale of my leaving certificate results: and the many repetitions of that event by which I tried to make you and Mum appreciate me: whilst all the while living a separate, lonely life: unfulfilled and frustrated of happiness. But this is my lot and whilst

I imagine I must accept it, it makes me discontented and hurts me that by being me, I hurt you. I do wish it were otherwise.

You must put pen to paper. Tell me how you feel now. You looked unwell during most of 1969 and I would hate to feel that I caused this. Tell me how [Michael's grandmother] Normie is now. I am lucky that my old age (like all my previous ages) has come on me prematurely. I am able by reason of time and distance to think of you and Mum and also Normie. I think of you constantly and appreciate and am grateful for all you've done for me. What a wonderful, happy childhood we had. It is a fund of warming memories.

Love, Michael

But Don still did not reply to Michael's letter. Instead, in July 1970, a letter from Jean arrived.

Dearest Michael,

I love you, I love you, I love you!!! No, I haven't gone mad, I just read your letter to Dad and we have just been sitting here quite silent, going over in our minds our memories of you as a little boy, as a baby, as a schoolboy as a uni student, as a man. Dear Michael, we love you, we miss you terribly.

Michael was not shocked or surprised by this letter from his mother. She was an emotional and spontaneous person and frequently responded like this in letters, especially while he was travelling so far away from home. It was not an indication that she had seen Michael's secret correspondence to his father (even though unbeknown to Don and Michael, that is exactly what had happened); he assumed she was referring to one of his other letters. Michael continued to wait and hope for a letter from Don. There had never before been a period in Michael's life when he had not seen or spoken to his father for so long. It was another three months before Don Kirby finally wrote to his son.

8/10/70

My Dearest Michael,

Well Maffekin has been relieved and reinforcements are rushing in with the necessary to help you along a few more miles of your shoestring tour de force.

At long last the Commissioner for Taxation has decided to send me my tax rebate which I am forwarding onto you with my compliments in the hope it will take you to some magnificent part of the British Isles.

I'm sorry you misunderstood my letters and saw them as a refusal to appreciate your problem. I know now that anything I say or have said in the past, present or future will always seem platitudinous and unrealistic because in my inadequate way I'll be out of my depth in finding the right words to express myself as I feel. But I do understand, Michael, and would like you to discuss your life with Donald and David who would also understand and no doubt be better equipped logically to help you than I.

I'm aware that I have no right to ask but I beg you now that you are in London to see someone professionally qualified to advise you a course of action. I will never believe that it's incurable. Yes I know it's easy for me to talk but if you want a change badly enough treatment will bring it about.

[. . .]

Always,

Dad

The words that he had been waiting for had finally arrived: 'I do understand, Michael.' Those four words were enough. The rest of it, the attitudes expressed, were no more than he expected. They were the prevailing attitudes of the time among people of his father's generation. As to his suggestion that Michael seek treatment, that was never going to happen. Since he had first compiled the twenty pages of notes on homosexuality in the mid 1960s, and underlined the police's stated rate of success in treating gay offenders – 90 per cent – Michael had read more widely. He had seen the mischief that medical, psychiatric, electric-shock and chemical intervention caused. He knew treatment never worked and it certainly was not an option in his case. He would eventually tell his father as much.

Michael had finally made it clear to his father that Johan was a fixture in his life. No matter what Don said or did, Michael was not going to suddenly stop being gay and Johan was not suddenly going to disappear. At that time he was in London, staying with his brothers David and Donald, and through tears he revealed all to them and, in another letter, to his sister Diana. The relief was enormous. It was a cathartic experience for Michael to have at last confronted and accepted his own sexuality. It was the most highly charged and emotional moment of his life. At last he could dispense with the burden of secrecy, at least as far as his immediate family were concerned, and the misplaced guilt that he had been living with. His siblings were supportive and loving, as they always had been. By the beginning of the 1970s, homosexuality was accepted by much of the younger generation of Australians and it was now decriminalised in the UK and other parts of Europe. They loved Michael for who he was and his sexuality was a part of that and couldn't be separated. His father too would now tolerate the situation, if not yet fully accept it.

Once Johan had moved into the Kirribilli flat – and that happened straight after their first meeting – Michael's life started to move in directions he had never imagined were possible. Johan began to change Michael and Michael changed Johan, and together they were different people. For the first time in each of their lives, they were totally happy and totally relaxed about who they were and the possibilities that life held for them. They were in love. Everything was transformed, from the smallest of details – the two men had to shift the two single beds in the apartment together every evening and then apart in the morning so that the housekeeper did not suspect anything untoward – through to the biggest of decisions about their lives together: would they remain in Australia? Perhaps like so many other high achievers of his generation Michael should bite the bullet and leave Australia with Johan for the real world of London, Geneva or The Hague. Robert Hughes, Clive James and Germaine Greer had all made that choice and Geoffrey Robertson would soon follow.

There were parts of Michael's life that he had already decided to leave behind. He knew that his days as the consummate student politician were past, but he had found it hard to cut the remaining ties. Johan, with his trademark frankness, told Michael what he thought of a man, now thirty years old, a barrister, still chairing meetings of disputatious teenage students. He was in danger of looking faintly ridiculous.

So in September 1969, Michael Kirby, a little reluctantly, ended his student life once and for all. He saw out the last year of his post as university senator, and handed his seat over to the new generation of student representatives, epitomised by people like Jim Spigelman and Geoffrey Robertson. The students were truly sad to see him go – he had been a loved fixture at the SRC and the union for most of the decade. He had been taken for granted for so long and now that he was really going, many couldn't accept it. If there had been a particularly difficult dispute, Michael had always been there to resolve it. If students faced legal charges, Michael would represent them; if the SRC wanted to fund a political campaign, Michael would advise on its constitutionality. It is the nature of student affairs, of course, that students come and go. Michael started late and just took a bit longer than most to go.

There was a vigorous send-off from the University Senate and his swansong was to attend a women's dinner held in his honour. A few present were tearful, and whether the women knew he was 'unavailable' or not, they all knew that he was about to leave the university for good. One or two felt betrayed years later when they found out that Michael Kirby was indeed gay.

Michael began to feel entirely secure in his relationship with Johan and, quite unexpectedly, surprising even himself, he suddenly let go of other aspects of his life that up until that moment had seemed locked in place. His move to the Bar had been a professional and financial triumph but it had demanded a life that continued to be solely focused on work: 'Before long the table in my chambers was groaning with briefs. The weekends of work became longer.'

David Kirby saw Michael close-up in action as a barrister in those years and although he never ceased to be amazed by his brother's work ethic, he also saw that Michael was not entirely happy. 'His first years or first year and a bit, maybe, he did a lot of workers' compensation and some common law jury work. And he became somewhat dissatisfied with that, even though he was making a fair bit of money.'

With Demo, Michael had tested his theory that there was more to life than just work, and with Johan he found the confidence to put that theory into practice. In May 1969 the two went along to the Sydney performance of *Hair*, the musical, with a young Marcia Hines in the lead. Together they occasionally revisited the Bottoms Up Bar in Kings Cross 'for old times' sake' and frequently took in the drag show at the Purple Onion Cabaret in Kensington. On one night there they danced with the doyen of ballet, theatre and the silver screen, Sir Robert Helpmann. In June they holidayed together in Fiji during the mid-year law break. Michael had never before spent quite so much time involved in extracurricular activity. It was as if he intended, all in one go, to make up for everything that he had missed out on during the years of celibacy and a dour Protestant workaholic existence. By the end of the year, with the encouragement of Johan, Michael had made the biggest personal decision of his life, and it had nothing to do with work. With Johan by his side, Michael Kirby was to begin an adventure like none other he had ever experienced.

6

An Experiment in Leisure

It was a surprise that he did take time off, but this was a time in his life when he was beginning to embrace the fact that he would pursue a relationship and love. And once he opened himself up to that, then he opened himself up to other things, including leisure. Now, he didn't readily take to leisure – he managed to work seven days a week. But he did *experiment* with leisure, and he did so in the unusual way of going for holidays for a year. But even when he did that, he packed the kombi van with a library full of books, and researched everything before he arrived anywhere. And so it was an educational journey, as his life has been a educational journey.

David Kirby

Michael and Johan sat side by side in the car as it remained motionless on the side of the Bruce Highway. Michael was in the driver's seat, his hands gripping the wheel, his knuckles white, a small bead of perspiration running down his temple. Johan took a deep breath, climbed out of the car and hurried round to the front and then the rear. He removed the two L-plates and then climbed in the driver's side as Michael scrambled across to the passenger seat. As the car had been heading up the highway on their trip to Noosa, a large truck had approached from the opposite direction. As the heavy vehicle got closer, Michael, behind the wheel, had closed his eyes. That's all – simply closed his eyes. The car slowly veered to the right and Johan was forced to take hold of the steering wheel and bring it back on course. They both agreed that perhaps it was not such a good idea to try to teach Michael to drive. Johan was a fine driver, Michael could navigate.

Johan had travelled extensively as a young merchant seaman to ports in Canada, the United States and even China. When he joined the service he was still a boy, not much more than fifteen years old, and it was the adventure of the foreign lands and exotic peoples that had excited his imagination. He had never lost that adventurous spirit. In 1968 the London *Daily Express* and Sir Frank Packer's Sydney *Daily Telegraph* sponsored the London–Sydney Marathon, an automobile rally with a rich prize of more $21 000. Seventy-two cars entered the competition and raced the specially designed course of more than 11 000 kilometres across eleven countries in less than two weeks. In a dramatic end to the race the French team in a Citroën, the leaders by an unbeatable margin, suffered a tragic head-on collision with two drunk locals in a Mini Minor less than 250 kilometres from Sydney. In the end the race was won by a Hillman Hunter with an Austin 1800 in second place and the

Australian team, in a Ford Falcon, coming in third. The race was covered extensively in the Australian media.

Johan, along with many other Australians, was excited by the possibilities opened up by the race. The fact that three cars common throughout the suburbs of Sydney like a Hillman, an Austin and a Ford could travel such long distances under such arduous conditions and survive the trip was inspiring. It had also demonstrated that there was an overland route that conventional vehicles could traverse through Central Asia to Bombay. Many young Australians were already shipping kombi vans to Asia or Europe to do the 'hippy' trek. Johan decided this was something he could do and wanted to do: the overland route of the car rally, but in reverse – Singapore to Europe.

Initially, Michael was sceptical. He had no doubt Johan was right about the practicality of such a trip – indeed, if anyone could do such a thing it would be Johan. But his reservations were about the obvious issues. What would he do about his legal practice? It was only a couple of years since he had gone to the Bar and perhaps the whole career would evaporate if he left it now. Then there was his flat . . . But the more he thought about the idea of the trip, the more it took hold in his imagination. Looking back, Michael remembers it as all Johan's initiative:

> He wanted it, he's an adventurer and I thought, 'I'm not sure this is a good career move', but then I thought, 'Well why not?' Everyone around me at the Bar said this is the end of civilisation, you will never get your practice back, you're so busy, stay here, keep working, slave away, never have any fun. But

> don't forget, during my twenties I'd really not had a lot of fun, so this seemed to be a perfect idea.

Some important things in Michael's life seemed to all coalesce at the same time. He had become a little bored with his practice – of course he was working as hard as ever and was totally committed to his work, but it was not giving back to him the feeling of achievement and reward that he had found with his long years of student politics. Forming a close bond with Johan allowed him for the first time to look back on the past decade of his life and accept that he had been running away from the things that most people take for granted: love, domesticity and even leisure. David Kirby, who knew Michael better, perhaps, than anybody else, realised that his personality demanded that he dive headlong into any venture that he undertook. There was no holding back for Michael. If it was worth doing, then it was worth doing fully, methodically and all-encompassingly.

> He was just a machine. And the amazing thing is, when he was a barrister, he would do cases in the order in which the briefs came in. Some would be fat, some would be thin, some would be easy, some would be hard. He would do them one by one, no matter what was involved. He would sit there and do it until it was finished. And it may take him twenty-four hours or it may take him fifteen minutes. Normal people, such as me, would get briefs, and then think, 'Well, I'll do a few warm-up briefs' and so I'd shuffle them. I'd get the easy ones that I could knock over without too much effort, and I'd do

> those. And more often than not, you'd run out of steam by the end of that. And the hard ones get postponed. But he didn't do that. He just used to do one case after another. Didn't care how long it took.

Once he had been convinced by Johan that the trip was a good idea, Michael threw himself into it as if it was another brief. This wouldn't be a few months' distraction, it was going to be a very significant logistic exercise and an open-ended odyssey. He would do the countries one by one as they came.

They bought a white VW kombi in Sydney, a fully equipped Caravanette Mark IV, and shipped it to Singapore. Just after Christmas 1969 they flew to Singapore and set off. Johan had seen to it that the van was stocked with all the practical requirements for such an expedition – spare fan belts, radiator hoses, provision for extra water, petrol and oil, tools and even snow chains, which would be essential later. Michael packed a library. 'It was a bit of an adventure and a bit of a worry,' Johan recalls, 'because I was the only one who had a driver's licence and the only one with a practical sense – he was theoretical, and so there was a little bit of pressure on me. But if we were in a tight spot, I relied on his gifted mouth to get us out of it, which he did.'

With the aid of his library in the back of the van, and before they arrived at any particular location, Michael would make sure he was already an authority on the history and customs of the locals. Johan enjoyed reading the history just as much as Michael. 'The combination of reading history at the very location where it happened was always appealing to us. Whether it's First and Second

World War battles or the beginning of the Raj and the whole episode of the Raj, reading it at the location was very interesting.' This preparation was to prove of important practical assistance on more than one occasion.

From Singapore, the two men drove as far north as Bangkok. They saw the beauty of the untouched beaches in Thailand. For the first time in each of their lives they had a total freedom about where and when they would go and what they might do. It was all entirely a decision for Johan and Michael to make at their leisure. The local industry in places like Phuket and Krabi was still mainly connected to the rubber plantations. Beaches were, by and large, deserted of western tourists, but it would not remain that way for long. In some places, groups of holidaying US servicemen reminded them of the war only a few hundred kilometres away in Cambodia and Vietnam. In good time they drove back down to Singapore and then shipped the van again, this time to India.

With a population in 1970 of 555 million people, India was an endless source of stimulation. Just the sheer mass of people confronting Michael and Johan on arrival at Madras was awe-inspiring. Vibrant colours, constant noise and extraordinary smells were everywhere. In the Koyambedu Market, hordes of shoppers pushed past the stalls of fruit and vegetables, the perfumed spices and the other more pungent smells. Men in blue and white and orange shirts and dhotis touted for business. Michael and Johan were enthralled by it all. They came to love India and they could not see enough of it. 'We spent about five months looking at every nook and cranny,' Michael recalls.

On 22 January 1970 Michael wrote a long letter to his parents and grandmother Normie. In his meticulous way he had planned out the entire trip. He enclosed the 'approximate itinerary' – an exhaustive list of about twenty-five locations to be covered over the next two and a half months, starting in Mysore, India, and ending up in Herat, Afghanistan.

Michael and Johan then pointed the kombi in the direction of Europe and whizzed through Afghanistan to Iran, stopping at the southern tip of the Caspian Sea before continuing through Syria, Lebanon and Turkey. By the middle of June they were in Bulgaria and, before long, lazing on the beaches of the French Riviera.

Christmas 1970 was spent apart from Johan. Michael, David and Donald were ensconced in Donald's house at 10 Roupell Street, London. Johan was in the Netherlands with his brother Fritz. It was cold and Michael was rather distressed by a toothache he couldn't shake, but the beautiful cover of snow across the whole city made up for it. He wrote to his parents and Normie.

I sent Johan the card you sent him here. He's now in Dordrecht and writes that 'your lovely parents sent me some money'. How thoughtful you are. You couldn't have given me a nicer present than to send something to him. Donald and I agreed that this was typical of your thoughtfulness. Johan has been a wonderful and can I say loving friend to me. He is absolutely without a mean or cunning thought in him. Being a slightly watered down version of David, I was very often difficult company in the small confines of that kombi as we meandered over Asia, but he was commonsense, practical and like you thoughtful. He reminds me every time of Dad. He is one of nature's real gentlemen. Would that I were so good. But I think that I learnt some things from him. He always spoke with gratitude of your welcome to him on Normie's birthday night and he never ceased to remind me of the luck I had in having parents who pressed me into education. His parents in wartime Holland were split by the war – his father in a concentration-type labour camp in France and his mother walking miles and miles for food for her children – but having survived the war they were washed out and never really encouraged his education. Although I think he would probably do better in Holland which is crying out for people, I have urged him to come back to Australia. And if he does I will have to try to get him a good job because he's bright and needs a bit of a help from me – just as I needed help from you. It's the least I can do. I have never had (outside my family) a more selfless friend.

It was a long and detailed letter running to eight pages and there was even a sketch of his swollen face with tears running down his cheek. On the very same day, Johan wrote to Michael's parents from Dordrecht.

Speak about hot conditions, how do I miss Australia now. The cold icy wind keeps my skin cracking and flaking by every step I do so I fear, quite literally, of falling apart. I consider to return to Australia within the next month or so. I don't know what Michael is intend to do but as he has shown so far more adjusting ability (the filth in India, etc.) than me, I'll be not surprised at the news that he is staying back in England.

As I gather from him he has been having a wonderful time with his brothers, with lots of reading and theatre-hopping and so, although out of his latest letter I gather he is suffering from a slight discomfort in the form of a toothache. But no doubt, knowing his mentality about these things, he has told you all about it himself sparing no gruesome detail, I guess.

But I should not contradict the general view of the Kirbys, that the Dutch have no sense of humour, with a humour at the expense of others. That wouldn't be good either.

Michael and Johan returned to Sydney at the beginning of 1971, after an amazing adventure that had lasted more than a year.

> Anyone who can live for a year in a kombi van with another human being can live a lifetime with them. And not only did we do that, but we loved it, and we read a whole range of books. We decided to do it again – and we did it again, in 1973. Probably if I had not been appointed a judge, that's what I would have done with my life – I would have gone on being a barrister for a time and then gone off and done these overseas trips. Which were a kind of epiphany or self-exploration.

In June 1973 they embarked on a second trip. They flew from Sydney to Germany, bought another kombi and began an extensive tour of Europe, which finished back at Donald's house in London. That was only the first leg; the two then set out to repeat the trip they had done in 1970 but in reverse. From London to Ceylon and back again.

They had now passed through Afghanistan three times and there had been several confrontations with the tribesmen, each of which had the potential to have gone terribly wrong. Johan was for all intents and purposes the leader of their expedition and so it was he who was often at the pointy end of these cultural misunderstandings. He never forgot the desolation between Kabul and Kandahar: 'Like a moon landscape, and all the people you saw had guns. So it would have been so easy to shoot, and there was no one there to question it. That gave you a bit of a feeling of fear but the landscape made up for it. It was so beautiful.'

Even in this desolate place Johan would stand up firmly for his rights. It was an admirable quality, but when the dispute happens to be with a number of heavily armed Afghan tribesmen who certainly do not understand English, things could end badly. Michael was more inclined to caution. The differing temperaments of the two men sometimes led to quarrels.

> At one stage we had had a disagreement and we didn't talk from Kandahar to Herat – which is an awful long way. But in the end I caved in, as I always have, and said I was sorry, even though I didn't quite know what I was sorry about. I think that's the reason why we've always stuck together – because I've always been willing to say I was sorry. Because generally I was in the wrong. Because I was very focused and preoccupied and slightly selfish and career-oriented.

Michael's honed diplomatic skills were required on several occasions where Johan simply expected the Afghans to immediately comply with his, as he saw it, quite reasonable demands. Even with the language barrier there was something about Michael's reassuring, judicial tone of voice that calmed the most aggressive tribesman or border guard.

> The Afghans are a very proud but rather wild people and everyone seems to have a gun. Johan was very Dutch. With the

> second kombi, the new kombi, it was a beautiful green one. He was driving across Afghanistan, I think it was between Kandahar and Iraq – though we were talking on this trip. And a child standing on the side of the road threw a stone at it. Johan pulled the car to a stop and found the stone had caused a dent in his beautiful car. Being Dutch, this was just something he could not understand and over my protest he just ran into the village after this boy. I said, 'You come back! They'll kill you.' But anyway, when he got into the village, the elder asked by sign language what it was, and he pointed. So they thrashed the boy, probably killed the poor little wretch. Johan came back to the car, justice having been dispensed. It was a very unwise thing to do in a country like Afghanistan.

On another occasion the two young men were confronted by some rather belligerent Afghan officials, who were armed with pistols and machine guns. This time they were at a border crossing. Johan had handed over their travel documents to a clumsy officer and the ubiquitous cup of sweet, milky, Afghan tea was spilt on his Dutch passport.

> He's a very courageous person, Johan. He picked a fight with the Afghan border guard because the border guard was dropping tea over his Royal Dutch passport, which he had then. And that was an offence to the notion that a Royal Dutch passport had to be treated with respect and not slopped. So he started ranting and raving and I said, 'Keep quiet, we may never get out of here.' But anyway, he's like many Dutch people – like most

> of them I know, he's very in your face, he's very direct. What you see is what you get, and it's something my family has had to get used to over the years, and me, but it's been good for us.

The other tourists in the queue were quite concerned about Johan's behaviour. They told him to calm down, that the guards would throw him in jail. Johan didn't calm down; he was angry and indignant. More than thirty years later he still remembers it in detail:

> The passport was dragged through the tea on the table in front of the official and when I made an objection to that, he got very stroppy and grabbed for his gun. Most of the other tourists had been subject to his rather cruel behaviour and were waiting for hours on end. He got angry and some of the soldiers had to restrain him, and Michael had to talk to him. Ultimately he threw the passport back after a quick stamp and we were across the border in five minutes flat – which was good in that aspect but a bit stupid on my part. It could have resulted in a year or so seeing Kabul from a different angle.

There were quite a few occasions where Michael was required to step in and resolve situations that might otherwise have resulted in a minor diplomatic incident. Johan was thankful for his companion's calm and persuasive manner under pressure, particularly in the case of the swaggering border guard. 'He started talking – his voice has a kind of authority in it and even this man responded to that, mad as he was, in charge as he was. But he thought, "Now I'd better not go all the way." So he realised, he pulled back. I wasn't aware of the consequences of that action but in retrospect I realised it could have been a bit more serious.'

Afghanistan had all sorts of treats in store for the travellers. The geography was unique and dramatic, from flat, rocky, empty deserts to the craggiest, snow-covered peaks. The cities like Kabul and Kandahar were bustling and colourful and seemed locked in a kind of medieval past. Side by side with this ancient culture, the Soviet Union's greatest engineers had set to work in the Hindu Kush. It had been fewer than six years since the grand opening of one of the world's most spectacular man-made tunnels, the Salang Tunnel. At 3400 metres, it was, at the time of building, the highest road tunnel in the world, running for 2.6 kilometres. Michael has this trip etched in his memory:

> We wanted to see the great Buddhas of Bamiyan, which of course were subsequently blown up by the Taliban. They were then magnificently in place, and so to get there you had to go north of Kabul and down through the Salang Tunnel, down into the Swat Valley and then up to Bamiyan. In the Salang Tunnel, which is huge, and very, very high, we nearly ran off the road – which would have been curtains for us. But in fact, by dint of a bit of luck and good driving, that didn't happen. Then we got down into the valley, but the road to Bamiyan was unpaved and Johan wouldn't take it because the tyres on the van were not suitable, so I never saw the Bamiyan Buddhas.
>
> But we saw the beauty of central Afghanistan, which is something most people have not seen – the wild country and the fact that just about everybody there has a gun. My heart

goes out to the soldiers from Australia and elsewhere who are there at the moment, because it's a big difference from India and from Pakistan. It's a country that never had a conqueror, not in modern times, anyway. Even Alexander the Great didn't conquer; he passed through and I think he passed through as quickly as he could.

On at least two occasions the kombi lost its traction on snow-covered mountain passes and almost came skidding off the treacherous roads. The drop on the side of these passes was hundreds of metres. Johan had prepared for such weather and packed snow chains in the van. Michael, on the other hand, was horrified that he might have to get out in cold and inhospitable conditions and somehow fit devices to the wheels. One incident took place near Erzurum in Turkey.

Mountain passes and snow are not a good look. We had to get out to put the snow chains on and I didn't like doing that at all, because I was not used to snow. He of course, being Dutch, knew all about snow, and he said, 'Stop complaining and moaning, just stand there and pull this!' So I would do what I had to do, but I didn't like it at all. He was, as usual, a very practical person. He's a good balance to my personality, because I'm rather ethereal and up there with the pixies. There's nothing ethereal at all about Johan and most people who can't stand me actually like him, because he's very European, very, what will I say . . . very dignified, intelligent and cordial. He's quite formal, quite a formal person with other people.

These two trips in the kombi vans cemented a lifelong love for travel and also strengthened their relationship. 'We both agree it was a wonderful time in our lives,' Michael says. 'We saw the world, we saw the commonalities of our world and of how, in the middle of Central Asia, human beings are still human beings.' In the years to come, he would regularly make twenty or thirty overseas trips a year while he was working full-time. These would all be on official business, but on top of that there was also time set aside for him and Johan to continue the journey they had begun all those years before.

Towards the end of the first trip Michael began to canvass the possibility of staying in the UK and working there or in Europe. Both his brothers were in London and some of his friends had also made the move from Sydney. Geoffrey Robertson was now in his first year at Oxford and he suggested Michael consider moving his practice. He could set up in London or, alternately, look for a position with the United Nations, the OECD or another international quango of some sort. Michael treated the suggestion seriously. He had been interested in international human rights law ever since his first overseas trip to Africa, in 1963. His recent adventures in India and Central Asia had extended that interest. He made a few inquiries, sent his CV out, but all of them came to nothing. So he rather ambivalently prepared for his return to Sydney.

Johan, for his part, never genuinely considered repatriation to Europe. He had become too attached to Australia and, like so many who had migrated after World War II, he considered himself an Australian now, and he was keen get back home. Quite soon after his return Johan took out Australian citizenship. Rather than swearing on the Bible, he heeded Lionel Murphy's call and made an affirmation of allegiance. On 11 August 1972 he affirmed allegiance to Her Majesty the Queen and received a copy of the Bible as a souvenir. Michael was no doubt pleased by both these things. Johan, on the other hand, valued only the citizenship itself; he had little time for the monarchy or religion.

Neville Wran QC, soon to be a Labor member of the NSW Parliament and with a thriving industrial law practice, wrote to Michael Kirby in late 1970, while he was still overseas. Wran was to save Kirby from the sense of terminal boredom that had descended on his own legal practice.

14th September, 1970

Dear Michael,
The decks have been cleared. We have a by-election in George's River on Saturday. It's a great shame you are not working for the Party.

I hope Afghanistant [sic] was all that you expected.

Looking forward to seeing you in the near future.

Kind Regards,

Yours sincerely,

Neville Wran

P.S. Everything turned out 100% NW

It may just have been a typo, but it also seemed somehow appropriate that Wran might have contemptuously misspelt 'Afghanistan'. He was appalled that a barrister like Kirby with a lucrative practice and a good political brain could willingly disappear into such an intolerably remote and unheard-of place.

Before his departure overseas, Kirby had spent the previous two years dealing almost exclusively with workers' compensation matters from the side of the insurance company. And before that, as a solicitor-advocate he had conducted workers' compensation cases from the side of the workers. He was very good at this sort of work but it no longer held any interest for him and he refused to let his career slide into mediocrity.

> At that stage, yes, I made an awful lot of money. But it wasn't particularly stimulating to me. It was very taxing. It really taught me self-organisation and the setting of standards and I always took my duties very seriously. But in a way, going overseas allowed me to clear the decks. When I came back I effectively let it be known that I was not going to do that work. So, I then moved into work very largely in the industrial field, in industrial cases, election disputes. I did a lot of work with Neville Wran, with Jack Sweeney, some little work – not much – with Lionel Murphy, with Bill Fisher. So I was really manoeuvring, working my way into an industrial practice, which I was very interested in because it was sort of tapping my knowledge in my economics degree and I was interested in industrial relations issues.

It was 1971, and time for a change. Wran stepped up to provide the important opportunity for Kirby to act as his junior. Wran was an incredibly hard worker – Kirby never saw him arrive after 6 a.m. and he was often in the office even earlier, at five-thirty or four o'clock. Sometimes after a very late sitting of parliament the night before.

> Sharp. Dedicated. Focused. Mastering the detail. Determined to win. Loved by his clients. It was an amazing experience for a young lawyer like me to have. He taught me a lesson that, in my opinion, provides a chief reason for his great success in public life. The devil is always in the detail. If you master the detail you cannot be snared by witnesses, outgunned by opponents or defeated by your own slips and mistakes.

Working closely with Neville Wran, Kirby got a strong sense of his own strengths and weaknesses. While he was sure he could match Wran any day on the level of hard work and that ability to master the detail, he realised that the raw political instinct and the passion for the cut and thrust of battle were not his strong points. Kirby was a very good barrister and getting better all the time, but he found it stressful. Johan had already observed that Michael didn't really enjoy working at the Bar. They both knew that he wanted appointment to the bench. How or where that was going to come from was unclear. When Kirby asked Wran if he had ever considered a judicial appointment, Wran shot back, 'Only if I had a terminal illness.'

All great Queen's Counsel know that their ultimate success depends on preparation. Those who walk into a courtroom and appear to present their case effortlessly belie the reality of hours of hard work that went before. Neville Wran was no different. Kirby's aptitude for work, and plenty of it, was already legendary but Wran set out to teach him 'the real meaning of hard work'. On one occasion the two went into competition to see who could get to work and master the brief first. Wran arrived at his customary early hour, but he had misjudged Michael Kirby: the junior barrister was already hard at work and had prepared strong tea and biscuits to boot. Wran had made the right decision – nothing is more valuable to senior counsel than highly competent junior counsel. Every day, Michael Kirby, behind the scenes, helped make Neville Wran look good.

Michael and Johan had always wanted to move from Kirribilli to the eastern suburbs. This was for several reasons: it would be closer to the legal precinct for Michael, they ultimately wanted to find a house with water views, and Johan wanted to have a pet cat, which wasn't possible in a flat. Until they could afford a house, they decided they would first look for an apartment in the right general area.

> Every now and again I would see Bruce Holcombe and occasionally Roger Lakeman. Some time in 1972 Lakeman telephoned me with the news that a very good home unit in Darling Point Road was for sale, which he would recommend to me. I remember that I went through that unit in Eastbourne Towers with Lakeman and Johan. Perhaps he wondered who Johan was. Perhaps he knew. The purchase did not go ahead. Subsequently he pointed us to Ranalagh, further down Darling Point Road. Lakeman was always eagle-eyed about property. I knew that anything he recommended would be a good buy.

So they kept the Kirribilli flat as an investment and moved to the eastern suburbs. Johan was now working for the pay section of the Australian Broadcasting Commission in Gore Hill. He was kept busy with his own full-time work, all the arrangements necessary for the rental of the Kirribilli flat and the purchase of the new apartment, the move itself and the setting up of their new home.

Michael was heavily dependent on Johan to ensure that the domestic issues of his life were all in order and that everything ran like clockwork. All the while, the very fact of their relationship was known only to their close family members. Homosexuality was still criminalised in New South Wales and most states of Australia; anyone with an axe to grind might have destroyed Michael's career at the Bar.

Only a few in the legal profession had put two and two together, and Johan and Michael remained very discreet. Johan never attended any work functions and if Michael's colleagues were ever invited back to the apartment, Johan knew that he would have to make himself scarce. These were the days before answering machines, and calls to the home number could not be screened. Johan would never answer the home phone in case it was a professional contact of Michael's calling or, God forbid, a journalist or the occasional female admirer. This meant the two had to develop a code. If the phone rang three times and then ceased, Johan knew the next call would be from Michael and he could answer it. For his part, Johan was not so concerned, but he knew the implications for Michael's career if he was ever outed: 'He had far more to lose than I had.'

On top of his work as Wran's junior, Kirby was also taking a range of other cases: in the NSW Court of Disputed Returns as junior to Maurice Byers QC, and matters of corporate law in the NSW Supreme Court. One notable case in the Supreme Court, *Ampol v. Miller*, involved a phalanx of QCs and barristers. Kirby was on the winning side, and almost all the lawyers involved later went on to become judges, some of them on the High Court. This placed Michael in the top ranks of his profession. He was also appearing in the High Court, where his fortunes were mixed. In only his second appearance there, in *R. v. Forbes* for the Boilermakers' Union, he scored a victory. This led to further work as he began to get a reputation as an accomplished junior.

On 10 October 1972, Liberal prime minister Billy McMahon announced in parliament that the federal election was to be held on Saturday, 2 December. The excitement in the ranks of the Labor Party was palpable; this was the election that, after twenty-three years, they knew they would finally win. Opposition Leader Gough Whitlam immediately jumped up to respond. 'The second day of December is a memorable day; it is the anniversary of Austerlitz. Far be it from me to wish, or to appear to wish, to assume the mantle of Napoleon, but I cannot forget that the second of December was a date on which a crushing defeat was administered to a coalition – a ramshackle, reactionary coalition.'

There followed a near-perfect campaign for Labor and there were few people who believed that McMahon had any chance of retaining government. In the last week of the campaign, Whitlam addressed the National Press Club in Canberra. He had the journalists in the palm of his hand. He had already moved from campaign mode –

every policy had been so thoroughly enunciated, now he talked as though he were already prime minister. McMahon's ineptitude, by contrast, had him doing a street walk in a die-hard Labor electorate and waxing lyrical over the 'delicious Chiko Rolls'. Don Dunstan captured the excitement for Labor supporters at the time:

> Well, we all saw it as a period of great opportunity. There was so much that needed to be done, there were so many inequities, inequalities, unfairnesses, within the community, so many things that needed to be righted. The position of Aborigines, the position of women, position of minority groups, the lack of anti-discrimination legislation, as far as minority groups were concerned. All of those things needed to be done, and we saw a great opportunity in it.

On 2 November, exactly one month out from election day, Michael Kirby had gone into the High Court once more. He was in the role of junior to Whitlam's shadow attorney-general, Senator Lionel Murphy QC. It was testament to both Murphy's extraordinary capacity for hard work and his commitment to the cause that even though he was one of the four leaders of the federal parliamentary Labor Party, in the middle of a historic election campaign, he still took time out to appear in court. Wran had handballed the case to him because he was too busy with state political matters and Murphy took it all in his not inconsiderable stride. They faced up to the Chief Justice Sir Garfield Barwick once more, but this time Kirby was out of luck. It was a highly charged political moment, with Whitlam and Murphy about to depose Barwick's former colleagues in the parliament. The workers' compensation case was over what now seems a trifling sum of $576, but to the injured and impecunious Sydney bus driver at the centre of the matter, it offered the possibility of rehabilitation. Barwick led the Court in a finding against Murphy and Kirby and overturning the win Wran and Kirby had secured in the NSW Court of Appeal. The unanimous judgement from the High Court was in favour of the employer.

There were strong views held on both sides of politics in Australia and sometimes tempers ran hot, but through it all, Kirby was always amazed by the way Australians changed the colour of their governments at the ballot box in a an orderly and peaceful way. Generally there were no demonstrations, violence or military force, just a calm and sensible transfer of power. 'For all the faults of our system, which are many, we could at least turf them out. We could get rid of them. It's a wonderful thing, peacefully to change a government.' Every three years the people entered into the equation and their judgement was final: the government elected by the people was supposed to remain for the duration unless the prime minister decided to go to an early election.

At a federal level in Australia, nevertheless, this change of power had not occurred since 1949. The last time Kirby had witnessed the Australian Labor Party winning a federal election he was a seven-year-old, sitting at the feet of his father and listening to the radio announcements of results in the 1946 victory of Ben Chifley. That seemed an awfully long time ago now; in fact, it had been twenty-six years. With change so rare in Australia, many adult Australians had never known any other situation and could be forgiven for thinking the nation was a kind of Menzian one-party state, and for all practical purposes it was. The Liberal–Country Party Coalition, with the aid of a significant gerrymander, had come to believe that they were the rightful government and, before Whitlam, the Labor Party had sunk into a continuing depression, believing that they would always be in opposition.

On Tuesday, 5 December 1972 Gough Whitlam was sworn in as the first Australian Labor prime minister in twenty-three years. He was in a hurry to institute his policies and had an unequivocal mandate to do so. During the first thirteen days of the Whitlam Government, Australia changed forever. The staggering list of his announcements left heads spinning.

- Recognises China
- Grants independence for Papua New Guinea
- Returns Wilfred Burchett's passport
- Immediately ends national service
- Withdraws troops from Vietnam
- Releases all draft resisters
- Reopens equal pay case
- Scraps the imperial honours, replaces with Australian honours
- Orders NSW Government to close Rhodesian Information Service
- Ends wheat exports to Rhodesia
- Contributes to UN South Africa Fund
- Removes sales tax on the contraceptive pill and all contraceptives
- Stops the prohibition on advertising of contraceptives

- Provides $0.3 million for international birth control
- Stops leases on NT Aboriginal reserves
- Approves grants to Aboriginal NGOs
- Begins Aboriginal land rights grants
- Establishes special schools for Aboriginal children
- Applies curfew on Sydney Airport
- Bans racially selective sporting tours
- Releases the film *Portnoy's Complaint* with R-rating
- Releases funds for expansion of tertiary education
- Provides $4 million arts grants
- Establishes the Australian Schools Commission
- Provides $2.5 million rice aid to Indonesia
- Agrees to ratify international convention on nuclear arms control, racial discrimination and labour
- Prepares to release thousands of secret or unpublished government reports
- Appoints Elizabeth Evatt to Arbitration Commission (first female federal judge)
- Makes numerous ambassadorial announcements or appointments
- Announces preference for Australian-made goods in government purchases

Michael Kirby watched all this happen with great interest. In the run-up to the election he had handed out voting pamphlets for the ALP, even though he had, by now, let his membership lapse. Many of the reforms were things that he had championed during his years as a student politician, especially the issues of racial and gender equality, the removal once and for all of the White Australia policy, and the position of Aboriginal people. When Senator Lionel Murphy QC was sworn in as attorney-general and began his own thorough program of legal reform, Kirby was impressed.

> Well, I think the steps towards the establishment of the Family Court, and the setting up of that court, the ridding of Australia of the old family law, the establishment of the Law Reform Commission – I like to think was an important development. The setting up of legal aid, and the attempts to bring the security forces, the services, under public review, the moves to abolish the appeals to the Privy Council, continuing the efforts that had begun in the previous government. There were so many things that he did, and that he started. The moves towards administrative law reform, the *Trade Practices Act*.
>
> When one thinks of it, it's really a most dazzling set of achievements. That in so short a time he should be able to do so much, because it's the whole lesson of our system of government that ministers, elected governments, can generally only move as fast as the inertia of the public service.

Much of what Whitlam did he did for the first time and therefore his legislation was always liable to be tested in the courts. It was easier for conservative governments who, by their very nature, rarely attempted legislation that did not carry with it a long line of precedents. The new prime minister was determined that his program of legislative reform would not be blocked by the Australian Constitution as had so often been the case with the policies of past

Labor governments. Lionel Murphy played a crucial role in devising the legal strategies that would ensure that the new reforms would eventually become law, and he enlisted the services of Michael Kirby in the battle to get the Government's bills past the High Court.

Although a federal opposition had not come to power since the 1940s, it was common at a state level for oppositions to make promises that were not kept after attaining government. Whitlam and Murphy would have none of that. The policy implementation was breathtaking and as a result the Whitlam Government was popular, especially among its Labor supporters. Not withstanding this popularity, the Liberal–Country Party Coalition Opposition vowed to get rid of Whitlam from day one. Unable to control the numbers in the lower house, the Liberal Party, first under Billy Snedden and then Malcolm Fraser, set out on an unwavering strategy of frustrating Whitlam's legislative agenda. First it was done by blocking certain Bills in the Senate, and later by blocking supply so that the Government would not have any money to pay public servants. This was a tactic that had not been used before and it was highly controversial. Under Section 53 of the Constitution, the Senate cannot amend supply Bills. Rather than test this section, the Opposition simply refused to vote, thereby effectively shutting down the Government.

With six important Bills stalled by the Senate, Whitlam decided to call a double dissolution election on 18 May 1974. Under Section 57 of the Constitution, a deadlock between the two houses of parliament can be resolved by both houses voting together in a joint sitting after a double dissolution election. Although Menzies had called a double dissolution election in 1951, he did not invoke the powers of a joint sitting – until 1974 no Australian government had ever held a joint sitting to pass its stalled legislation. On 11 April the Whitlam Government added another important achievement to its list of 'firsts' by calling the election which returned the government and thereby led to the joint sitting.

On the eve of this historic coming together of both houses of the Australian Parliament, the Liberal Party, in the form of two senators from Victoria, Magnus Cormack (a former president of the Senate) and James Webster, rushed to the High Court. They issued a writ for an injunction to stop the joint sitting from proceeding. Four days before parliament was scheduled to sit, Chief Justice Sir Garfield Barwick and the Full Court heard argument from the Government, led by the attorney-general Senator Lionel Murphy QC and supported by the solicitor-general Sir Maurice Byers QC in *Cormack v. Cope*. Jim Cope was the Labor Speaker of the House. Counsel for the Liberals included Daryl Dawson QC and William Deane QC, both later to be appointed justices of the High Court. Appearing with them was Murray Gleeson, Michael's old law school chum, soon to take silk and eventually to be appointed chief justice of Australia many years later.

Again Michael Kirby appeared in the High Court as junior to Lionel Murphy. This time, though, it was not a bus driver's compensation case, but one of the most important and historic constitutional hearings ever to come before the Court. The Liberal–Country Party Opposition dismissed what the governor-general, the parliament, the prime minister and the Government all took as given – that the parliamentary process had concluded, the election had returned the Government, and the Bills were to be moved.

Cormack and Webster based their case on the hope that, because a joint sitting had never occurred before, the Court could well find procedural flaws in the application of Section 57 of the Constitution. Perhaps it was more than a wishful hope: Sir Garfield insisted from the bench that the 'courts have a right and a duty to ensure that the law-making process is observed' and there were various technical requirements that had to be fulfilled before a double dissolution election could be called and a joint sitting initiated.

The case began in Sydney on Friday, 2 August 1974 and continued on Monday 5 August, the day before the joint sitting was scheduled to take place in Canberra. Murphy and Kirby wrapped up their case and at precisely 5.15 p.m. the Court's orders were pronounced. All six justices agreed not to issue an injunction to prevent the joint sitting but gave different reasons for their decisions. These ranged from Douglas Menzies' view that such matters of parliamentary process were simply not justiciable, through to Barwick's that an injunction at this late stage was practically impossible and that any Bills passed could be challenged later (which in the event is exactly what happened). Having won the case, Murphy raced to catch a flight to Canberra, the joint sitting went ahead, and the stalled Bills were passed the very next day.

This one historic win in the High Court of Australia ensured that some of the most important of Whitlam's reforming bills passed into law. Without it, there would have been no universal and free healthcare – the Medibank legislation was the first one on the list. Two more of the Bills were also very close to Whitlam's heart. They were designed to reshape the electoral system to remove the entrenched structural unfairness caused by gerrymander. Whitlam's 'one vote, one value' legislation meant that all Australians now had equal power at the ballot box, whether they were in country electorates, which invariably supported the Country or Liberal parties, or in the cities. The Australian Capital Territory and the Northern Territory had previously had no Senate representation, but Whitlam's Bill introduced Senate representation for all Australians, no matter where they lived. These reforms created the modern democratic nation that Australians now take for granted. There was one further Bill passed, the *Petroleum and Minerals Authority Act 1973*, but it was later struck out on a technicality, in a case that came before Sir Garfield Barwick. This area of Australian law, defining how the government deals with mining and energy resources, continues to be vigorously debated to this day.

Clyde Cameron, former shearer and Australian Workers' Union official, was now labour minister. During the first days of the Government, Whitlam had asked Cameron to reopen the equal pay case, which had last been heard in 1969. Cameron did so and briefed another of Michael Kirby's fellow Sydney University alumni, Mary Gaudron, now a successful barrister, to present the Government's case. Gaudron was an inspired choice. Her skills of advocacy were equal to any of her peers. When the Commonwealth Conciliation and Arbitration Commission sat to hear the reopened equal pay case, they were faced with a situation that they had never faced before – a woman stood before them as the barrister presenting the Government's case. Just as importantly, the Government was now, unlike the previous Liberal–Country Party Government, arguing in support of equal pay for equal work regardless of gender. It was an exquisite moment where the absurdity of the existing discriminatory situation was writ large. Gaudron won the case and by April 1974 she had taken her place as only the second woman, after Justice Elizabeth Evatt, to be appointed to the Commission itself as a deputy president.

Mary Gaudron, at thirty-one, was four years younger than Michael Kirby and he still thought of her as the young, rather bolshie girl he had known at Sydney University Law Society meetings. Kirby couldn't reconcile this image with the now Justice Mary Gaudron of the Australian Conciliation and Arbitration Commission, the youngest person ever appointed to a federal bench. It was a slightly unsettling feeling and it made Michael focus even more intently on the possibilities of his own judicial appointment.

After the stunning victory in *Cormack v. Cope*, Kirby continued to work for the attorney-general Lionel Murphy. Murphy was consistently the butt of the most scurrilous gossip and innuendo, involving Sir Frank Packer's *Bulletin* magazine and ABC-TV's *This Day Tonight*. Michael offered opinions on defamation matters and began to think Murphy might soon find him a judicial post. But when the call came, it wasn't from the attorney-general. In November 1974, Clyde Cameron asked Kirby if he would consider joining Gaudron on the bench of the Arbitration Commission.

There was some concern about a drop in his income – as a barrister he could earn twice the yearly salary of a judge. Everyone at the Bar thought he would be mad to take the job. The Arbitration Commission wasn't even a real court, as far as the black-letter lawyers were concerned. Silks like Neville Wran and Michael

McHugh (who Michael Kirby had had a little to do with and who became a mentor for Michael's brother David) thought he would die a death at the Commission. But Kirby was excited by the prospect. 'It was a really important body in Australia. It decided the national wage and the quarterly adjustments and issues like Aboriginal employment, awards, equal pay for women – a whole range of very important things. That was an area that I had done a lot of work in and I was interested in, because it combined law with economic concerns.' He talked it through with Johan but they both knew elevation to the bench was what Michael had always wanted, and the opportunity might not come along again.

The press greeted the announcement of Kirby's impending elevation to the bench in a misleading way. An article appeared in the *Sydney Morning Herald* with the headline: 'Judge not my friend – Cameron'. It was indicative of the increasing press hostility to any appointment of the Whitlam Government, and ironic since, at the time, Cameron certainly believed Kirby was a Liberal.

> The Minister for Labour, Mr Clyde Cameron, yesterday gave special references to Mr Justice Kirby at a ceremony to welcome him as a member of the Australian Conciliation and Arbitration Commission. 'The press will be glad to know the judge is not my relative or friend,' he said. 'He is not a member of the ALP, he hasn't led any demonstrations, he has not been active in the left-wing or trade union movement. I hope it will recognise that his appointment was for his sheer ability and because of his qualifications.'

Tom Hughes QC spoke at Kirby's swearing-in. Hughes, the brother of Kirby's old Sydney University chum Robert Hughes, was a former minister in the Menzies Government. The speech famously made mention of Kirby's 'urbanity'. This was recorded incorrectly in the transcript as 'vanity' and remains uncorrected to this day.

> It also gives me great pleasure on this occasion to be able to speak in substantial unison with my old friend and political adversary, Mr Clyde Cameron, because I seem to recall that on those occasions when I happened to disagree with him, and they were perhaps not infrequent, I always came off second best [. . .] I speak with complete confidence in saying that Your Honour will have as distinguished a career in your new field as Your Honour was having (and would have continued to have) had you stayed at the Bar. Your Honour is possessed of tenacity, versatility and vanity [sic] – a very rare mixture, indeed, when to that mixture is added intellectual brilliance.

On 13 December he took up his position as deputy president and for the first time wore the title that would follow him throughout his life – Justice Michael Kirby. (Another judge was appointed to the Commission on the same day, Dr I. G. Sharp. Sharp stepped down as head of the Department of Labour and Immigration to go to the bench, and he was replaced by none other than Dr Peter Wilenski.) Michael Kirby joined Mary Gaudron, she the youngest person and he the youngest man ever appointed to a federal court.

> I was appointed, I was welcomed. I remember quoting Sir John Kerr during my welcome speech about the importance of industrial law to the fabric of Australia. He'd been very much involved in the industrial law field and was very good at it and he was a judge of the Commonwealth Industrial Court at the time. I remember Tom Hughes, who was then the president of the Bar, came and welcomed me on behalf of the Bar. So, I was there, settled in, in December 1974, to be a judge of the Arbitration Commission. I recruited my first associate. I was then set up over in Temple Court and I assumed that that would be what my career would involve.

This was the point in Kirby's career that he had always hoped for and worked towards. It had only been six years since he had left behind student politics and made the decision to turn his back on the path to parliamentary office. At just thirty-five he was now on the bench and he could look forward to a career as a distinguished deputy president, and perhaps one day even president, of the Arbitration Commission. And then who knew where that might lead?

He was convinced that he had made the right decision, to move from the daily stress of the Bar to the more sedate and predictable life of a judge. Indeed, way back at Fort Street, he had always looked to the framed photographs of the old boys who had gone on to sit on the High Court or NSW Supreme Court, who had become the most eminent of jurists. Little did Michael Kirby know what the following month held in store; there would be nothing sedate or predictable about the years ahead.

7

The Great Communicator

> There's a great thirst for knowledge about the law. There is a problem that a lot of lawyers find it a bit difficult to explain things in simple terms. So my talent, for what it was worth, of explaining things simply and cutting away the exceptions and the qualifications and the nuances and just explaining the issues as well as I could, made for an interesting engagement on the part of people. The law doesn't belong to lawyers. It's not boring. The law is interesting. The big issues of law are the big issues of life. We sometimes need people to be interlocutors and communicators. That's certainly what I tried to do, and I don't regret it for a minute.
>
> *Michael Kirby*

Climate scientist and mathematician Edward Norton Lorenz coined the term 'butterfly effect' to describe how even tiny changes in non-linear dynamics can deliver unexpectedly large effects elsewhere in the system. His important contribution was the recognition that all things are interconnected in strange and interesting ways. In the peculiar and arcane world of the NSW bench and Bar, every little change, no matter how trivial, was noted and weighed. The fact that a judge's horsehair wig sat slightly askance on his Honour's head might have unimagined ramifications in chambers in some faraway corner of the system. How much more so, then, would be the fallout from the death of a High Court judge.

Mr Justice Douglas Menzies of the High Court of Australia, Sir Robert Menzies' cousin, an independently minded and yet highly conservative judge, collapsed and died at the NSW Bar Association's annual Bench and Bar Dinner in Sydney on 29 November 1974. He was only sixty-seven. Michael Kirby was at the same function, standing in the same queue waiting for his meal. 'He died at the feet of Tom Hughes in the Bar common room, just three people in front of me on the receiving line.' This, suddenly and dramatically, offered an unexpected opening on the High Court bench. Justices of the High Court were at that time appointed for life and some, like Sir Edward McTiernan, then eighty-two, stayed on for a very long time before contemplating retirement. In that context, Menzies was still in his prime and might have remained for another decade at least.

Lionel Murphy was at the same dinner and it was his duty as attorney-general to immediately start the search for a replacement for Menzies. Within a few days he asked Kirby for his CV. The hairs stood up on the back of his neck. Was it possible that Murphy was considering him for elevation from the most junior member of the humblest commission to the highest judicial bench in the land?

Justice H.V. Evatt, the youngest-ever appointment, had gone to the High Court at the age of thirty-six; Kirby was just thirty-five. Admittedly, Dr Evatt had been a Labor member of state parliament and one of the leading KCs in Australia before his elevation. It seemed unlikely that the Government was considering appointing Kirby from three weeks at the Arbitration Commission straight to the High Court. But if not, what was Murphy up to?

Kirby was half expecting a phone call from the attorney-general at any moment but it didn't come. So he turned his attention to the immediate task of settling into his new job as a deputy president of the Australian Conciliation and Arbitration Commission. His colleague Justice Mary Gaudron had been listed to hear cases involving meat-workers. It was a pretty rough-and-tumble industry and she was expected to visit abattoirs and butcheries. Kirby was more fortunate; he was allocated the maritime industry, an area Johan had told him a little about, and one suited to his temperament – he wasn't required to put on gumboots and tramp around stockyards.

> It wouldn't have been my scene, I suspect – I hadn't escaped the medical profession to end up in the slaughterhouse with the Arbitration Commission. But I'd been given the extremely clean, but highly disputatious, maritime industry. So, I'd been going on inspections on ships in the Gulf of St Vincent, being 'piped on board'. I had sort of mental images of myself as the Lord High Admiral of the modern Australian Arbitration Commission.

On the first working day of 1975, Kirby came face to face with none other than Senator Lionel Murphy in the lift of the Temple Court building. Murphy was heading up to the attorney-general's offices and Kirby travelled only a few floors with him to the Arbitration Commission on level seven. In that short trip, Murphy revealed to Kirby why he had asked for his CV: he wanted Kirby to head up the new Australian Law Reform Commission. Such commissions did exist in the individual states but there had never been one at the federal level. Murphy had secured passage of the Law Reform Commission Bill through parliament in late 1973, with the support of the Opposition. On 23 October of that year he told the Senate:

> The Government is concerned to see that the system of law under which people live is responsive to the social needs of our time. The rules which govern the relationship of persons with each other and with the government should reflect current values and philosophies. This concern is reflected in the importance the Government attaches to law reform. The Bill is also an expression of the Government's view that except where local circumstances justify different treatment, people wherever they live in Australia should be subject to the same law. For this reason, many questions of law reform must be dealt with on a national basis.

The ALRC had been on the books for more than a year but it had not gone into operation. Murphy had made the appointments of the part-time commissioners, and now all that remained was to appoint a full-time chairman to run it. The suggestion was a bolt from the blue for Kirby. He had only just got his first judicial appointment and was hardly going to relinquish that for some quasi-governmental executive position. 'I'd only got through the first batch of my modest disclaimers before the lift arrived at seven, but he would take no negatives, and he ultimately insisted that I come up to his chambers.' Murphy proposed that Kirby could take leave from the Arbitration Commission, as Justice Elizabeth Evatt had done to run the Royal Commission on Human Relationships. He could maintain the title and prestige of Justice Michael Kirby, but also be the inaugural chairman of the new ALRC. Michael was unconvinced, telling Murphy: 'Well, you really should get somebody older because the profession won't like this young person coming in.' Murphy was adamant. 'No, I don't want any of those old fuddy-duddies. I want you. I want a young person with new ideas.' Kirby stepped out of the lift a little shell-shocked. As the doors closed, Murphy smiled. 'Come up and see me later.'

Kirby walked back to his office and mulled over the idea. It was typical of Murphy to formulate such a proposal. There were certainly many others as qualified as Kirby and the more senior judges and practitioners would not take kindly to a young smart alec coming in and telling them what they should be doing. Strangely enough, that aspect had a certain appeal, but even so it didn't feel quite right to move on from the Arbitration Commission after such a short tenure. Geoffrey Robertson, Kirby's old Sydney University chum and now high-flying London barrister, was coincidentally waiting for him in his office on a social call.

> Michael said, 'I have a terrible decision to make. The attorney-general wants to make me the chair of the Australian Law Reform Commission, and I am too young. I have only been a judge for a couple of weeks.' I said, 'Michael this is a terrific opportunity for someone of your talents to actually give back to Australia a real law that isn't just based on ancient English common law.' I knew Leslie Scarman, who was the doyen of law reform in those days. I explained to Michael just what Leslie had managed to do with the English Law Reform Commission, and he could do much more with his terrific ability to communicate.

The phone rang and it was Murphy. He asked Kirby to come up to his office straightaway. Kirby hesitated, telling Murphy he had someone visiting. Murphy asked who it could possibly be, and before Kirby could prevaricate further he told them both to come up. Like many a judge before him, Kirby was unwittingly caught in a trap. It was a pincer movement between the dogged and unrelenting advance of Lionel Murphy QC and the smooth advocacy of Murphy's 'junior', Geoffrey Robertson. Kirby didn't stand a chance. Robertson remains immensely proud of his role in the appointment.

> I said, 'Look, Michael thinks he's a bit too young and raw to take this position, and I think it would be terrific for him, and for the country.' And Lionel gave one of his sort of lopsided Cheshire cat grins and said, 'Right, it's decided then.' And he sort of ambled over to his fridge. This was about eleven o'clock

> in the morning. It was full of French champagne, of course. So he poured a couple of glasses and I don't think Michael drinks very much, certainly not at eleven o'clock in the morning, and Lionel Murphy proposed a toast to Mr Justice Kirby: 'your first step to the High Court of Australia'.

In Murphy's mind it was all decided. He had gone into overdrive to put the finishing touches to a series of projects he had initiated as attorney-general, and chairman of the ALRC was high on his list. He was in a hurry to tie up loose ends and he had a very good reason.

Murphy had been attorney-general for barely two years and in that time he had vigorously shaken up the legal profession, the churches, the security services and virtually every establishment enclave in the country. Internationally, he had taken the French to the World Court and personally led the case that put a stop to above-ground atomic testing in the Pacific. This early use of environmental law set precedents used from Nicaragua to the Antarctic. When he introduced free legal aid, the profession was aghast; this was the way to communism – the government dictating to the practitioners and the public who their lawyers would be and even how much they would be paid. Actually, it was an early recognition that justice can never be served if much of the community simply cannot afford legal representation.

Murphy also identified a strong feeling in the community that if a marriage had irretrievably broken down, then after a period of two years a divorce should be granted automatically. With an antagonistic Senate and a conservative Opposition saying no to everything, the Government ran it as a conscience vote and somehow Murphy cajoled and persuaded enough members to get it through. With this reform he led the democratic world, the USA eventually adopting 'no fault' divorce in all fifty states. He introduced the *Racial Discrimination Act 1975* and the Human Rights Bill 1973. He brought the police and the security services under tighter control and introduced a *Trade Practices Act* to outlaw unfair and unconscionable actions by retailers and other businesses big and small. His list of achievements was extensive. And there was so much more to do. Lionel Murphy was a larger-than-life figure in the Whitlam Government, and he relished the job of attorney-general. The possibility that he would suddenly and without warning drop from public view was unthinkable, but that is exactly what happened.

Unbeknown to anyone but a small group of cabinet ministers and Prime Minister Gough Whitlam, Murphy had been persuaded to take the vacancy on the High Court left by Justice Menzies' death. Michael just assumed the rather unusual approach with the ALRC chair was the consistent behaviour of Murphy the iconoclast, but in fact it was the behaviour of a man whose time was quickly running out in the job he so loved. For his part, Michael Kirby still had to consult a small group of people who were close to him before he made his final decision. The first on his list was Johan.

> He always rang me. Always. I was the first person to be informed of any of his career moves and I've always supported him in that. I was the first one to say, 'Oh yes, do that. If that's what you want, if that's what you need – do it.' It meant that he was his own boss, which is also important for him. It fits in his nature to hold the middle chair. And that was a very good

> appointment because he was imaginative, he was reaching out, and that was a perfect vehicle for him to do so.

Kirby then spoke to his parents and his brothers and sister. They all supported him. 'I accepted, rather reluctantly as I look back on it, the job which really gave me a chance and put me on the national scene of the law in Australia, and without which I wouldn't be sitting here as I am now. After forty days and forty nights in the Arbitration Commission, I was moved to the anteroom to the bankruptcy judge's chambers. That's where we started the Australian Law Reform Commission.'

The first year was a blur of activity, beginning even before Kirby had officially taken the job. Murphy had set the tone with his urgent appointment and by early February 1975, just ten days before moving to his new role as High Court justice, Murphy rang Kirby from the ALP National Conference in Terrigal. Under the *Law Reform Commission Act*, every inquiry had to be referred to it by the government of the day, and the attorney-general had a set of references for the new ALRC. Kirby was yet to formally take up the chairmanship and he suggested that Murphy might have to put the references in writing as required by the Act. Murphy would have none of that; he didn't have much time left and he was like a man on a mission: 'No, no, no, I am about to go. And this is what I want you to do . . .' His instructions to Kirby included references on technology and the law (Kirby later marvelled, 'How prescient this was in 1975'), and the impact of transnational corporations on the law and on society. In the end, the new Attorney-General, Kep Enderby, didn't give a reference on transnational corporations, but the one on technology did eventually arrive. Much of Murphy's agenda was nevertheless set in train.

The Whitlam Government had given Kirby a reference to inquire into police powers of arrest, search and seizure, conduct of investigations, rights of persons detained, their access to bail and legal representation and to humane and dignified treatment. Many of these issues were matters that Kirby had confronted himself, at the coalface, when acting for the NSW Council for Civil Liberties nearly ten years before. *Corbishley* was a case in point. An important consideration was the fact that Whitlam had already introduced legislation for a new Australia Police (later the Australian Federal Police), combining the ACT and Northern Territory police forces, the Commonwealth Police and sections of the Department of Customs and Excise into one organisation. This new federal police force would have an expanded role and the Government was keen for it to be established on a solid footing, utilising the world's best practice in policing. It was also significant that the report was to be framed within the context of the Government's commitment to the International Covenant on Civil and Political Rights. These sorts of international treaties and norms were, as far as Gough Whitlam and Lionel Murphy were concerned, essential considerations in the development of Australia's domestic law if it was not to remain a parochial backwater.

The first big report Michael Kirby guided through was *Complaints Against Police*, tabled on 7 August 1975. He had held hearings in every capital city and received more than 120 written or oral submissions, with many judges, practitioners, police officers and academics participating. Six commissioners conducted the inquiry, including Gareth Evans, then a law lecturer at Melbourne University; Gerard Brennan QC, a barrister from Queensland with a criminal law practice; and John Cain, a prominent Victorian Labor lawyer and son of the last Labor Premier of that state. At the time in Australia there existed no way that a member of the public could initiate a complaint against any member of a police force and have it investigated and determined by an independent body. The report recommended that a police tribunal should be created, and that the newly established Australian Ombudsman, another of Murphy's innovations, should oversee complaints.

The second report, an interim report called *Criminal Investigation*, was tabled in parliament on 8 November 1975. The main findings called for legislation guaranteeing safeguards to stop improper use of powers of arrest, questioning and bail; and for a procedural code covering all members of the proposed Australia Police. Failure to act within these guidelines would, on the face of it, make any evidence gathered inadmissible.

Gareth Evans took leave from his academic position at Melbourne University and became a full-time commissioner for one month to write this report. The second important contribution Evans made to the ALRC was to suggest that the commission be media-friendly and get the message out to the wider community, not just the legal fraternity, and at the same time have a mechanism whereby members of the general public could contribute. Lawyers and especially judges tended to be very wary of any media attention, often with good reason. Judgements and cases were frequently misunderstood, trivialised or sensationalised. Kirby agreed with Evans, and made himself available for interviews and backgrounding, presenting his reports in an attractive and readable form and releasing media statements, while at the same time having community hearings.

Kirby ensured that these open hearings had all the trappings and theatrical touches of a courtroom. In that way he elevated what were essentially public meetings to apparent judicial status. Mr Justice Michael Kirby presiding. But at other times, depending on the nature of the inquiry, Kirby also presented himself as only one part of the proceedings and would simply sit down on the same level as the other lawyers and the general public. In the later hearings on Aboriginal customary law, for example, all the participants sat outside in a big circle under the Northern Territory sun.

Within a year Kirby had become a regular feature in newspapers, on radio and on television: 'Something that led Gareth Evans to assert that I had to be pushed into the public media but that, having embraced it, I did so with an excessive enthusiasm.' ('Coming from him, I think that's a little bit rich,' Kirby suggests.) ABC-TV interviewed Justice Michael Kirby – young, smart, handsome – in front of his legal books behind his desk in the Elizabeth Street offices of the ALRC. His voice was smooth and authoritative, articulate and persuasive, moderate and sensible. The *Four Corners* program went to him for comment first on privacy, then on the handling of police complaints from the public.

> Kirby: There's a certain want of frankness about the procedures that are available. Police, generally speaking, don't advertise the procedures that are there. Secondly, when the procedures are

> followed, often the person doesn't know how the investigation is conducted. It's conducted by senior police officers, generally speaking, it's conducted by the very people who are over the police constable or officer complained of. These are the two issues: knowledge of the system, and when the system is known its obvious fairness or unfairness.
>
> Reporter: Does what you have said point to substantial malpractice in the police forces when it comes to dealing with complaints made by the public?

Kirby's response came back immediately, calm but firm, and with just the slightest trace of a wry smile as he spoke the first sentence:

> What I have said doesn't point to substantial malpractice. What I have said points to a system which is not on its face an independent, just one. And what the commission proposed was a system which would introduce independent elements and be manifestly just and be seen by policemen and members of the community alike to be a just and fair one.

There was another reason for getting the work out there into the public domain: it made it much harder for the government of the day to relegate the report, as was so often the case, and do nothing about it. As Kirby observes now:

> It became a kind of insurance policy against neglect and indifference once the reports were in, because if you'd been

> burrowing away in a closed room, nobody would know about it, no one would care. But if you'd raised expectations and involvement and commitment, then it became harder for politicians to just ignore the product. And the ALRC has had a very good record by world standards in the implementation of its reports and has been useful to successive governments, whatever their politics, in helping parliament to tackle big topics which otherwise would tend to get neglected because they're not specifically political.

On Tuesday, 11 November, only three days after the tabling in parliament of his second report, Michael Kirby was hard at work in his Sydney office. A call came through from Justice J.T. Ludeke, a fellow deputy president of the Arbitration Commission. Justice Ludeke told Kirby the most dramatic political news since federation: the governor-general, Sir John Kerr, had just dismissed the prime minister and the entire Whitlam Government.

Kirby was surprised but not shocked by the fact of the dismissal. He had heard enough conversations over luncheon in the Bar common room to be well aware that in some circles Kerr would be applauded for his actions. Kirby knew Kerr quite well; he had appeared before him a number of times when Kerr was a judge in the Industrial Court and he had always seemed to Kirby to be a bit bored in that role (in Kirby's words, 'the job didn't seem big enough for him'). Michael Kirby had no doubt that Sir John as governor-general had the strict legal power to sack the government, but he was offended by the way Kerr did it.

He didn't observe the conventions which bound the representative of the Crown. Those conventions require that the Crown and its representatives would always be candid with the prime minister. Sir John's task was to warn Mr Whitlam that if he could not guarantee supply then he would have to see if an alternative prime minister could guarantee it, and if not, he would have to dissolve parliament and have an election. But instead of doing that, he was engaged in negotiations behind Mr Whitlam's back. Mr Fraser was summoned to Government House and was waiting in a comm car at the back under a tree whilst the prime minister of the country was coming, unbeknownst to him, to be sacked, up the front steps.

This wasn't, in my view, the honest, honourable, direct way the Crown acts. Being correct has always been quite an important value to me. The excuse given at the time was that had Sir John Kerr alerted Mr Whitlam to what he was thinking of doing, Mr Whitlam might have gone to the Palace to have Sir John Kerr sacked and that he, Sir John Kerr, was seeking to immunise the Queen from possible involvement in local politics. However, the Queen, even by 1975, had been Queen for a long time – twenty-three years. There is little doubt what the Queen would have done. If the fear of Sir John was that he would lose his job, that was not a proper consideration. Soldiers die for the Crown every day or every second day, and therefore, he should not have taken that into account in my view.

The year ended even more tumultuously than it had begun. The Labor Government was gone after three short years and three increasingly enervating elections. They had been under enormous pressure from the outset with an Opposition who never accepted Whitlam's legitimacy, a public service whose allegiance still lay with the Liberal Party – they had known nothing else since 1949 – and a press, led by Rupert Murdoch, whose daily fare was gushing, tabloid-style anti-Whitlam vitriol – so much so that even his own journalists went out on strike in protest. The depiction was of a government that lurched from disaster to disaster.

Under the circumstances it was extraordinary that Whitlam achieved as much as he did and ironic that Malcolm Fraser, the new prime minister appointed by Kerr, went on to lay claim to so much of the Whitlam legacy: the Racial Discrimination Act and the end of the White Australia policy, the establishment of the Federal Police through to multicultural Australia and a host of other initiatives. Even some of the big-ticket items like free tertiary education survived Fraser, although diminished to varying degrees. The major piece of legislation that was yet to pass into law when Kerr stepped in was the Human Rights Bill. Fraser had voted against it and he never reintroduced it. Australians are yet to get that basic protection.

Kirby had admired the ordered, peaceful and democratic change of government in 1972. He had never known it to be any other way. How different things were now. The troops were on alert, a national strike was expected, though it never eventuated. A spontaneous mass demonstration greeted Malcolm Fraser outside Parliament House as the governor-general's official secretary read the proclamation dissolving both houses of parliament and calling an election. At the same time the 'victorious' Liberal National Party opposition, now the first undemocratically installed government in Australia's history, drank champagne on the upper balcony at the front of Parliament House and laughed as they looked down on the protestors below. It was an unedifying display of gloating that even some of the Liberals themselves later regretted.

With Whitlam's departure, the ALRC, a Murphy initiative, could also easily have disappeared, especially if it had come to be seen as simply a government-controlled organisation. Initially Kirby had wanted to set up his offices in the attorney-general's department in Canberra. The department head, Sir Clarrie Harders, strongly advised him against this course of action, arguing that the ALRC should be seen to be at arm's length from government. Kirby accepted this advice. Throughout 1975 he made sure he consulted widely, speaking to the shadow attorney-general Ivor Greenwood and his successor, in the new Fraser Government, Robert Ellicott. It had occurred to Kirby that the new government might harness some of the criticisms he had sustained: that he was too young and inexperienced; that the very idea of law reform was a waste of time (these had come mainly from very conservative sections of the judiciary in Victoria and Queensland). He knew they might abolish, de-fund or sideline the ALRC:

> Partly because, I suppose, of my Anglican institutional upbringing, I did believe in neutrality. I did not believe in being partisan. So, I made it my business to see the Opposition. I think that was a factor in making sure that when November '75 came, that the Law Reform Commission survived.

Ellicott was an old Fort Street boy and cousin to the chief justice of Australia, Sir Garfield Barwick, another Fortian. The chief justice saw Kirby as being too close to Lionel Murphy, and there was never much of a rapport between them. 'I'm sure that he was very suspect of my appointment and my capacities. But he was very correct to me. I've always had, shall we say, a correct but not a warm relationship with Sir Garfield Barwick.' Attorney-General Ellicott was more open-minded – Kirby thought him forward-looking – and the two formed a good working relationship, although not a close one.

Ellicott did not like the idea of Gareth Evans remaining on as a commissioner. Although Evans had been there from the beginning, had a keen intellect and was an extraordinarily hard worker, he had also run unsuccessfully on an ALP Senate ticket in 1975. Evans was not reappointed by Ellicott, but replaced by Sir Zelman Cowen, another law academic from Melbourne University and highly respected. (Cowen was also to be the next governor-general, appointed in 1977 to bring a 'touch of healing' to the office Kerr had left in such poor health.) With Cowen on board it was becoming difficult for even the most strident critics of the ALRC to completely dismiss the commission's findings.

The next decade was to be most exciting, creative and demanding of Kirby's life. Not only did he shape and run an organisation that had never existed at a federal level before, but the new body also shaped him. He was a judge and yet not a judge. A political figure and yet completely nonpartisan. An outspoken advocate and yet with no power to implement any of his findings. More than anything else,

Kirby became a highly respected, and even loved, national figure. His power to communicate to all Australians and to explain even the most complex legal problems to a lay audience was peerless. Geoffrey Robertson was certain of how Michael Kirby would be remembered.

> The great thing about Michael, looking at him as a great member, if you like, of the human race, is his ability to synthesise principles in a way that very few if any others can. A way that has provided the basis for progress in medical science, in judicial organisation, in genome therapy, and in so many areas where he's used the skills that first became apparent during his ten years as a law reform commissioner to provide international organisations with the principles, the codes on which they can work and progress. I don't see Michael Kirby as a great radical. In fact, we often jokingly argue about our differences of opinion. He believes you've got to walk before you can run, and he's provided at least the running track for doing that in many areas. And I think this is his great contribution to international society.

Two references given to the ALRC by the new attorney-general Robert Ellicott were to lead to significant reports for the shape of law both in Australia and internationally. The first was on the issue of privacy, and the second was on human tissue transplants. In an address to the Australian Computer Society in Melbourne on 12 November 1976, Kirby quoted Jimmy Carter. In response to a journalist's question, 'How would you sum up the campaign?

What have been the important themes?' The US President-Elect had nominated 'additional openness in government. Strip away secrecy. Have a greater respect for personal privacy.' At a time in Australia when no ordinary person owned a computer or would even imagine that they could or should do so, Kirby was discussing issues that would still be controversial more than thirty years later:

> Intellectual property: patents, copyright and trade secrets, throw up difficulties when the computer dimension is added. Is a computer program susceptible to copyright? Is it a 'literary' work? These and many like problems are now appearing at last in the law journals of this country and overseas. My concern at the moment is with privacy and the problems for the preservation of proper bounds of privacy in the computer age.

ALRC Report 22, simply titled *Privacy*, was published in two volumes and went to more than a thousand pages. It was the most comprehensive and wide-ranging document of its type that had ever been assembled. Its final publication was not until 1983. The production of this one report covered almost the entire time Kirby was to be in the job of chairman of the ALRC. As early as 1978, and as a result of his knowledge in the area, Kirby was called on to act as Australia's representative at the Organisation for Economic Co-operation and Development on an expert group on privacy protection. At the time, the OECD member countries included most of the developed Western European nations, the USA, Canada, Japan, Australia and New Zealand. Michael Kirby impressed the group and was immediately elected to chair it.

In 1978 the world was increasingly moving towards globalisation and most of the members of the OECD were developing laws that would allow for and regulate the free flow of data across international borders. Kirby's expert panel was formed in order to address a number of related issues including removing impediments, ostensibly aimed at protecting privacy, to such legitimate international activities as airline bookings. And allied to this, to see that national governments didn't unreasonably restrict flows of data under the cover of privacy protection. Kirby's group was tasked with pointing the way towards making the myriad of different national 'laws on data protection harmonious or (at least) compatible'.

As Australia's official representative to this international body, Kirby had now begun a career of involvement in international affairs that would see him traverse the globe, at his busiest, on an almost weekly basis. He now had official diplomatic status when he left the country and could speak with authority not just on matters of Australian law but also on implications and developments all over the world. Since he was not acting at all in his role as a judge, even though he retained the title, he had a certain freedom in his commentaries to slide into even quite contentious political areas.

The *Privacy* report recommended the introduction of a full-time privacy commissioner with statutory guidelines for dealing with invasions of privacy. New legislation was suggested to regulate listening devices and optical surveillance and to prohibit telephone tapping and illegal interception of the mail. The report recommended that all Australians should be able to access their own personal information and it should become a right enshrined in federal law. Finally, the report looked to the future, highlighting developments including cable television, personal computers and global satellite surveillance. Many of the topics raised went on to become everyday issues but in 1983 they were generally unknown to the public. Kirby's work in this area was truly groundbreaking, not just in Australia but internationally.

The importance of privacy protection was of obvious personal interest to Kirby. He was now more recognisable than at any other time in his life and with public recognition came problems, especially for a gay man living with his partner – even in the exclusive and secluded harbour-side Sydney suburb of Rose Bay. Johan and Michael remained cautious. From time to time they holidayed in the US, sometimes in Palm Springs, 160 kilometres from Los Angeles, and sometimes sampling the gay scene in San Francisco. Johan had always liked following the sun, and Southern California was even more consistent in that regard than Sydney with its sudden subtropical downpours. They would visit the Jewish restaurants, go out for Jell-O or to Sizzler for a steak, and just sit in the sun and read books. 'He liked it, and therefore I liked it,' Michael explains.

> I wasn't ever, because of my fair skin, quite so enamoured of sitting in the sun and in fact, what I did in that department wasn't good for me, but he loves it. To some extent you could let your hair down there more than you could in Australia – more than I could in Australia. But every day or so we would be in a restaurant and someone would come over and recognise me, because I was then the chairman of the Law Reform Commission, so you knew that you were never really

> unknown. A lot of Australian tourists were there, especially in San Francisco.

Paradoxically, while Michael and Johan were jealously guarding their own private life together, he was increasing his high profile as a 'celebrity judge' in the media. In early 1980 Michael Kirby appeared on the John Laws radio program on Sydney's 2UE, one of the highest-rating programs in the country. Laws had his own special brand of music and talk and was an early adopter of the 'shock jock' persona. The talkback host lauded Kirby and each surprised the other with their attitudes – Laws supporting action on police complaints and Kirby claiming no evidence existed to support the efficacy of random breath-testing on reducing the road toll. But there was one area where Kirby would not go.

> Laws: Has the Law Reform Commission looked closely on the law on homosexuality, for example?
> Kirby: No, we are a federal commission and we work to areas that are specifically assigned to us.

Laws persisted. 'Have you given any consideration to those sorts of laws? As a human being, what's your attitude to the laws that are existent in most states?' Kirby brushed it aside: 'Well, I think it is important for me to confine myself to the matters that are given to the commission.' Laws wouldn't let it go. 'You don't want to be involved in that one?' Kirby calmly responded, 'As a citizen, of course I have my own views, but I don't think my views as a citizen are any more valuable than the views of any other citizen.'

Michael Kirby was a handsome, successful, high-profile 41-year-old bachelor who had never been romantically linked to a woman. Laws had done some asking around and most people, of course, had their suspicions. As Johan later put it in his uniquely understated way, the thought that people did not know about Michael's sexuality, that even close friends and colleagues could be unaware, 'Well, that would surprise me.' The 'Don't ask, don't tell' formula was strictly followed. Even John Laws obeyed the rules, eventually ending the line of questioning with: 'We shan't press the point, that's not that important.'

By the end of the decade, Michael Kirby was easily the best-known judge in Australia. This was ironic, since he had actually only acted as a judge for little more than a month at the end of 1974. Nevertheless, Justice Kirby was famous, in large part because he knew how to use the Australian media. Professor Henry Mayer, the authority on politics and the media in Australia, would walk into his first-year lectures at Sydney University holding up a copy of *New Idea* and *The Australian Women's Weekly*. 'How many of you read these magazines?' No hands would go up in the packed lecture theatre, the students sniggering at the thought. Mayer would screech back at the shocked audience: 'You must! You must! You must!' These magazines had an enormous circulation among ordinary working Australians; they could be a hundred times more influential than a program on ABC Radio. Kirby never attended Mayer's lectures but he had learnt that lesson.

In late 1977 *The Australian Women's Weekly* carried a double-page spread: 'You and the law, how to make it, not break it.' Here Michael Kirby is described as 'one of Australia's most influential judges', trying to 'make the law better'. Several cases from the files of the ALRC were recounted, including the young mother bankrupted over a bill of $96.40, a Queensland man who could get no employment because a police record wrongly listed him as a convicted criminal, an Italian man who was charged for calling police 'bastards' when in fact he was using the Italian word *basta*, meaning 'enough'. In this article Kirby asked Australians to have input into his inquiries. The article finished with the exhortation, 'Address your experiences and your ideas to: "The Law and Me", care of *The Australian Women's Weekly*.'

The editor of the *Women's Weekly* was a young and dynamic journalist, Ita Buttrose, who had become a senior executive in the Packer family's cut-throat business of magazine publication in Australia. Ita Buttrose and Michael Kirby were to become good friends. He appeared again in the popular publication in January 1982:

> Should parents be able to choose the sex of their child? What is the definition of brain death? Such fundamental problems cannot be ignored with medical science surging ahead in its researches in genetic engineering and tissue transplants. JUSTICE MICHAEL KIRBY, Chairman of the Australian Law Reform Commission, explores the implications of these complex questions.

Kirby thought it was important to get the message out as widely as possible. The reference that Bob Ellicott had given him on human tissue transplants back in 1976 had been tabled the following year but it had not lost any of its relevance. Indeed, there seemed to be daily advances in medical science and the law was barely catching up. Kirby ended his piece in the *Women's Weekly* with:

> I am just a lawyer. My concern is that our legal system should be ready to provide answers to the questions I have mentioned. I hope that future generations will not say of our time: 'Yes, Australians then reaped benefits from a lot of very inventive scientists, but they were not imaginative enough or just couldn't be bothered to sort out the moral and social problems which their scientific advances produced.'

The ALRC report *Human Tissue Transplants* advocated that the definition of death in Australian law should be based on brain function and not solely in relation to heartbeat or circulation. This is now the accepted definition. The recommendations of the report were embraced nationwide, resulting in new Tissue Transplant Acts federally and in every state and territory. The report also emphasised that payment of any kind, or any kind of trade and commerce in human body parts or tissues, should be outlawed.

> That was a most important project, not only for its subject matter but also because it demonstrated that difficult questions, involving health, law and ethics could, in an enlightened modern democracy, be tackled in a public way. It showed that we could achieve results in legislation, not just a report consigned to the 'too-hard drawer' or public debate leading nowhere.

Michael Kirby's optimism that Australian society and the law could deal with difficult and perplexing issues of ethics and medical science was to be tested. He had seen the interaction of the law and the medical profession up close during his years as a compensation lawyer and he knew it was always going to be hard work. But in 1981 the first reports of an unexplained illness, especially among the gay community and also affecting intravenous drug users in Sydney, started to appear. Within a year both Michael and Johan were aware of friends and acquaintances who were getting sick; by the end of the decade, it was as though a whole generation of their friends, sometimes very close friends, had died of the horrible wasting disease. The medical profession was unable to explain what was happening and the term Acquired Immune Deficiency Syndrome, which did no more than describe the observed condition, was coined. Kirby could not sit back and watch this horrible affliction claim the lives of so many otherwise healthy young gay men and do nothing about it. He couldn't stand by as Christian religious extremists and even Australian politicians proclaimed the disease as a public good, ridding the world of 'immoral sodomites'. He did not understand a Christianity that was so full of hate and he would not accept it.

Kirby knew that he was not only morally bound to do something but he also knew that he was almost uniquely placed to do it. He was the most outspoken authority on medicine, ethics and the law and he was widely respected in the Australian and international community. The issues raised by what was slowly being recognised as a global pandemic were fascinating and urgent. There was one problem. As far as the general public were concerned, Michael

Top *'I think of you constantly and am grateful for all you've done for me. What a wonderful, happy childhood we had.'* Michael Kirby and his father, Don, 1951.
Bottom *'Dear Mum... Thanking you for everything.'* Clockwise from top: Michael, Donald, David, Moppie (on all fours), Diana and Jean Kirby, 1954.

Left Michael the photographer: *'Well, maybe I'm trying to capture life before it all disappears.'* **Right** In the famous Fort Street High School prefect's blazer, with sister Diana, 1955.
Bottom Michael's grandmother, Normie, and Uncle Jack Simpson, the national treasurer of the Australian Communist Party.

Top With mother, Jean. *'At a critical moment in a young person's life they have to hide their reality from those who are their greatest source of love and strength.'*
Left At Sydney University: *'I was a non-sexual being.'*

Right Leaving Sydney with fellow delegate John Clark on a National Union of Australian University Students delegation to Nigeria and twenty-five other countries in Africa and Asia, January 1963.
Bottom Pro bono honorary student solicitor, Sydney University.

Left *'My first love':* Demofilo Solera, 1968. **Bottom** *'This was a time in [Michael's] life when he was beginning to embrace the fact that he would pursue a relationship and love.'* With David Kirby, London, Christmas 1970.

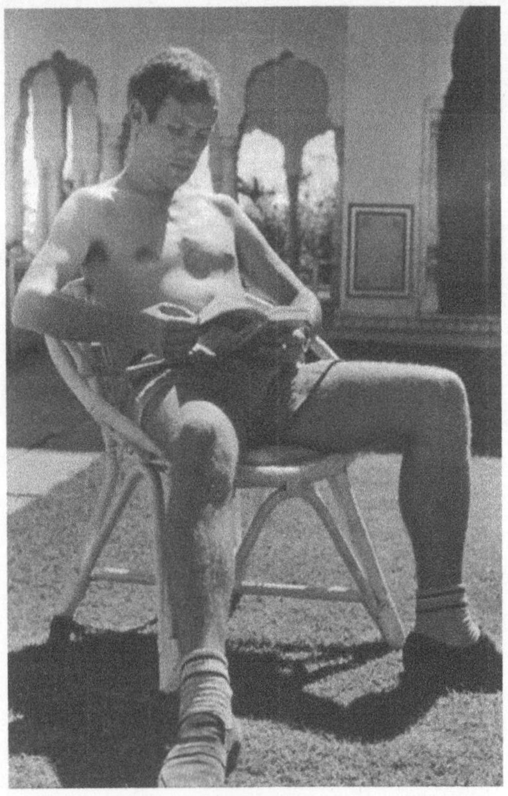

Top *'Anyone who can live for a year in a kombi van with another human being can live a lifetime with them.'* With Johan van Vloten, Sydney, 1969.
Right A rare moment in the sun, India, 1970. *'I wasn't ever, because of my fair skin, quite so enamoured of sitting in the sun and in fact, what I did in that department wasn't good for me…'*

Michael and Johan in India, 1970.

'In a very short time I was introduced to [Michael's] parents. Let's say within two or three weeks.' Dining with Jean and Don Kirby.

Bottom left Senator Lionel Murphy QC, Attorney-General 1972–1975, High Court Justice 1975–1986. **Bottom right** Neville Wran QC MLA, Labor Premier of NSW 1976–1986. Wran wrote to Kirby in 1970: *'It's a great shame you are not working for the Party.'*

Photos courtesy Film Art Doco

Working on weekends in the president's chambers, Court of Appeal, Sydney Law Courts.

Top Lunching with Gareth Evans at Kirby's High Court chambers in Canberra. **Bottom** In the Sydney chambers with Geoffrey Robertson QC. In the background, just a glimpse of the photographic collection: King Sihanouk, Lord Denning and the Dalai Lama.

Left Celebrity judge: Cartoon on page seven of the *Sydney Morning Herald*, 27 May 1977, headlined: 'The man reshaping the laws of our nation'.
Bottom At radio station 2GB in Sydney, September 1984 – the month Kirby was sworn in as president of the NSW Court of Appeal.

Top Johan, Jean and Don in courtroom number 1, High Court, at Michael's swearing-in ceremony, 1996. **Bottom** *'If in the end of my life I look back and say, was there one thing you did that really helped humanity, it would probably be going to Cambodia…'* UN special representative on Cambodia, 1993–6.

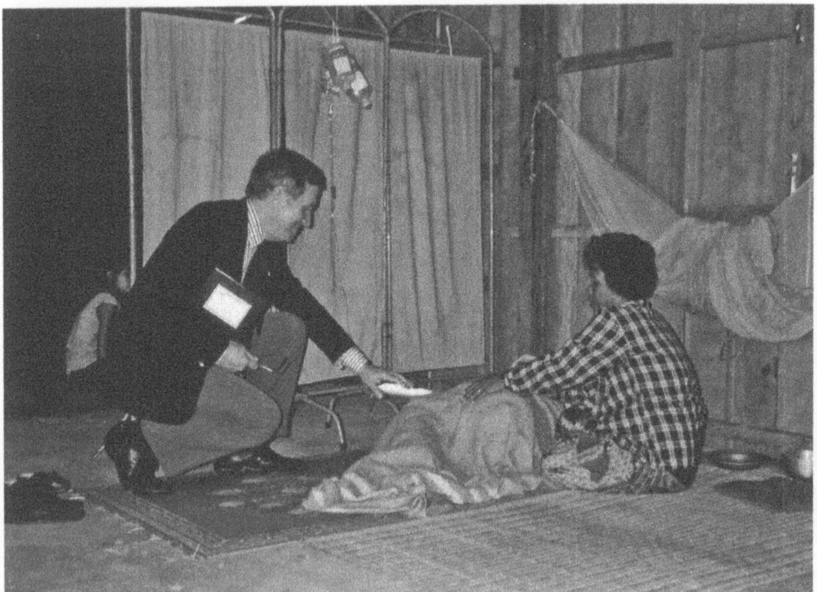

Top With Tony Abbott, fellow constitutional monarchist and good friend, High Court, Canberra, 1997. **Bottom (l–r)** Justices Mary Gaudron, Michael McHugh, Michael Kirby and Kenneth Hayne, and Chief Justice Sir Gerard Brennan, Hobart, March 1998.

Top to bottom With Prime Minister John Howard at the unveiling of the Garfield Barwick Plaque, High Court, Canberra, 9 August 2001; exchanging travel stories with Gough Whitlam and Johan, 25 November 1999; with Shadow Minister for Health Julia Gillard at the Archibald Prize luncheon, 2006 (portraits of both were finalists).

Top Standing in front of the Sydney Street house in Concord, with Don Kirby and Johan, 2002. **Bottom** Johan relaxes at home, 2005.

'Underneath everyone's dark suits is a bright golden outfit, which they're just waiting to get into.' On stage with Elf Tranzporter, Victorian Arts Law Week, May 2007.

Kirby was a bachelor, and as far as he was concerned, he wasn't planning on revealing his homosexuality any time soon. To tackle the controversy that was AIDS as a closeted gay man would surely be to court disaster. Somehow Kirby needed to find a formula of words, if it was possible, that would allow him to take action and make comment without totally revealing his own personal situation. Perhaps simply by associating himself so closely with the AIDS crisis he would be making a public statement of sorts, from which he could not then resile. And if that was so, maybe it was not such a bad thing. At any rate, he certainly did not intend to curtail his public speaking. In fact, he intended to be even more outspoken.

In every year since 1961 the ABC has called upon a prominent Australian to present its landmark series of radio lectures, named after the former chairman of the ABC Sir Richard Boyer. In previous years the Boyer Lectures had been given by Professor Zelman Cowen, Dr H.C. 'Nugget' Coombs, Justice Dame Roma Mitchell, Professor Manning Clark, ACTU president Bob Hawke and Professor Bernard Smith. This was a rollcall of some of the most respected and influential people in the country. In 1983 Michael Kirby joined the list. His topic was 'The Judges', and it was the first time a prominent judge had spoken in this way about the profession. It brought judges into the minds of hundreds of thousands of Australian radio listeners and asked them to think about a sphere of government most people hitherto knew little or nothing about.

The first of his lectures began with the enticing invitation, 'Come with me into the world of the judiciary . . . behind the purple curtain.' During the next six weeks he ranged over topics as diverse as the Lindy Chamberlain conviction and the Tasmania dams case. The lectures attempted to answer the questions:

> Who are our judges? How are they appointed? What work should be committed to them? How do they perform their duties when policy choices must be made? What of complaints against judges? What role, if any, do they have in the reform of the law? What is the future of the judiciary?

From the first lecture, Michael Kirby caused a stir. The rather innocuous question he began with, 'Who are our judges?', was to lead in directions the very conservative, almost all-male profession (only three women out of 330), almost entirely of British stock, in some cases from the same one or two select private schools, did not like. Kirby quoted Justice Lionel Murphy: 'A proper balance throughout our legal system is overdue.' There was only one issue that was designed to antagonise judges more than questioning the make-up of their ranks, and that was questioning their competence for office. Kirby did not shy away from this contentious area. In his fourth lecture he asked if it was appropriate that judges who might have become incapacitated, or who had misbehaved in some other way, could only be called to account by removal by a joint sitting of parliament. Should there be a complaints mechanism? He decided, whatever the mechanism was to be, it should balance two competing requirements: 'the preservation of judicial independence, including even the protection of original and unorthodox judges, and the provision of adequate redress for citizens with a legitimate grievance'.

'The Judges' was an enormous success. It thrust Kirby onto the national stage once and for all, and secured his place as an important legal thinker. There was still the old rump of judges who muttered about his very credentials to comment on a judiciary of which, in their eyes, he had never been a real member. But these voices had gradually begun to recede into the background. Kirby was increasingly perceived as the calm, rational, dispassionate advocate for sensible and overdue change.

Throughout his period as chair of the ALRC, Kirby's relationship with Lionel Murphy developed from no more than a professional acquaintance into a close personal friendship. Murphy, who was a naturally outgoing person, found the High Court isolating, so different to the cut and thrust of parliament. He would often ring colleagues to discuss legal points or to simply have intellectual conversation. Fellow judges were sometimes contacted by Murphy and as time went by, phone calls to Kirby started to become a weekly routine. The chief justice Garfield Barwick had no time for Murphy, and he and the other judges on the High Court often joined together in majority judgements, while Murphy, initially at least, was a sole radical dissenter. It didn't make for a very congenial atmosphere, and Kirby wondered how one could survive in such a tension-filled environment. Nevertheless, Murphy survived and by the early 1980s was more often than not in the majority.

> Lionel was a sort of counterpoint to my own life. He was a very unconventional man, he was a very gregarious man,

> he was a person who was given to very unusual things. He would ring you whilst you were in the middle of your own labours and he was in the middle of some case in the High Court, and he would be very anxious about this or that line, and he would talk about it to me, as another judge, about the issues and problems that were concerning him. Then he would go off to talk about nuclear physics, and then he would be talking about the latest issues of biotechnology. He was a very friendly man, and a very unconventional person, for a lawyer. Most lawyers are fairly conventional people and most judges are extremely conventional, and most of the judges of the highest court are even more so. But Lionel Murphy was a very unusual human being, and his love for his fellow man and woman shone through.

Michael often saw his friend at legal functions – the swearing-in of the new silks, the retirement of judges, Bar dinners. In May 1980, Murphy, aware of Kirby's affection for the constitutional monarchy and his love of the great historic occasions, invited him to the grand opening of the new High Court building in Canberra. To Kirby's delight, he was introduced to the Queen. It was to be just one of many such meetings throughout his life. Within a few years Michael Kirby was officially recognised: the Queen's New Year Honours list in 1983 included his name. He was appointed a Companion of the Order of St Michael and St George, which carried with it the post-nominal letters CMG. Kirby had always appreciated Prime Minister Malcolm Fraser's reintroduction of the Imperial Honours system after Whitlam had moved to abolish it, and he accepted the honour with pride. Murphy, by contrast, had eschewed Fraser's offer of a knighthood early in his term on the High Court.

On the last day of 1982, one of the inaugural commissioners of the ALRC and now justice of the High Court, Sir Gerard Brennan, wrote to Michael's mother, Jean. The two had come to know each other over the years, meeting at ALRC functions or at the High Court when Michael and Jean had been visiting Lionel Murphy. He congratulated her on her son's recent award. 'He is so manifestly the beneficiary of his mother's personality and abilities, and the honour bestowed on him honours those who have formed him: chief among whom, of course, is you.' Jean immediately wrote back to Sir Gerard to thank him. 'MDK received quite enough letters of congratulations. You were the only one to write to me. We are all very proud of him though I am sure you know he has to be put in his place by his family at least once a week.'

With the election of the Hawke Labor Government in 1983, several things started to fall into place for Michael Kirby. The now Senator Gareth Evans, the new attorney-general, appointed Kirby to the bench of the Federal Court of Australia. No one could say he wasn't a real judge any longer. Kirby was happy to accept the position – indeed, delighted to be elevated from the Arbitration Commission. He would continue as the full-time chair of the ALRC and keep up his many international engagements, but would now also occasionally sit on matters in the Federal Court. Perhaps sometime in the near future he might consider resigning from the ALRC and moving back to the bench as a full-time judge. But for the time being, Kirby was very pleased with this state of affairs, and he would now be busier than ever.

If it had been a NSW state judicial position as opposed to a federal job, it might have been a more difficult decision. Whitlam had overseen the removal of discrimination against homosexuals at a federal level back in 1973, but homosexuality was still a criminal offence in New South Wales in the early 1980s. A NSW judge at that time might very well be forced to convict or sentence gay men for what was, anachronistically, still a crime. (Of course, many NSW judges, lawyers and politicians were gay and it hadn't stopped them accepting their positions.)

Late in 1982, attempts to decriminalise homosexuality had failed in the NSW Parliament. Michael Kirby was beginning to get irritated by the lack of action. New South Wales was his home state, Sydney his home, and he was tired of the years of pretence, secrecy and the cover-ups. He and Johan had the right, like any other citizens, to live their lives without discrimination and persecution. How many more years did they and thousands of others in Australia have to endure this nasty oppression? Shortly before his appointment to the Federal Court in 1983, Kirby accepted an invitation to give an address to the NSW Gay Business Association. His topic was homosexual law reform. Only a few days before his address, the NSW Police had raided a gay club in Sydney.

Kirby explained to his audience that as a federal officer his remit was to act on references given to him by the federal attorney-general. No reference on homosexual law reform had been forthcoming, so any comments he made were his own personal opinions. He went on to detail the confused situation under NSW law:

- It is a criminal offence for a male person to perform certain homosexual acts.

- Yet it is not and never has been an offence for a female person to perform homosexual acts.
- A person can be sent to prison and be criminally stigmatised for pursuing his sexual orientation.
- Yet despite this enunciation in the criminal law, other persons, including most employers, may *not* discriminate on the grounds of a person's sexual preference.
- Because of reform of rape laws, it is in some cases more serious to perform consensual indecent acts with a male person than it is to perform an act of rape itself.

Things would not change for another year. At the state election in March 1984, Neville Wran and the ALP were returned to government. Unexpectedly, the Premier indicated he intended to decriminalise homosexuality. It had not been an issue at the election but it was a reform that was well overdue. In Victoria, South Australia, the ACT and, of course, federally, homosexuality had been decriminalised. The fabric of society had not disintegrated. Far from it, the scurrilous notion of police and officers of the state peering into people's bedrooms had been thrown out in those states and the country was better for it.

In May of that year the NSW Parliament finally passed legislation decriminalising homosexuality. In practice, it didn't change Johan or Michael's life that much but there was certainly a sense of relief. The fear of a criminal sanction, however remote, that had hung over Kirby's head ever since he was eleven was now gone forever.

One month later, the NSW attorney-general, Paul Landa, rang Kirby with a proposal: would he consider appointment as president of the NSW Court of Appeal? Kirby was excited by the offer – the presidency was the second-most senior judicial position in New South Wales after the chief justice of the Supreme Court and a highly sought-after appointment. Michael McHugh QC, the barrister who had warned Kirby all those years ago not to take the job at the Arbitration Commission ('you will sink like a stone'), had been considered a very likely choice, and Justice Bob Hope, a current member of the Appeal Court, was thought to be next in line for promotion. It was a great accolade for Kirby, and an important recognition of his achievements to date and his skills. Once again in his career, if he was to accept the position, he would be coming from outside to trump people who were considered, at least by a large section of their peers, to be more senior and deserving. By now, that did not concern Kirby in the slightest. Other matters were more pressing, as far as he was concerned. He wanted to continue his work on international bodies and to continue, where appropriate, to speak and act publicly on issues that he deemed important.

He knew that if he were to take the position, then his life would change dramatically. Working full-time as a very senior judge he would not be able to have the kind of flexibility that the ALRC had afforded him. He would be far more confined in the matters he could discuss publicly and he would be locked to his office, with much less freedom than he currently enjoyed. It would be a diet of work, work and more work. In the end, though, the offer was too good to turn down. He decided life would change dramatically, but it would be for the better.

Before he had been approached, there was talk in legal circles that the job might go to Kirby, and two or three judges of the

Appeal Court invited him up to chambers for a cup of tea. It was a rather awkward meeting, the judges present making it clear to him that they thought he was not the best qualified person for the job, should he be offered it, and that it should go to their colleague, Bob Hope. The strong suggestion was that Kirby should stand aside. It was water off a duck's back. He politely drank their tea, told them it was academic since there had been no offer of apppointment, and left. It was only later, when he heard that two of the judges were complaining around the traps that the job was going to 'that sodomite Kirby', that he felt hurt. Every little homophobic barb had its effect and they could not simply be dismissed or laughed off. When it came from people Kirby considered his colleagues and even friends, it was particularly cruel. Kirby remembered his father's letter warning him to be aware of what so-called friends might actually be saying behind his back. Nasty gossip and innuendo could destroy a life and bring down the tallest poppy.

As Kirby prepared to begin his new life as the president of the NSW Court of Appeal, his friend Lionel Murphy began a most public and tragic decline. It started with the publication of transcripts of illegally taped conversations between the judge and his lawyer. Murphy, along with Gough Whitlam and Jim Cairns, had been dragged through the Queanbeyan Magistrates Court on a private prosecution, wholly politically motivated, over their actions when in government. That case was thrown out by the magistrate but during the hearings and in the aftermath, Murphy's phone calls were tapped by corrupt officers of the NSW Police. In what was perhaps the single most damaging act of journalistic irresponsibility in the whole 'Murphy Affair', as it became known – and there were many – *The Age* ran the following exchange, taken from purported transcripts of those illegal telephone interceptions. The two men were allegedly making small talk about their social engagements over the weekend: 'The solicitor asked: "Did you have a good time?" The judge replied: "If you can call getting tired and drunk and fucking everything a good time, yeah . . ."'

But *The Age* had transposed the statements. It was the judge who appeared in the transcripts asking the question and the solicitor who made the salacious remarks. *The Age* published a correction *weeks* later but the damage was done and Murphy's reputation destroyed.

Murphy was subjected to years of intense and unrelenting media attacks, which culminated in a criminal prosecution launched by the Director of Public Prosecutions 'to clear the air'. He was charged with attempting to pervert the course of justice over a series of private communications with the NSW Chief Stipendiary Magistrate Clarrie Briese in the early 1980s. Some in the legal profession felt that the charges were ludicrous, that the alleged comments were no more than professional discussions between a High Court judge and a junior judicial figure, and of the sort that happen every day between judges. Many others in the notoriously conservative profession had no sympathy for Lionel Murphy. Unfortunately for Murphy, the jury in his first trial were misdirected by the judge and he was convicted.

During that trial, Kirby agreed to give character evidence for Murphy. It was unusual – judges generally avoid going into the courts, unless they are hearing the case themselves. If a judge gives evidence in a case, they put themselves in a position where their evidence may be contested or disbelieved, which could bring the judiciary into disrepute. But Kirby believed strongly that Murphy was entitled to the support of his peers, and since Murphy was a very senior judge, his peers would be senior judges. In the nasty partisan atmosphere swirling around at the time, it was a brave step. Neville Wran was convicted of contempt of court for saying that he believed Lionel Murphy was innocent. In Murphy's own words it was a topsy-turvy time, like something out of *Alice in Wonderland*, where 'the judge says first the verdict, then the trial'.

Murphy appealed the conviction and secured a new trial, and the second jury acquitted him of the charges. But what had begun essentially as a media and political campaign to get him off the High Court bench continued unabated. Murphy was driven to his grave by the stress of the unrelenting claims and counter-claims against him. Cancer took hold of his body. Just three months after the judge had been acquitted, Michael Kirby spoke at his state funeral at a packed Sydney Town Hall.

> Never in all the years I knew him did I hear him utter a single uncharitable word about those who hated or assailed him. Even in the recent years of trial he was full of charity and kindliness. His concern was not for himself, but for others, for Ingrid, for his family and for principle, as he saw it. His injunction to us today would be, I am sure, to set aside entirely petty hatreds and recriminations. It would be to lift our sights to the way in which we can all, individually, each one of us, contribute to a kindlier and more sensitive world.

> Lionel Murphy had enthusiasm in the old Greek sense. When I spoke to him, shortly before he died, he was full of courage and fight. It is true that his warm and resonant voice had lost some of its power. His prodigious energy was flagging, but he had lost none of his optimism and dedication. And none of his faith in the law, in the independent judiciary and in a better world.

In these his early years at the Court of Appeal, Michael had to face a series of tragedies, and it was a sad time in his life. Within a few months his father's indomitable mother Norma died, Michael's own mother Jean had a heart attack and had to undergo a bypass operation, his brother David's wife, Marie-Line, died of cancer, and many of his and Johan's friends succumbed to the AIDS virus.

At this cheerless time Kirby drew on his own 'optimism and dedication'. He decided to make a big statement. To the chagrin of some of his colleagues on the Court of Appeal, he agreed to speak at the first National AIDS Conference in Melbourne. If he was not coming out of the closet by making this appearance, he was opening the door wide and saying, once and for all: 'Here I am!'

8

Holding the Middle Chair

> It is vital that scientist and social scientist, politician and media reporter, AIDS patient and ordinary citizen should all recognise the challenge to our species which is presented by AIDS – but also the opportunity. In ten or fifteen years time, when we look back on this grim moment, each one of us will wish to feel that we have played our part, however small it may be, to contribute, in a decent but vigorous way, to the response to this threat to humanity. Ask not for whom the AIDS bell tolls. It tolls for us all.
>
> *Michael Kirby*
> *Speech at the WHO/Australian*
> *Inter-regional Ministerial Meeting on AIDS*

Like prisons and horror movies, the most disturbing thing about a hospital ward is the soundtrack. Groaning, coughing, vomiting, interspersed with sporadic clinical announcements over the public address system. A cold and emotionless voice is heard – 'Code red, code red, level seven' – then buzzers and electronic pulses and more announcements. Sometimes the most unsettling are the quiet, distant sounds. A muted sobbing drifting through the ward from an anonymous patient or a distressed family member. That is just the basic daily routine; it never gets any better than that. Michael Kirby heard all these things as he took the long walk through a Sydney AIDS ward and saw a whole floor of young men wasting away.

Peter was only in his forties and had been quite an athlete at Fort Street High School with Michael, although a few years younger. Peter contacted his old school friend and the two went to dinner. Peter wanted to ask Michael a favour: would he speak at his funeral? Michael looked at the apparently healthy young man opposite him and he knew what was coming. Peter explained: he was HIV-positive. Michael tried as best he could to reassure his friend. Of course he would speak, but such a eulogy would not be needed for many years to come, Peter would be fine, a cure and even a vaccine would be found soon, and anyway, the probability of progressing to full-blown AIDS was low. Peter relaxed at these comforting words and he seemed relieved, but through the smile Michael could see the fear in his eyes. Michael was frightened as well.

Less than six months later Peter quickly became very sick. He was diagnosed with lymphoma. Michael went to see him in hospital.

> Peter's concern was how he could tell his colleagues that he would not return next week to work. He had already braved that journey once and told his parents. To the fear of death was added, for him, the hurt of embarrassment and stigmatisation,

> even of loathing among some at the mention of the fearful acronym. I composed a letter for him. It just said, accurately, that he had been diagnosed with cancer and would need chemotherapy. He would probably not be back this semester. It was a great relief for him when he signed the letter. He wanted to act professionally and honourably.

Peter died in hospital shortly after this meeting, and Michael, who was then in India for a conference of judges, heard about his death in Bombay. He never did speak at Peter's funeral. No matter how much Michael wanted to be there for every friend or acquaintance that was struck down, he could not – the magnitude of the tragedy was just too great. But there were important things he could do, and his work continued apace.

The Hawke Government's health minister, Neal Blewett, had crafted a response to the AIDS epidemic that was immediate and effective. The first that most Australians knew about AIDS was in the form of the confronting 'grim reaper' advertising campaign. Prime-time television audiences saw the grim reaper, a ghastly figure with a skull and a black scythe, send bowling balls of death towards unsuspecting babies, children, men and women. The deeply sinister voice of actor John Stanton could be heard:

> At first only gays and IV drug–users were being killed by AIDS, but now we know every one of us could be devastated by it. [Close-up of a crying ten-year-old blond girl with plaits.] The fact is that over 50 000 men, women and children now carry the AIDS virus, that in three years nearly 2000 of us will be

> dead, that if not stopped it could kill more Australians than World War II. But AIDS can be stopped and you can help stop it. If you have sex, have just one safe partner or always use condoms, always! [Title card: AIDS. PREVENTION IS THE ONLY CURE WE'VE GOT. FOR INFORMATION PHONE THE AIDS LINE (008) 042161.]

It was controversial but highly effective, and along with advocacy for the use of condoms and provision of needle exchanges for intravenous-drug users, Australia led the world in a compassionate and commonsense approach. Nevertheless, there were sections of the community that reacted very poorly. The Opposition health spokesman, Wilson 'Ironbar' Tuckey, a former Western Australian publican who had earnt his nickname after a conviction for violently assaulting an Aboriginal patron, suggested that homosexual men had only themselves to blame for AIDS. Around the world the reaction was often similar. The US Government banned HIV-positive people from entering the country (a ban only removed by Barack Obama in 2009; more than fifty countries still have entry restrictions in place) and opted for punitive policies of blaming the victims rather than adopting strategies for prevention. It refused to implement the three most effective strategies: needle exchanges, sex education and promotion of condom use.

Michael Kirby was outspoken on the issue, naming particularly unhelpful government responses as HILs – Highly Inefficient Laws. HIL I was the extreme proposition, seriously advocated, that the entire population be tested for AIDS. The expense and waste involved in this idea can only be imagined. HIL II referred to the mandatory testing of specified groups in the community, and HIL III was the issuing of mandatory certificates at state or national borders (declaring that an individual had been tested and was AIDS-free). Kirby utterly rejected these ideas. 'The whole thrust of effective social policy and lawmaking,' he insisted, 'must be to promote the spread of information and of measures for prevention of infection.'

Sitting as the president of the NSW Court of Appeal, Michael Kirby saw many cases go through the system where the judges were required to deal with AIDS as it affected human rights, discrimination, criminal law, negligence and even insurance law. At the same time he had quickly become one of the most well-recognised commentators on the AIDS crisis. Some in the legal profession saw a conflict of interest and politely suggested to Kirby that now he was the second most senior judicial figure in the state, he must give up his program of lectures, speeches and international commitments. There is a fundamental responsibility of judges to maintain strict silence in relation to cases that *might* come before them, let alone cases that they are presently hearing, the obvious reason being that if a case were prejudiced by a judge's words then it would have to be reheard. If three or more judges are hearing a matter, as on an appeal court, then there is the added possibility that the judge's remarks could be seen to be an attempt to influence his fellow judges. Again the case would have to be reheard, at enormous expense and inconvenience. Both scenarios risk the public losing confidence in the system. Some of Kirby's fellow Court of Appeal judges also believed it was inappropriate for the president to be regularly speaking on the same bill as homosexuals, sex workers and illicit-drug users.

> I was very respectful to them because they were all older than I and very experienced judges and I didn't want to do anything at all in my work as president of the Court of Appeal that would damage the court of which we were all members. But I pointed out that my years in the Law Reform Commission had given me particular insights into some issues, including medico-legal ones, and that this was a very big issue for Australia nationally, and that I had been asked by Jonathan Mann [leader of the World Health Organization's global AIDS program] to be involved and that I thought I could make a little contribution.
>
> Anyway, we hit a compromise: that I would be more careful but that I would continue doing it. It was a little awkward because I could see their point of view, but I just also could see the importance and urgency of which I was being reminded repeatedly by the infection and death of friends.

This tension between Kirby's judicial function and his public persona and activities was to be an ongoing issue. He accepted outside appointments that were uncontroversial and suitably judge-like: chancellor of Macquarie University, member of the executive of the CSIRO. But there were a host of others that were considered inappropriate in more conservative circles: trustee of AIDS Trust Australia, where he joined his friend Ita Buttrose; member of the NSW Ministerial Advisory Committee on AIDS; commissioner of the WHO Global Commission on AIDS; chairman of UNESCO Expert Group on Rights of Peoples; and Australian delegate-general to the Conference of UNESCO. These represent only a tiny fraction of the organisations he was a member of or a delegate to, and the papers and symposiums were legion (more than 800 written, published or delivered from 1984 to 95), all on top of his full-time work as the president of the busiest appeal court in Australia.

Kirby later maintained that only once while a judge of the Court of Appeal did he put a foot wrong in terms of the conflict between his public persona and judicial responsibilities. It did not occur because of an unintended slip; quite the contrary – it came about because he felt it was his duty to highlight the issues in a case, even though it was still to be decided by the Court of Appeal on which he sat.

In May 1987, sitting with his two brother judges of the NSW Court of Criminal Appeal, Michael Kirby saw the prisoner brought into the courtroom by two guards. Kenneth Bailey was appealing against the severity of his sentence on the major grounds that he was suffering from AIDS. There is an established legal principle that if a prisoner is suffering a severe illness, then a reduced sentence could be in order if the illness is likely to make the sentence more onerous, or, in the worst case, result in the prisoner dying in jail. It is an uncontroversial legal principle but in the heightened atmosphere of fear and even panic that existed in these early years of AIDS, everything was potentially controversial. Adding to the volatility of the case was the fact that the prisoner had been convicted of rape (although the victim had not acquired the AIDS virus).

Justice Kirby wrote his judgement in the *Bailey* case but did not release it to the public; that would have to wait until the other two judges on the panel had also written their judgements. He then flew to the United States and spoke at the Third International

Conference on AIDS in Washington DC. He began by detailing the outline of Bailey's case, which he had heard only two weeks before. He described the scene in the courtroom and the atmosphere of dread and the powerful tension. In a forceful opening he compared the NSW authorities' treatment of this AIDS-infected prisoner to events in Washington the night before, when police had broken up a demonstration outside the White House. The Washington Police wore yellow gloves, as though AIDS protestors might infect them by their very touch. Kirby's words were a dramatic way of describing the raised level of discrimination, fear and prejudice that was in the community. He went on to detail the three grounds on which the prisoner had sought a reduction of his sentence: that there was a high likelihood that his condition would develop into a serious and probably life-threatening one; that the stressful prison environment would lead to an accelerated worsening of his health; and finally, that his agreement, while in prison, to be tested for AIDS and the resulting positive test had meant that his life was now much more difficult – he was isolated from fellow prisoners and stigmatised.

Kirby then made a statement to the conference of the kind he might have made from the bench many times before, and indeed he may well have said something similar from the bench in this matter. The difference was that he was not in the courtroom, but in a public meeting, and the other two judges on the case were yet to finish their deliberations.

> I cannot tell you the result of this appeal. Although my judgement has been written, the decision still awaits the judgements of the other members of the Court. Behind the issues relevant

> to this particular prisoner were, of course, considerations of the way in which the legal system will respond to the challenge of AIDS. Candour requires me to say so. If some recognition were not given to the impact of a positive test for AIDS in the case of this prisoner (and on the consequent intensity of his punishment) might this not discourage other prisoners from volunteering to take the HIV test? On the other hand, the courts must reflect the opinions of the community in matters of punishment, at least to some extent. As much recent evidence shows, in the matter of AIDS those opinions are often grounded in ignorance and fear, bordering on panic.

The paper was subsequently reported in the *Sydney Morning Herald*. Perhaps he did not expect the worldwide reach of the Fairfax press to catch up with him Washington. He had revealed nothing that was not already available to any member of the public interested in this case and he did not even mention it by name (although it was in the footnotes of the written speech). His purpose was not to influence his two fellow judges but instead to highlight issues that he saw as fundamental in the AIDS debate. Within the international AIDS community his uncompromising speech was received very well, but to his fellow judges in Sydney it was seen as a direct attack on their independence and totally unacceptable. For the first time in his career, it seemed, he had walked headlong into calamity.

On his return to Sydney, Kirby was immediately confronted by the other two Court of Criminal Appeal judges who had sat with him on the *Bailey* matter, the chief justice of NSW Sir Laurence Street and Justice Jack Slattery. They were furious. They felt his public remarks on the case had the effect of 'subtly pressuring' them towards his view, and that he must now remove himself and discard his judgement. Kirby refused. He was convinced that technically he had done nothing wrong. It was the stubborn streak he had inherited from his father: once he had made up his mind there was no going back. Nevertheless, he was in an embarrassing position – precisely because he had referred to this case in the Washington conference, he now felt compelled to stick to his judgement and allow it to go through. To remove himself would be tantamount to betraying the position he felt so strongly about: that those with AIDS should not suffer discrimination.

Unfortunately the simple proposition that Mr Bailey, a prisoner with AIDS, should have his sentence reviewed because of his illness, was somehow lost in the internal judicial quarrel. Kirby found in favour of Bailey and the other two judges decided to make a statement – they submitted a joint, one-paragraph dismissal of his appeal. The case then went to the High Court where, although recognising the principle, 'Generally speaking, ill health will be a factor tending to mitigate punishment only when it appears that imprisonment would be a greater burden on the offender by reason of his state of health or where there is a serious risk of imprisonment having a gravely adverse effect on the offender's health', the High Court justices sent the matter back to the NSW Court of Criminal Appeal to be reheard. The new hearing was listed by Street for three judges from the criminal division, one of whom was Justice David Yeldham, a judge of the common law division and one of Kirby's fiercest critics. Yeldham would not have thought it was proper for a judge to speak out in the way Kirby so frequently did.

This time the appeal was unanimously dismissed.

This had been a most unsatisfactory episode. Kirby knew that on this occasion he had overstepped the mark. On reflection, he accepted that Street and Slattery had been right from the outset. At this realisation anyone else might have withered, stopped the public engagements, the AIDS work, the UN committees, and retreated into their shell. Not Michael Kirby. He had tested the limits of reasonable public commentary for a judge. If he had not overstepped the mark, then he would never have reached the limits of what might be proper. Having now learnt his lesson, Kirby was not going to repeat the mistake, but he was also not going to stop the behaviour that had led to his transgression. Laurence Street and Michael Kirby resumed a good working relationship and the affair did not damage their close rapport, both personal and professional. Street, who liked Kirby and admired his international activities and even his outspokenness (where appropriate), wrote to him not much more than a year into Kirby's presidency, in December 1985:

My Dear Michael,
I write to thank you for so many things that I am embarrassed by my tardiness [. . .] above all your unfailing help and support throughout the year – I value greatly the unreserved warmth of our personal relationship and I am proud indeed of the significant lift that your leadership has given to our Court of Appeal – a lift in both professional stature and authority as well as in the whole atmosphere that now pervades that Court in both its internal cohesion and collegiate philosophy as well as its public face in the Courtroom in dealing with the profession and litigants. The changes you have wrought have been truly admirable and I congratulate you on

having achieved so much in such a comparatively short reign. I am looking forward with keen enthusiasm to the future – and thank you again for everything.

Sincerely, Laurence

Michael Kirby's inclusive administrative approach, his preference for consensus decision-making and his phenomenal work ethic gradually won over the judges of the NSW Court of Appeal. In the beginning, at his swearing-in ceremony, although the standard kind words were said, the real story was told by the number of vacant seats left by senior members of the Bar and some of the justices of the Supreme Court, who thought Kirby was not the right choice for president. But as the years flew by he became more and more respected. His mother Jean had always said, 'Kill 'em with kindness.' This was his motto, and it seemed to be working.

> The Court of Appeal was happy because it was a very, very busy place. Everybody was so busy, you just didn't have time to allow your ego to dominate, you just had to get through the work. In my last year as president of the Court of Appeal in New South Wales I signed off on 480 opinions – that's a big output and they were reasoned and explained. We were very collegial, we met every week or fortnight over the raisin toast and the coffee in the morning, we would talk about the cases past and the cases yet to come, about some of the issues, about the running of the court, about sharing the workload. I would endeavour to share the cases fairly between the judges, and assign the writing of the lead opinions to the judges fairly,

> and all in all I think we had a very strong court, of diverse opinions, but a mutually respectful place and that was a great strength of the Court of Appeal at that time.

Shortly after the *Bailey* matter in 1987, an appeal from the United Kingdom Government came before the Court of Appeal, consisting of the Chief Justice Sir Laurence Street, President Michael Kirby, and Justice Michael McHugh, who had joined the Court not long after Kirby. It was perhaps the most celebrated case to come before the NSW Court of Appeal during Kirby's tenure as president. In the media it became known merely as *Spycatcher*.

Peter Wright, who had worked for decades as a Cold War counter-intelligence officer for British security service MI5, decided to retire to Tasmania in 1976 and write his memoir. It had been his job to uncover spies, double agents and traitors within the British security services. Wright was now the epitome of the disgruntled former employee. He was angry that his full thirty-six years of service for the British Government was not reflected in the pension he received on retirement. MI5 had used a technicality to exclude his first fifteen years of work for the Admiralty, and consequently his pension benefits were greatly reduced. On top of this, he had waged an ongoing and bitter internal battle with his employer.

At the heart of this dispute was Wright's claim that the long-time head of MI5, Sir Roger Hollis, was a spy for the Russians. This allegation had never been proved and the British Government never accepted it, but Wright was convinced there had been a cover-up, that throughout the 1950s and '60s, Britain's most senior security official was a communist spy. Fuelled by indignation, Wright decided that his memoir, eventually entitled *Spycatcher*, would set the record straight and supplement his meagre pension. Publication was to be in Sydney through the Australian division of William Heinemann. So it was in Sydney that the British Thatcher Government immediately injuncted the book, claiming that Wright's memoirs breached the *Official Secrets Act (UK)*.

Later described as 'a thoroughly unmeritorious piece of litigation', by the time the *Spycatcher* case had reached Kirby's attention on the NSW Court of Appeal, it had already wended its way from none other the Geoffrey Robertson QC in London to the young lawyer, barrister and Liberal Party aspirant Malcolm Bligh Turnbull, the NSW Supreme Court and now the NSW Court of Appeal. Its ineluctable path would only terminate in Canberra at the High Court of Australia. Kirby's old friend Robertson had passed it on to Turnbull; all the other Australian lawyers contacted by the book's publisher had given opinions that the case was impossible to win in the UK, and even less likely to succeed in Australia. Robertson was otherwise inclined and suggested to Turnbull that he would have a good chance of success in New South Wales.

Malcolm Turnbull had only practised as a barrister for a few years, and had since taken leave from the Bar to work as a solicitor for Kerry Packer, subsequently founding his own firm, Turnbull McWilliams Solicitors. Kirby had first met Turnbull when he turned up to the Elizabeth Street offices as a 22-year-old journalist to do a story for *Bulletin* magazine on the new head of the ALRC. Turnbull was now thirty-one years old, having lost none of his boyish charm or bravado as he took on the combined might of the British and Australian governments in what he later described as 'the greatest adventure of my life'. '*L'affaire Spycatcher* raised a great many serious issues about official secrets, the rule of law, and democracy generally. But it was also an enormous lark and I enjoyed every minute of it,' Turnbull wrote a few months after the litigation ended.

In some respects the *Spycatcher* case was a David and Goliath struggle. As Justice Michael Kirby looked down from the bench on the first day of proceedings, the odds definitely seemed to be stacked against Turnbull. On one side of the Bar table, appearing for the attorney-general of the UK and the Australian Government, were four QCs in wigs and gowns: Bill Gummow QC, not far off appointment to the Federal Court, Theo Simos QC, Bill Caldwell QC and Dr Gavan Griffith QC, the Commonwealth solicitor-general. It was a significant array of heavy hitters made worse because the Australian Government had decided to join with the UK Government in the action, having determined that it was in Australia's national interest to suppress British secrets.

On the other side of the table was Malcolm Turnbull, in a business suit. Because he had taken leave from the Bar to set up a firm of solicitors he was not even entitled to wear wig and gown. Turnbull was ably assisted by a team of three: his wife, Lucy Turnbull, a law graduate still not admitted to practise and so not permitted to sit at the Bar table; his mother, Coral Lansbury, not a lawyer at all but a fiction writer who loved courtroom intrigue; and as an unofficial member of the team, Lucy Turnbull's godfather, The Honourable Antony Larkins QC, then a retired Supreme Court judge. Larkins was the man who had moved Michael Kirby's admission to the Bar years earlier. Kirby was amused to see Turnbull valiantly holding the fort with the rather unconventional team behind him, and Larkins, the very distinguished, elderly, old-school advocate who still wore a monocle, unnerving the opposition by snoring loudly through the monotone of their opening address.

In an inspired move, Turnbull called former prime minister Gough Whitlam to give evidence in the *Spycatcher* trial. Two of the gravest allegations in Wright's book were that the British security services had plotted to overthrow the Wilson UK Labour Government, and had earlier conspired to assassinate the Egyptian President Gamal Abdel Nasser. Whitlam refused to countenance such illegal activities and when in office, a decade earlier, had curtailed the abuses of the Australian security services ASIO and ASIS. He called for the *Spycatcher* book to be published as a matter of national interest.

> I think it is very much to Australia's advantage that [the allegations contained in Wright's book] should be published and at the same time it should be known that Australian governments in the last fourteen years have not condoned those activities, which are in breach of Australian domestic laws or international law as accepted by Australia.

In a two-to-one verdict, with Michael Kirby and Michael McHugh finding in favour of Peter Wright and Sir Laurence Street dissenting, Malcolm Turnbull won his case before the NSW Court of Appeal.

The *Spycatcher* trial was replete with a series of particular ironies. If it had gone through the NSW courts only twelve months earlier, the British Government would still have been able to appeal it to their own Privy Council. (Prior to 1986, the British Privy Council, under certain circumstances, remained the final legal court of appeal for Australian courts. Gough Whitlam had ended appeals from the High Court to the Privy Council, but could not abolish the power of the states, if they wished, to bypass the High Court of Australia and appeal to the British directly.) There seems little doubt that a court in Margaret Thatcher's Britain would have found against Peter Wright and upheld the Official Secrets Act (UK). But in 1986 the Hawke Government had passed the *Australia Act* and as a result, all but one of the last vestiges of constitutional connection to the British Crown were gone. The last remaining link to Britain was now only the Queen herself. A further irony was that the case was presented by a confirmed Australian republican, Malcolm Turnbull, to a court that included Justice Michael Kirby, president, a confirmed Australian monarchist.

In nearly sixty pages of closely worded reasoning, Kirby provided a fascinating history of the case, outlined the relevant law, and tackled every major issue raised by Turnbull. Most importantly, he upheld the established legal principle that a foreign public law (the UK Official Secrets Act) could not be enforced in an Australian court. The British had argued that Wright was subject to an implied contract when he signed the Official Secrets Act and therefore had breached that contract by writing his book. However, Kirby's judgement (later supported by the High Court), found that no implied contract existed and that although he may have been in breach of the Official Secrets Act, as a foreign public law it could not be enforced in Australia.

> When Vladimir Petrov defected to Australia from his service in the Embassy of the Soviet Union in Canberra in 1954, can it really be suggested that the proper law officer of the Soviet Union could have sued in our courts to enforce here a duty of secrecy and confidence which Mr Petrov undoubtedly owed to the KGB but renounced in Australia . . .

Kirby's implied comparison of the UK attorney-general to a Kremlin apparatchik was not received well back in London. Heinemann, having secured a win in the NSW Court of Appeal, immediately published the book in Australia and, after the enormous publicity of the case, it was quickly a bestseller, making Peter Wright a millionaire and cementing Turnbull's reputation as an extraordinary advocate.

When Kirby went to London a few years later to speak at a conference, organised by the Campaign for Freedom of Information and aimed at revising the UK Official Secrets Act, the gulf between Australia and the UK was clear. British public servants were compelled to sign the Act and could be ordered to maintain strict silence on any aspect of their work. Australia had now enjoyed freedom-of-information legislation for more than a decade and a focus on open government since Whitlam's attorney-general, Lionel Murphy, first flagged it back in 1973. Kirby wryly noted, 'Civilisation as we know it has survived.' The *Independent* newspaper ran an article headed '"Spycatcher" judge condemns British official secrecy'. The article quoted Michael Kirby: 'Ask not what advantage your country derives from your gaining access to information necessary for your political decisions to be informed. Ask rather by what right your country may deny you such access? And who is it, on behalf of your country, who is doing so?'

Perhaps the greatest irony in the whole affair was that Wright's book, far from revealing secrets, really did not contain anything that was not already on the public record. Malcolm and Lucy Turnbull had examined every page in forensic detail when they still hoped the British Government would come to a negotiated settlement, and found that there was nothing in *Spycatcher* – certainly nothing of a sensitive, security-related nature – that had not already been revealed in other books such as Chapman Pincher's *Their Trade Was Treachery*, published six years before. This was hardly surprising, since Wright had worked on that book for Pincher. The Turnbulls joked that if their findings had been made public, the book would have gone straight to the remainder tables on the day of publication.

The next time Kirby and Turnbull faced off was on opposite sides of the republican debate a decade later. Again it was Kirby's judgement that prevailed, although this time at Turnbull's expense. Then the chairman of the Australian Republican Movement, Turnbull argued that the Queen should no longer be the Australian head of state. The final model put in a referendum to the Australian people to amend the nation's Constitution replaced the Queen with an Australian President, to be appointed by a two-thirds majority of both houses of parliament.

In 1992 Michael Kirby, along with Liberals like Tony Abbott, became a founding member of Australians for Constitutional Monarchy (ACM). The organisation was a reaction against the recent change to Labor policy calling for a republic by the centenary of federation in 2001. Kirby asserted that the existing constitutional arrangements worked well and should not be changed: 'If the system ain't broke, you don't fix it.' His support for the monarchy was seen as paradoxical, at conflict with his rather liberal, even radical, outlook in many other matters. But his views in relation to the monarchy, as with any other area – human rights law, AIDS, law reform generally – were soundly based (as he saw it) and firmly held. It was not just any monarchy that he supported, but the Australian constitutional monarchy in particular. In fact, his true affection was for the existing monarch, Queen Elizabeth II, a woman whose fortunes he had followed since he was a boy and for whom he had always had the utmost respect. Perhaps it was like his penchant for photography, an attempt to freeze the Australian Constitution in time, in a moment he knew and liked. Once Her Majesty had left the scene, things could very well change. It was not that difficult, even for him, to imagine a situation where, under His Majesty Charles III, Australia might decide to make the change.

> I am willing to concede that in the long run some changes to our constitutional monarchy may occur in Australia. The moves from colonies to dominion and from Commonwealth to a fully independent country continue apace. Our country, like every nation, is on a journey. If Europe is any guide, the journey will probably take us to an enhancement of regional relationships rather than a retreat into the isolation of the nation state. And our region, in the coming century of the Pacific, offers us the opportunities of a special relationship with our neighbours if we can harmonise our national role with our geography.

Another overarching reason why Michael Kirby emerged powerfully in support of the monarchy was that, as the debate developed, the media in Australia, largely under the control of Rupert Murdoch, but also the Fairfax press and even the ABC, were not prepared to give equal space to each side of the argument. By founding the ACM, Kirby threw his weight behind the side he felt had been unfairly ridiculed and dismissed. He also resented the rather scurrilous, and in some cases certainly illegal, activities of the British media designed to reveal highly damaging and entirely private information about the royal family. His comments in early 1993 were prescient, given the Murdoch phone-hacking scandal of eighteen years later.

> Some people – based upon taped eavesdropping of private conversations and snooping photographers – have formed a different view about the Prince and Princess of Wales and other members of the royal family. I pass over how such intrusions came about; how they passed into the hands of a voracious media; how suddenly elements in the media turned upon members of the Family; and how intercontinental media interests played off each other like modern brigands. The role of the modern media in manipulating public opinion – even in constitutional fundamentals – must be a source of grave concern to all serious observers. It is virtually impossible to get published in Australia serious opinions in defence of our constitutional system. This is in itself astonishing and disturbing.

It was hard to argue against Kirby's view that our constitutional arrangements – with the exception of 1975 – had functioned well and continued to do so. There were certainly risks in changing the system. An elected president of Australia for example (an idea which became popular but was not the model proposed) would be the only politician directly elected to the job by all the voters of the nation. By contrast, the prime minister is simply, say, the member for Lalor, and becomes prime minister by virtue of a vote in the party room. No one – not even Bob Hawke or Kevin Rudd, as they found out to their everlasting disappointment – is voted in as prime minister at a general election. Therefore it was not hard to imagine destabilising conflicts, under that proposition, arising between the prime minister and the directly elected president: questions of who had the superior mandate from the people, for example, something that could not be envisaged under the current system of prime ministerial appointment of the governor-general.

Kirby's view was a complicated and nuanced one. He was no haughty advocate for a 'Bunyip aristocracy', 'protecting' the nation from too much democracy. He also identified a nineteenth-century nationalism behind the moves towards a republic and, as a committed internationalist, he thought that kind of jingoistic rhetoric was retrograde. He feared the development of a kind of 'cult of the President', where the stretch limousines, police outriders and luxury palaces became a daily reality in a country that currently saw such a phenomenon only once a decade when the Queen herself visited.

> I have always looked on my appreciation of the constitutional monarchy in Australia as fundamentally an anarchistic view of the Constitution. It is a view of the Constitution that doesn't have, essentially, a head of state. It has an absent head of state

and gets by perfectly well without a head of state. Heads of state can cause a lot of trouble, particularly if they're in competition with heads of government. Therefore, I don't think it is a bad system. That wasn't my original idea. My original idea, like most Australians of my age, was one of reverence for the royal family, particularly for the King, who had been there when Britain and Australia came through the war victorious, which was no certain thing, and respect and affection for the young Queen. You've no idea what Sydney looked like when the Queen arrived in 1954. The whole place was ablaze with banners and welcomes. So people of my age began with a real affection and respect for the royal family.

That has been partly eroded in popular esteem by various factors, but I have allowed that to, as it were, pass me by, because I began to see that when I became a lawyer and later in public office that the system of constitutional monarchy gives a solution to a problem which is inherent in a parliamentary democracy. Parliamentary democracies are good for majorities. They look after majorities. They spend their whole time searching for what majorities want. They are not so good at looking after minorities. I happen to be a member of a minority, therefore for me, the ideal of a good, functioning polity is one that respects and protects minorities whilst proceeding in a democratic majoritarian way. The constitutional monarchy, in its theory, should do that.

In the end, the referendum, which called for a President, appointed by parliament, to replace the Queen, was not carried by the

Australian people and the monarchy remained. The result was probably as much to do with in-fighting between republicans as anything else. A faction of republicans calling for a directly elected President entered the debate and muddied the waters. The result did not come anywhere near the required majority of overall votes and a majority of states in favour, although according to opinion polls, most Australians still overwhelmingly supported a republic.

Previously, every time there was an announcement of the resignation of a justice from the High Court of Australia, Michael Kirby waited on tenterhooks for a phone call. But by entering the debate as a monarchist so vocally, Kirby did not endear himself to the Labor Government, or to Prime Minister Paul Keating, who had championed the 'yes' vote. Michael became convinced that his judicial career was now stalled. He had watched Mary Gaudron go up in 1987, only to see his more junior Court of Appeal colleague Michael McHugh leapfrog over him two years later. Now it certainly appeared as though that last remaining step, a seat on the High Court, was probably out of his reach once and for all. Even close Labor friends like Barry Jones and Neville Wran were at a loss to explain Kirby's position on the Queen, and all the lobbying in the world by that most persuasive of supporters, Gareth Evans, to get Michael onto the Court wasn't having the desired effect. In 1994 he told his friend Ita Buttrose's *Ita* magazine:

> I'm perfectly content [on the Court of Appeal] but lately my life has turned to international activities . . . I don't think it's

> necessary to constantly agonise over what will come up. I think worldly ambitions are so insignificant. As you get older they become less important, and I have plenty of opportunities to do that. Who knows what the future has in store?

There was no doubt that Kirby's work for the UN and his international human rights advocacy was increasingly important and enormously rewarding. But it was also possible that he had decided to accept it as a kind of consolation for the judicial appointment he now, in his early fifties, thought he would never have.

There were three figures in Kirby's professional life to whom he owed everything: Lionel Murphy, who gave him his first real break by appointing him to the ALRC; Neville Wran, who saw in a young junior barrister a skill and work ethic that he later rewarded with the second most senior judicial appointment in New South Wales; and, Gareth Evans, close to Michael as a student politician, side by side with him at the ALRC. Now, as foreign minister in the Hawke Government, Evans asked Kirby to take up a position in international affairs that would lead to his greatest humanitarian work: special representative of the United Nations Secretary-General on Human Rights in Cambodia (1993–1996).

Michael and Johan hadn't made it as far as Cambodia on their kombi trip in 1970 but they'd got very close. The border was about 200 kilometres from Bangkok and they had certainly seen the US service personnel. They were not aware, then, of the secret US bombing campaign that had begun on Michael's thirtieth birthday, some ten months before they had arrived in Thailand, and which was to continue for four years. The US forces dropped 540 000 tonnes of bombs, killing close to a million Cambodians, leaving many more horrifically injured and obliterating countless acres of farmland and forest. At he end of the American war the Khmer Rouge took over driving the entire 2 million inhabitants of Phnom Penh into the countryside at gunpoint in a crazed attempt at agrarian reform. Within four years, as many as 2.5 million from a total national population of 8 million people had died as a result of these policies – either starved, worked to death, tortured or murdered. The terror did not end until the Vietnamese invaded in 1978 and set up a new government. It would be more than a decade before Cambodia finally achieved a level of peace and stability.

Since Eleanor Roosevelt's work which saw the promulgation of the Universal Declaration of Human Rights by the United Nations General Assembly in 1948, only one World Conference on Human Rights had taken place – in Iran in 1968. By the time of the second conference twenty-five years later, in Vienna in 1993, there was a great deal to be done. The conference called for the establishment of a high commissioner for human rights and reaffirmed the need for action to protect the rights of women, girls, indigenous peoples, migrant workers, children and the disabled, and the importance of human rights education and the absolute prohibition on torture. There was also the strong recommendation that the UN must find more effective ways of monitoring the progress of reforms in member states. As a result, the use of special rapporteurs and special representatives of the secretary-general became increasingly important. These were high-profile individuals who were appointed independent from government but with the agreement of the national authorities to enter countries and conduct fact-finding missions on matters of human rights.

Kirby interpreted his mandate as the special representative on human rights in Cambodia very broadly. He was unafraid to highlight the shortcomings of the Cambodian Government, seeing that as a vital part of his role. Soon after his appointment in November 1993, he arranged meetings in Geneva and Paris with all the national and international organisations relevant to his human rights mission: the UN Educational, Scientific and Cultural Organization (UNESCO), International Labor Organization (ILO), World Health Organization (WHO), UN Development Programme (UNDP), UN Children's Fund (UNICEF), and the Office of the UN High Commissioner for Refugees (UNHCR). Later he had more meetings in Phnom Penh and Battambang in Cambodia itself, on the first of seven missions to the country.

It was an overwhelming experience: almost every institution taken for granted in the West – a judiciary, police force, prisons, a system of hospitals and health care, schools and universities, local and national government infrastructure, electoral and voting mechanisms – was either non-existent or severely degraded. On top of this chaos there was ongoing conflict in remote areas with the remnants of the Khmer Rouge, simmering tensions with the Vietnamese, including pockets of ethnic cleansing of Chree Thom tribes who had been pushed into Vietnam, and looming problems of spreading disease, particularly the unchecked AIDS virus.

Michael Kirby tackled each of these issues in a characteristically methodical and painstaking way, travelling widely throughout the country and speaking directly with the people at every opportunity. Gareth Evans had chosen wisely; he knew from his close observations of Kirby as ALRC chairman that he had an unparalleled aptitude for this sort of work. Kirby had seen plenty of suffering, even among some of his closest friends as their lives were cut short by AIDS, but the catastrophe he confronted in Cambodia was like nothing he had ever experienced before. He visited the hospitals where patients were still suffering, and the massacre sites where thousands of human skulls and bones were stacked in massive piles or interned in mass graves. It was on a scale that can be understood in theory, but when actually confronted in reality, it was almost incomprehensible.

Having completed three missions to Cambodia, he submitted his report to the UN General Assembly in New York on 23 November 1994. The UN Secretary-General was not expecting Kirby to write the seventy-page report himself; the usual practice was that reports of this kind were prepared by the UN and that special representatives would only have an overseeing role in their production. That notion was contrary to Kirby's thinking: his fierce independence, sustained over many years as a judge, would never be surrendered so easily. He highlighted twenty-two areas of concern, ranging from the ongoing war with the Khmer Rouge, the laying of land mines by both sides in the conflict, forced disappearances, abductions of foreigners including the Australian tourist David Wilson, 'ethnic cleansing' and general political instability; through to issues of education, employment, sustainable environment, courts and judges, prisons, media freedom, immigration, minority rights and human rights, and non-government organisations. He detailed eighteen specific recommendations on the rights to health, work, fair and open trials, the right to be elected, and on protections for vulnerable groups including women, children, the elderly and minorities.

Special Representative Kirby's forthright report ruffled feathers in the Cambodian Government. They allowed him to continue his work, but access to government and high-level cooperation from the two prime ministers gradually deteriorated. One of the most difficult issues was the right to health and, in particular, how to deal with the AIDS virus, about which the Cambodian Government was in denial. Kirby reported that since his first mission, 'there has been no significant change. A national committee on AIDS has been established and it is about to launch a national survey to determine the extent of the disease. The infrastructure and delivery of health services remain poor.' But by the time of his last report in 1996, he was pleased to reveal progress in a number of areas. The first one he listed was health:

> The health budget of Cambodia for 1996 was increased by 60%. The country is working closely with UNAIDS and with WHO in the attack on HIV/AIDS, and also malaria, and other health problems. The First Prime Minister accepted the position of Chairman of the National AIDS Committee, as previously recommended by me . . .

Most remarkably, Kirby managed to conduct this emotionally and intellectually exhausting program of activities while still performing his duties as president of the Court of Appeal. His first trip to Cambodia was over a few days during the Court vacation in January

1994, the second from 26 to 28 May, and the third during the mid-year break from 16 to 30 July. These were followed by four more missions, the last of which was in April 1996. Cambodia was only one of his international destinations over this period. On 10 May 1994 he attended the inauguration of President Nelson Mandela in Pretoria; on 30 May that year there was the UN Commission on Human Rights meeting in Geneva; then trips to the Solomon Islands, where he was president of the Court of Appeal (in his spare time), to Maryland to attend the Human Genome Project Working Group, and to Portugal for an inter-parliamentary conference on East Timor. Few people in public life, short of the prime minister or foreign minister, could maintain such a demanding regimen of international engagements. On 1 June 1995 he wrote to his parents from Lisbon:

Dearest Mum & Dad,
Today I spoke in the Portuguese Parliament about East Timor. It was such a great speech the local equivalent of Graham Richardson offered me a safe seat – party no option. My UN meeting in Geneva went well. Not much time to look around. Just hard work. Johan has to have the holiday for both of us.

There were the inevitable criticisms from some quarters that it was inappropriate for the president to be taking on such a challenging 'second job'. But whatever the critics said, Kirby was not going to curb his gruelling schedule – he enjoyed it too much and felt the work was too important to stop. It was one of the most intensive and active periods of his working life.

> If in the end of my life I look back and say, was there one thing you did that really helped humanity, it would probably be going to Cambodia and insisting that HIV/AIDS was a human rights issue and within the remit of the United Nations, against quite a lot of local opposition. Nobody wanted to talk about sex, nobody wanted to talk about sex workers, nobody wanted to talk about condoms. But we insisted, I insisted, and ultimately – with some support from King Sihanouk, interestingly enough – it was accepted to be a human rights issue. The consequence of that, in part, and of all the effort of the Cambodian people themselves, was to cut the rate of sero-conversion, which was leaping up. That saved lives.

When, on 1 May 1996, Michael Kirby did resign as the UN special representative on Cambodia, it was because of a conflict with his work as a judge. Yet it had nothing to do with the NSW Court of Appeal.

For Kirby, Thursday, 14 December 1995 began as just another day tending to matters of administration of the busiest appeal court in the country. But by late in the afternoon when he opened a meeting of the Court of Appeal users' committee he was aware that something was afoot. There had been a call from the cabinet office of the federal government, simply wanting to know where Justice Kirby would be at approximately 6 p.m. that day. When Kirby inquired as to why this information was required, the officer replied that the attorney-general, Michael Lavarch, wished to speak with him. It had been four months since Prime Minister Paul Keating had announced that High Court Justice Sir William Deane had agreed to become the next governor-general, but there had been no subsequent announcement about who was to replace him on the Court. The last time a federal attorney-general had rung Kirby in similar circumstances was in 1974, when Lionel Murphy had called just after the death of Justice Douglas Menzies of the High Court. At that time, Kirby had (rather presumptuously) thought that the attorney-general was ringing to offer him that seat on the High Court. Now, twenty-one years later, Kirby quivered as the very same thought flashed through his mind and, with it, Murphy's prediction that his appointment to the ALRC was but his first step to the High Court of Australia.

> To be frank I thought, at that stage, that my moment had passed. I had seen Justice Gaudron, Justice McHugh and then Justice Gummow appointed. Given the nature of the High Court as a national court, given the number of Sydney people on it, given my age (I was then fifty-six), I thought that I'd reached my use-by date. Always the bridesmaid, never the bride. But in life you can never say never. It wasn't so.

It was to be a day that he would remember in technicolour for the rest of his life. Michael's brother Donald was also a member of the users' committee, representing the Law Society of New South Wales, and he was sitting opposite Kirby. At precisely 6.10 p.m. there was a knock on the judges' conference room door, which in itself was unusual. Kirby's young associate came in and, unaware of its significance, handed a yellow Post-it note to the closest member of the committee, so as not to disrupt Kirby's running of the meeting, and then left. The note was passed, hand to hand, judge to judge, down towards Kirby, whose eyes were fixed on it as he spoke on some entirely abstruse matter of court operations. After what seemed like an eternity, it was finally placed safely into his hands. Michael looked at Donald, took a deep breath, and opened the note. It simply read: *Ring Michael Lavarch*.

> My brother describes the colour going from my face because I knew that at that moment my life had changed, and that's the way it happens – the judge has nothing to do with his or her own appointment. The appointment is made by politicians who are elected by the people; it's the one moment of a democratic component coming into the judiciary, and once it happens the politicians have to get out – they don't have anything after that. So I went down and he said 'I have the honour to invite,' and I said 'I have the honour to accept.' I didn't allow too much of the water to flow under Sydney Harbour Bridge.

On Friday, 2 February 1996 Michael Kirby sat for the last time as president of the NSW Court of Appeal. He had been in that office for eleven and a half years and over that time the Court had changed enormously. The Court had also changed him. Of all the judges of the Supreme Court that had rather begrudgingly accepted the upstart into their ranks, only ten now remained. Of the members of the Court of Appeal itself only two remained from the bench that Kirby had joined in 1984, and he noted that the majority of the existing bench had appeared before him as counsel in the Court of Appeal. It had been a thoroughgoing change. A court that had been renowned among barristers as a vitriolic 'torture chamber', where it was not unusual for judges to delight in skewering unsuspecting counsel, had, under Justice Kirby, long since become a pleasant and collegiate environment. The welcoming ceremony way back in 1984, muted by the absence of some of the Supreme Court justices, had been replaced by a farewell ceremony where practically all the justices of the Supreme Court of New South Wales – for the first time in living memory – joined a jam-packed courtroom to say goodbye to Michael Kirby.

There was emotion in Kirby's speech, especially when he acknowledged the support of his family. As with every function of this kind throughout Kirby's judicial career to this point, Johan did not attend. Kirby could only refer to him obliquely: 'My family and loved ones sustain me in all that I do. But some debts are too intense, enduring and private for words on a public occasion such as this.' Even though acceptance of homosexuality had come a long way, it was certainly likely that if, before then, Kirby had come out as gay, he would never have gained the ultimate promotion to the High Court. Johan himself was certain this was true. Now Kirby had secured the job he had always wanted, perhaps it was time to reconsider his position. The construction of words that he had used so many times before – 'my family and loved ones' – now seemed tired and inadequate. It was getting close to the time where he should once and for all be able to refer to his partner of almost twenty-seven years, directly and honestly. The man who had shared his life since 11 February 1969 – Johan van Vloten. Kirby ended his farewell speech: 'Each one of us must strive to make a contribution. Judge mine in this Court with charity. Look to the future.'

Four days later, at 10.17 a.m., the imposing number one courtroom of the High Court in Canberra was full of judges, lawyers, politicians and dignitaries as Michael Donald Kirby was sworn in as the fortieth justice of the High Court of Australia. There was no beating around the bush in Kirby's speech. First there was reference to the radical Lionel Murphy and, in the same breath, the great conservative chief justice of the High Court Sir Owen Dixon's famous words, 'There is no other safe guide to judicial decisions in great conflicts than a strict and complete legalism.' Kirby went on to show how Australia had changed since Dixon's 1950s. That strict legalism had not served the interests of all Australians that well. For Aboriginal Australians, women, gay people, Asian Australians, communists, conscientious objectors to the Vietnam War, homeless Australians, and so on, the 'good old days' had often meant harsh and unjust days. He even made direct reference to the case of *Crowe v. Graham* (1968), his first appearance in the High Court before Garfield Barwick. The case of censorship of a 'mildly erotic' poetry magazine. That kind of 'strict and complete legalism' would have no place in the court presided over by Justice Michael Kirby.

Again Michael thanked his family; this time, though, something was different. There in the front row of the public gallery seated next to Jean and Don and Michael's sister, Diana, and David's wife, Judith, was Johan. As he said the words of indebtedness – 'To my family and loved ones, who sustain me and criticise me every day' – Judith nudged Johan. 'That means you,' she said. From that day on, Johan would no longer be an invisible partner, and the days of 'Don't ask, don't tell' were numbered. But Johan was still not named. That step was still to come.

Walking into his new suite of offices on the first day – native Australian wood panelling everywhere, an extraordinary view across Parliament House to the Brindabella mountain range, his own private balcony – Michael Kirby savoured the moment. This was to be his home for the next thirteen years. Of course there was his home in Sydney with Johan, but this would be Kirby's spiritual home. These were the chambers only just vacated by Justice Sir William Deane and around the corner and down the corridor were the chambers of Justice Lionel Murphy. Kirby had visited him there often. Voices echoed through this building. Voices of judges, counsel and litigants long gone.

If he needed to be reminded that his was a temporary appointment, to end at the age of seventy, if not before, if he needed to be reminded of number twenty-one in his list of consolations, the transience of life, then what happened next did so in a shocking way. He settled down at his desk and inserted a cassette tape into the dictaphone. On the tape he heard the voice of his long-dead predecessor, Sir Keith Aickin, dictating his reasons in *Onus v. Alcoa of Australia Limited*. The tape had survived the thirteen years that Sir William Deane had occupied the room. Would he too, one day, only be a scratchy memory on an old magnetic tape?

Michael Kirby thought of all the justices in his long lineage. He had succeeded Sir William Deane, who in turn had succeeded Sir Ninian Stephen. The line went all the way back to Sir Isaac

Isaacs. Those three being the only High Court judges to have been elevated to the office of governor-general. He reflected on this for a moment, then told himself it was just an odd coincidence and didn't think of it again.

Kirby often lamented that he arrived at the High Court too late to be a part of its greatest historical phase and most significant legal bench – the Mason Court (1987–95). Anthony Mason was the chief justice at a time when the High Court was asked to decide the *Mabo* case. *Mabo* had its origins in barrister Barbara Hocking's Master of Laws thesis and the question she posed: 'Does Aboriginal Law now run in Australia?' The majority of justices had resoundingly answered 'Yes', at least in as much as they recognised native title rights. It overturned 200 years of a legal fiction that Australia was 'terra nullius', an empty land belonging to no one.

But if the *Mabo* decision was to define the Mason Court, then the *Wik* decision in Kirby's first year of office would be no less significant for the court led by Mason's successor, Chief Justice Gerard Brennan. Nineteen respondents assembled in courtroom number 1 in the High Court in Canberra on 11, 12 and 13 June 1996. Twelve Queen's Counsel represented the parties: the Wik and Thayorre Aboriginal peoples versus the State of Queensland, the Commonwealth, Comalco Aluminium and sixteen other respondents. Kirby sat on the long bench with his six fellow justices, Brennan, Dawson, Toohey, Gaudron, McHugh and Gummow. What was to become known as the *Wik* case was about to begin. It would determine whether native title claims could succeed over leasehold properties. Freehold land – the form of legal land title most people held over, for example, their residential homes in Sydney and Melbourne – extinguished native title but there remained a legal question mark over whether native title still existed over pastoral leases. In Queensland and the Northern Territory, for example, these leases could run to millions of acres with peppercorn rental and often had traditional native peoples still living on them. *Wik* was to be a landmark case with huge ramifications, legally and politically.

Two days before Christmas the judgements were handed down. In a majority decision, Kirby, along with John Toohey, Mary Gaudron and Bill Gummow, found that pastoral leases did not automatically extinguish native title, but that where there was a conflict between the two, pastoral rights would prevail. The practical result of the *Wik* decision was that Indigenous Australians could, by law, demand that leaseholders allow them access to their lands for hunting or ceremonial purposes – in effect, leave the gate unlocked. In every other respect the arrangements of the leaseholders stayed the same. This nevertheless unleashed a political backlash. Prime Minister Howard drew up a ten-point plan to roll back native title.

Criticism of the Brennan Court by the conservatives in the Howard Government and the state governments came thick and fast. Jeff Kennett, the Liberal Victorian Premier, said that *Wik* 'hasn't covered the High Court in glory and it has left the Australian community at the edge of an abyss.' Rob Borbidge, the Queensland National Party Premier, claimed parliament must always trump the courts: 'At the end of the day the parliament is the highest court in the land.' And John Howard pushed the line that only elected parliaments should be making these decisions: 'The perception has developed that some judges believe it is their role to give the parliament a hurry-on and do things that they think the parliament should have done.' His ministers and right-wing commentators categorised the High Court judges, particularly Michael Kirby, as activists. Perhaps the greatest irony was that Chief Justice Sir Gerard Brennan was included as a target. If these politicians had actually read the judgements, it was hard to miss the fact that the chief justice was in dissent in *Wik*.

All this noise simply went to show how little the Australian people really knew about the proper functions and the individual responsibilities of each of the three arms of government – the executive, the parliament and the judiciary – and it showed how easy it was for cynical politicians to manipulate this situation. They spoke as if the judges had a choice about which cases they heard, as though, in relation to politically sensitive matters, judges could simply leave the decision for the politicians. They behaved as if they had no understanding that the common-law system, the very basis of the British legal tradition that Australia had inherited, demanded that in some circumstances, judges make law. For hundreds of years, judges had been asked to make decisions that now form the common law that fills the law books. The *Mabo* and *Wik* judgements were common law decisions, they could not be ducked by the judges, and the result of their deliberations went to make up the judge-made common law of Australia as opposed to the laws legislated by parliament. If politicians did not like the judge-made law then they had to pass legislation to change it. That could be an unpalatable choice for politicians: it was often easier to simply attack the judges, undermining their position and independence in the eyes of the public.

In this instance, John Howard's attorney-general, Daryl Williams, refused to defend the High Court from the political attack, which was, more often than not, coming from the Government itself. It was the first time in Australia an attorney-general had backed away from the time-honoured tradition of defending the courts.

At the end of this first year on the High Court, and as if to underline Johan's fear that Michael would not have been appointed to the Court had his sexuality been publicly known, tragedy struck the Supreme Court of New South Wales. Retired Justice David Yeldham, a former colleague of Michael's and his strongest critic over the *Bailey* case, was named by NSW MP Franca Arena. The MP stood up in parliament and asked questions about the judge and an ongoing inquiry into paedophilia. 'What about former Supreme Court Judge David Albert Yeldham?' she said. 'Was he or was he not interviewed?' Arena raised his name under parliamentary privilege, thereby blocking the former judge from suing. Yeldham was a married man with children and grandchildren and he insisted he was not a paedophile. No evidence was ever provided that he was. However, his homosexuality was a complete secret to his family, friends and colleagues. Only a few days after Arena's speech, David Yeldham committed suicide. ABC-TV's *Four Corners* then ran a program on the former judge, which posthumously continued the destruction of his reputation: 'Tonight on *Four Corners*, the tragic double life of a man who betrayed the law, and the unanswered questions he left behind . . .'. All this because he had secretly had homosexual affairs.

Homosexual men were more susceptible to allegations of paedophilia because the age of consent for homosexual sex in NSW was eighteen, while it was only sixteen for heterosexual sex. So a youth on his eighteenth birthday could have sex with a boyfriend who was one day younger than him and the older boy would legally be a pederast. Thus even teenage sexual experimentation could be considered pederasty, but only if it was with a partner of the same sex. This discrimination caused a link between gay men and paedophilia, feeding into a heightened sense of moral panic. Homophobia was alive and well in New South Wales, and judges and other prominent public figures were not going to escape the attention of the tabloid press, religious zealots or unscrupulous politicians.

Michael Kirby had long known the discrimination at the heart of Australia's 'sodomy' laws, inherited, as they were, from the ancient British system. He also knew the horrible, perhaps irreparable, damage that could so easily be done through defamatory media and political campaigns – whether or not they had any factual base. In February 1973 he wrote to his brother David after having read Oscar Wilde's *De Profundis*, which he called 'a wonderful and moving protest that I had never read before. It is on your highly recommended list.' In 1897 Wilde was doing two years' imprisonment in Reading Gaol for gross acts of indecency. *De Profundis* was a 50 000-word letter to his lover, Lord Alfred 'Bosie' Douglas, written from jail. Michael was so affected by the book that he wrote out a passage in his letter to David:

As regards [. . .] the Relation of the Artistic Life to Conduct, it will no doubt seem strange to you that I should select it. People point to Reading Gaol and say, 'That is where the artistic life leads a man.' Well, it might lead to worse places. The more mechanical people to whom life is a shrewd speculation depending on a careful calculation of ways and means, always know where they are going, and go there. They start with the ideal desire of being the parish beadle, and in whatever sphere they are placed they succeed in being the parish beadle and no more. A man whose desire is to be something separate from himself, to be a member of Parliament, or a successful grocer, or a prominent solicitor, or a judge, or something equally tedious, invariably succeeds in being what he wants to be. That is his punishment. Those who want a mask have to wear it.

But with the dynamic forces of life, and those in whom those dynamic forces become incarnate, it is different. People whose desire is solely for self-realisation never know where they are going. They can't know [. . .] The final mystery is oneself. When one has weighed the sun in the balance, and measured the steps of the moon, and mapped out the seven heavens star by star, there still remains oneself.

Twenty-five years after he sent this quote to his brother, Kirby had succeeded in becoming what he wanted to be, and all that time, to the world outside his closeknit group of family and friends, he had worn a mask. The professional mask of the judge: the robes and the wig that hide the ordinary man or woman underneath; and another mask that hid the details of his intimate life, or as he had more dramatically described it, a door, firmly shut, with a sign: 'Do not enter.'

There was, though, an extraordinary dynamism to his world and in that regard he was unlike any judge before or since. In truth, the great paradox about Michael Kirby was that this thoroughly dedicated, dutiful, academic, erudite jurist who sat for hours every day in his chambers, grinding out judgements, was at the same time anything but predictable. He never did know, really know, where each day would take him or where his life would ultimately lead, and that sense of excitement about the unknown was the very thing that kept him going.

9

The Devil Made Me Do It

When I got in at about six o'clock in the morning, the phones were ringing and that was the first I had heard about his allegations. So I didn't feel that that was a good day in my life and it wasn't a very good day in the relationship between the High Court of Australia and the parliament.

Michael Kirby

Tony Blair had no qualms about appointing the former Conservative Party chief whip Sir Alistair Goodlad, as UK high commissioner to Australia in 1999. Goodlad took up the post with alacrity. Labour governments, it seems, frequently reward their opponents with top jobs. The converse is rarely the case. John Howard was determined to make the very most of all his appointments, especially to the important jobs, and that certainly meant every appointment to the High Court.

By 2002 Prime Minister Howard had made three appointments to the High Court, all of them noted conservatives: Justice Kenneth Hayne, a Victorian Supreme Court judge; Kirby's friend from law school Chief Justice Murray Gleeson, formerly chief justice of New South Wales; and Justice Ian Callinan, a well-known Queensland barrister who had prosecuted Justice Lionel Murphy. Kirby's remaining brother and sister judges on the High Court were, in order of seniority, Mary Gaudron, Michael McHugh and William Gummow. All of these three were from the Sydney Bar and all were Labor appointments. Kirby knew each of them well: Gummow was a black-letter lawyer and academic who had appeared before Michael in the *Spycatcher* case, and McHugh had sat on the NSW Court of Appeal with Kirby from 1984 until appointed to the High Court in 1989. Both had seemed to grow more conservative as the years passed. Meanwhile, Mary Gaudron, whom Kirby had known since university and whom he had joined on the Arbitration Commission, the most radical of all of them, was gradually withdrawing from the Court due to ill health; she would announce her early retirement by the end of the year. Kirby, who had begun in the majority on the *Wik* case, was becoming isolated on the bench.

On the night of 12 March 2002 all seven High Court justices and their wives and partners gathered at the private dining room in the High Court in Canberra with High Commissioner Goodlad and his wife, Cecilia Hurst, who was the granddaughter of the twenty-seventh Earl of Crawford. Johan was charming as usual, and, as the only other European at the gathering, helped make the guests feel at home. That he was there at all was a new development: partners were always invited to these functions – but 'partners' had always meant wives. It was only after Justice Gaudron's appointment in 1986 that an 83-year tradition was broken and husbands had to be included on the invite list. Gay partners took a little longer – nearly twenty years longer.

At any rate, the function was more Kirby's cup of tea. He has always enjoyed the social interaction of meeting new people and engaging them in conversation; his natural curiosity about how other people live and work was never far away. Sitting across the table from two titled guests, his monarchist tendencies came to the fore and he took the opportunity to inquire after the Queen and the royals. Johan, on the other hand, did not share Michael's particular interest in their aristocratic guests. He had only just finished the three-hour drive from Sydney and was tired.

As they quaffed the Australian vintage wines and made small talk, the acrimony that had developed among some of the judges towards Kirby was only just below the surface. He had been the last Labor appointee by the Keating Government in 1996, and since then the new Howard Government had sought to make what Deputy Prime Minister Tim Fischer freely described as 'a capital C conservative' mark on the Court. Justices Gummow and McHugh, although Labor appointments themselves, more frequently sided in their decisions with the three new conservative judges and rarely joined with Kirby. This inevitably left him to cut a rather lonely figure on the Court. It was not long before snide comments were made about his judicial approach – his so-called 'judicial activism', a term he hated. 'Activist: that's definitely code language,' he laments. 'That's code language of generally conservative people who don't want anything to change or anything to be different.'

Justice Gaudron would have seemed a natural ally – they remained personally close – but ironically, she was likely to take an even more radical position than Kirby on a number of major cases. And in many others, while her legal reasoning was different, she still often ended up voting with the conservatives. Kirby's situation was to dramatically worsen over the coming year as Gaudron retired and was replaced by Justice John Dyson Heydon.

On 30 October 2002, four months before his appointment, Heydon had made a speech (published in the right-wing journal *Quadrant*) that many saw as a public application for the job of High Court justice. It consisted of a long and pointed argument against what he described as 'judicial activism'. He suggested that judgements coming down from the High Court were not simply applying the law as it stood, but instead stating the law as the judge would like to see it, according to his or her particular political or social views. Kirby's name was nowhere mentioned in the speech but it was abundantly clear who Heydon had in his sights. When a copy of the speech arrived on John Howard's desk, the prime minister would have been impressed.

Five of his fellow judges seated around him in the High Court dining room, Gleeson, Gummow, McHugh, Hayne and Callinan, weren't just politically more conservative than Kirby, they felt a certain professional distaste for him as well. He was a self-promoter, as they saw it, always in the media, always pushing Michael Kirby; his was not appropriately judicial behaviour. Perhaps it was fortunate for Kirby, then, that nobody at that private dinner had the slightest inkling of what was taking place less than 2 kilometres away in the Australian Senate – a government minister was about to drop a bombshell designed to end Kirby's career and lead to criminal charges. Or if anyone did know, they certainly weren't letting on.

Not quite three years before this baneful night, Michael and Johan's long-term relationship had finally become public knowledge.

Late in 1998 Michael Kirby sipped tea in his High Court chambers. The long expanse of windows overlooked Capitol Hill and Parliament House and behind that the hazy mountains. Kirby thought it one of the most beautiful views in Canberra. He was putting the finishing touches to his entry for the 1999 edition of *Who's Who in Australia*. He had been doing this every year since first being appointed to the bench in 1974. His entry in the volume was one of the longest, if not *the* longest, and that was not about to change. Journalists were also fond of recounting, to their own amusement if no one else's, that under the heading 'Recreation', Kirby listed 'work'.

But this year his entry was notable for an entirely different reason. The abbreviation 'p' had never before appeared, and after it the date 'Feb 11 1969' and the name 'Johan A. van Vloten'. Michael and Johan had decided to formally and very publicly come out. It had been Johan's idea, and when he'd raised it with Michael they'd decided together that the time was right. Johan said to Michael, 'If we now state who we are and what we are, it makes it easier for people who are following us and also it takes pressure off you.'

Kirby was guaranteed a seat on the bench until the constitutional requirement that he retire at the age of seventy, and in 1998 that was more than a decade away. It was very unlikely that he would ever be appointed to the ultimate judicial post of chief justice of Australia – the Howard Government had only recently appointed the new chief justice, Murray Gleeson. Kirby had probably got to the highest point he would ever reach in the judicial hierarchy. It would seem that his career could suffer no damage as a result of the announcement of his and Johan's long-term relationship.

The legal position in Australia in 1998 was that homosexual acts between consenting adults in private was decriminalised in every state and territory and under federal law, although there remained differences over the legal age of consent. Ironically, the last state to do away with its punitive anti-gay laws now took one of the most enlightened positions. In the early 1990s, Tasmania, then under a Liberal government, refused to decriminalise homosexuality and, as a result, gay rights activist Rodney Croome began a long campaign that Michael Kirby publicly supported. Kirby went down to Tasmania, braved the placard-waving homophobes, and spoke at a public meeting: 'I didn't think it was right to be working hard for human rights in other countries and ignoring them here in my own.'

A case was brought to the United Nations Human Rights Committee claiming that the Tasmanian criminal laws against 'sodomy' were a breach of the International Covenant on Civil and Political Rights. When this idea of going to the UN was first raised with Kirby in the early 1990s, he advised against it. His view then was that such a claim would never succeed. However, it did succeed, forcing the federal government to act, and in 1994 it passed the *Human Rights (Sexual Conduct) Act*, banning any interference by any state with the privacy of people's sexual conduct, regardless of sexual orientation (privacy being as defined by the International Covenant on Civil and Political Rights). The Tasmanian Government held out for three more years before finally acknowledging in 1997 that its laws had to conform with the federal statute.

Understandably, there were few avid readers of *Who's Who in Australia*, and even fewer who would turn directly to Michael Kirby's detailed entry and read it diligently, right to the very end. And so a story that what would eventually be front-page news was initially missed by every journalist in the country. It was not until well into 1999 that it was finally picked up, first by the Sydney *Sunday Telegraph*, then by all the news media.

> The *Canberra Times* said, 'The biggest non-secret is out,' and that was what it was. It was not a big secret, but we passed the point of it being understated, to the point where to help people get over their phobias, we were out and about. I think it's been a good thing. Certainly lots of people, straight people, gay people, people with family members, they've said, 'That was a good thing you did.' If people don't like it, well, they've just got to examine themselves and examine the science. But overwhelmingly, I think it's been a good thing. Good for us and I hope good for Australia.

Initially it was a continuation of an odd situation where Kirby was out but he wasn't out. Michael and Johan's understated announcement was perhaps too understated. When finally the press did cotton on, there was a sense of relief for them both. They had now been together for forty years, hiding their relationship throughout that time. Once and for all, Johan did not have to worry about who was ringing on the home phone or who of Michael's friends or colleagues he could confide in. David Kirby was also relieved that Michael was now open about his sexuality. There had always been the risk that someone might out him for political or malicious reasons, and now that fear had passed. Kirby added two more things to his long list of speaking topics: gay, lesbian, bisexual, transgender and intersex (GLBTI) discrimination, and his personal life with Johan. In the past he had only really addressed the former in the context of AIDS and the latter had, of course, been taboo.

But not everyone thought this kind of public acknowledgement and acceptance of a prominent gay relationship was good for Australia. Since the demise of the Keating Government in 1996, religion had inexorably crept back into political life in Australia. In the early 1970s Attorney-General Lionel Murphy had proudly noted that a majority of parliamentarians now took an affirmation, rather than swearing the oath of office on a Bible. But by the end of the century it seemed every MP had decided they were believers, and there was hardly an affirmation in sight. In truth, only the minority had a strong connection to religion, and if they truly represented the Australian people, then fewer than 25 per cent of them would ever walk into a church.

From the mid 1990s Australia entered a conservative phase where religion and politics often came together in unexpected ways. John Howard even appointed a priest as the new governor-general, Anglican Bishop Reverend Peter Hollingworth. Less than two years into the job he was forced to resign after allegations that during his time as Anglican Archbishop of Brisbane he had failed to respond properly to complains of child sexual abuse within the church.

Whether in the office of governor-general, the High Court or the parliament, religion and politics have never mixed well in Australia. The ALP was kept from government for two decades after the Roman Catholics behind the Democratic Labor Party split and crossed over to support the conservatives, and after finally achieving office in 1972, Whitlam gained enormous criticism for introducing state aid to non-government religious schools. But the Howard Government seemed intent on taking Australia back – in some respects almost literally – to pre-Whitlam Government times. The prime minister introduced significant changes to the *Family Law Act 1975* to appease men's groups and Christian lobbyists, he moved federal legislation to override territory laws on euthanasia, he changed the *Marriage Act 1961* to ensure marriage could only be between a man and a woman, and Health Minister and former Catholic seminarian Tony Abbott (Kirby's good friend) refused to legalise the morning-after 'abortion' pill, RU486. Howard was criticised for forming links with extremist sect the Christian Brethren, while Treasurer Peter Costello, addressed the Hillsong Church and, along with other Liberal Party and National Party colleagues, was a member of the Christian faith-based faction the Lyons Forum, or, as their critics put it, 'the God Squad'.

For his part, Kirby had no illusions about the retrograde aspects of religion in combination with politics as it played out on both sides of the political divide. There were many religious people in the Labor Party who were just as socially conservative as anyone on John Howard's side. Nevertheless, while the ALP in opposition supported legislation like the amendments to the Marriage Act, it was the Howard Government in the driver's seat.

Deputy Prime Minister Tim Fischer – also a member of the Lyons Forum, a devout Catholic and later appointed by the Rudd Government as Ambassador to the Holy See – took every opportunity to attack what he saw as the activism of the High Court, the latest manifestation being the *Wik* decision. 'Those basket weavers on the High Court', he scolded from the dispatch box. And Howard's best mate and cabinet secretary, Senator Bill Heffernan, a man with his own strong religious views – especially on what the Bible describes as 'the abomination' of homosexuality – had cemented his place in the Government's ranks.

In mid 1999 Kirby spoke at a legal conference in London on 'The Legal Protection of Same-Sex Relationships in Australia', saying:

> Significantly, the principal reason given in the United States survey by those personally opposed to homosexuality is 'religious objections' (52 per cent). Yet even among the major religions in many Western countries, there has been a cautious shift to recognition of the need for change. Many commentators on the Pope's visit to the United States in January 1999 remarked on the 'sharp generational polarisation' on issues such as homosexuality, premarital sex and the ordination of women priests. In Australia some thoughtful commentators within the Roman Catholic Church (now the largest religious denomination in the country) have begun to talk of sexuality beyond the absurd proposition that sexual orientation should be tolerated but all of its physical and emotional manifestations prohibited.

Kirby was taking the initiative. Since the *Who's Who* entry he was now out and about and speaking regularly on the issue of homosexuality, urging tolerance and gay law reform. In February 2000 he accepted an invitation to address Riverview School. Situated on acres of prime real estate over looking the Lane Cove River on Sydney's north shore, St Ignatius College Riverview is one of Australia's oldest, most conservative and richest Catholic boys' schools. He had suggested that his topic would be homophobia. The Jesuit priests who ran the school agreed, as long as he broadened the theme. 'I gladly did this but warned that the main thing that I wanted to speak about was homophobia,' Kirby says. 'I was still invited.'

> As chance would have it, on the day before my lecture the Catholic Archbishop of Sydney, Cardinal Edward Clancy, issued a statement condemning the Gay and Lesbian Mardi Gras held in Sydney every March. He said that the Church recognised that there may be no responsibility on the part of homosexuals for their 'homosexual condition', but he went on to say that the Church 'teaches that homosexual practices are contrary to the moral law' so that homosexual people 'are required to exercise self-discipline and avoid such conduct'. They are called to a life without sex.

Leaders of both the Catholic Church and the Anglican Church in Australia had been teaching from the pulpit that homosexuality was 'an intrinsic evil'. Kirby would not stand for it and he told the boys at Riverview so. He called his talk 'Social Justice and Intrinsic Evil'.

> 'Intrinsic evil' is a very serious verdict. It goes beyond 'unfortunate' or 'undesirable' or 'misguided'. It is the kind of language that I believe inflames hatred by outsiders and self-doubt and loathing by those involved. I for one deny that, as a gay man in Australia today, I am 'intrinsically evil'. Boringly enough, I think I am quite a good man – kind to my loved ones, to other human beings and to animals. I have tried in my life to reach out to the needs of others, to act justly towards them and, where I can, to improve their lot. I respect the human rights of others. I do not think it is too much to expect that others will respect my human dignity.

He went on to tell the gathering of several hundred boys that homosexual acts between consenting adults were normal and must be respected.

> To demand a life of celibacy of the millions of homosexual people in this world – as some churches do – is not only totally unrealistic, it is completely unreasonable. Indeed, it is seriously unnatural. It amounts to an important rejection of an aspect of personhood which is impossible and wrong to demand of most human beings. In my experience, few if any gay and lesbian people choose their sexuality. It is like your gender, your skin colour or being left-handed. A bit like kicking with the left foot – although you can eventually choose your religion. From the earliest days of puberty, you just know that is how you are. And if that is how you are, that is how God meant you to be.

During the year 2000 he spoke a dozen times on similar themes. All this activity could scarcely have gone unnoticed. It was one thing to be gay and on the bench. But to some in the community, coming out and then openly proselytising for gay rights was too much.

The Junee farmer, recent past president of the NSW Liberal Party, senator, close confidante of Prime Minister Howard and now cabinet secretary, Bill Heffernan, began to compile a file on Michael Kirby. The minister's dirt team scoured Kirby's judgements, transcripts of his comments from the bench and his speeches, looking for any bit of (as they saw it) incriminating material. The cabinet secretary took particular interest in Kirby's frequent addresses to adolescent schoolboys. The minister's activities were no secret and they were not new. In 2000 the prime minister had been warned by the Labor Opposition that Heffernan was improperly using his office of cabinet secretary to conduct a campaign against gay Australians. Fellow senator Democrat Brian Greig recalls suffering repeatedly from uncomfortable, aggressive approaches by Heffernan:

> He often wanted to chat to me about gay stuff but it was always on his terms and it was always around, 'What are you doing about paedophilia?' I would raise an important gay rights issue in the Senate, again, and he would get all flustered and he'd physically walk across the chamber when I'd finished and poke his bony finger in my chest and say, 'You people have to do more about paedophiles.' Utterly fixated on it. It's all very odd.

In late 2001 Heffernan went to Howard and told him what he was up to with his Kirby dossier. Howard did not tell his friend to back off – far from it. Later, on *The 7.30 Report*, Howard said he merely gave a vague warning: 'I counselled him against any improper use of parliamentary privilege.' Howard apparently saw nothing untoward in the wider issue of his cabinet secretary using his office to try to bring down a High Court judge.

The minister ramped up the stakes and began to interview 'personally and at great length' a number of Darlinghurst rent boys (young male prostitutes). He also formed an association with John Howard's former long-time Commonwealth car driver Wayne Patterson. Under pressure from Heffernan, Patterson provided the senator with log sheets for travel in 1994 that purported to show Michael Kirby travelling to Darlinghurst, picking up a young male companion and taking him to his home in the eastern suburbs.

Heffernan contacted the NSW Police and handed over the material he had compiled against Kirby. Some weeks passed with no response and the senator was furious when the police eventually declined to take any action. His so-called evidence was fundamentally flawed. The rent boys were not credible witnesses and he had little else.

But this rebuff only served to spur the senator on. The dirt unit operating out of the office of cabinet secretary then broadened their inquiries, going through Kirby's NSW Court of Appeal and High Court cases. They separated out those that involved homosexual litigants, especially men convicted of sexual attacks on young boys. This approach was intended to reveal that Kirby was unable to keep his political views in favour of gay rights out of his judicial work and so was predisposed to treat gay men more leniently than other litigants. It also conflated criminal sexual violence, especially by older men against boys, with normal gay relationships. This kind of fishing exercise aimed at a High Court judge was certainly grossly improper and would have been expensive for the Coalition Government: in his last year as president of the NSW Court of Appeal alone, Kirby had handed down 480 judgements. But at the end of this long and detailed campaign, Heffernan came up pretty much empty-handed. There was no suggestion of any impropriety, of softer sentences handed down, of special pleading or a whiff of misconduct.

As Heffernan's team sifted through all the matters dealing with sexual abuse by men against boys, there was one case that had all the required elements – if only they could turn it to their advantage. During a special leave hearing in the High Court, Kirby had made some comments from the bench in a case involving a Catholic priest serving ten years for sexually assaulting boys in his care. Kirby was one of a panel of judges who unanimously gave the priest leave to appeal against the severity of his sentence but, as with all special leave hearings, no reasons for their decision were given by the judges. Nevertheless, this case went into the dirt file based on on a question from Kirby during the hearing as to whether the priest's vow of celibacy could be considered as a factor, given he may have been a 'situational paedophile'. This was interpreted by some religious figures as an attack on the Catholic Church. It could also be dressed up and presented, to those who did not understand how the appeal system worked, as Kirby showing favour to a convicted homosexual paedophile. In using the words 'situational paedophile', Kirby had left himself open to this kind of attack, even though his question and comments, when read in full, did not offer his definitive view on the matter. Heffernan called it 'legalese', implying that the priest was somehow a 'victim . . . locked in a vow of celibacy'.

The truth is that in granting special leave, no decision is made about the case itself – the justices are simply agreeing to hear the case, usually because they recognise that an important point of law has been raised and needs to be resolved. Using Kirby's words from the bench in this way was a classic case of selective quotation out of context. In the end the appeal was granted, with three High Court judges agreeing to send the prisoner back to the NSW Supreme Court for resentencing. One of those judges in agreement with Kirby was Justice Ian Callinan. Needless to say, Heffernan nowhere refers to Callinan's judgement in this case.

While Senator Heffernan's dirty dossier remained locked in a Liberal Party filing cabinet it was relatively harmless to Kirby. But Heffernan was not going to let it rest; since the police had found nothing in the criminal allegations, the senator was now focused on doing the most damage to Kirby with the material he had.

At 8.43 p.m. on Tuesday, 12 March 2002, while Kirby was dining with his High Court colleagues, Heffernan's course was set.

NSW ALP senator George Campbell was about to resume his seat after speaking for more than twenty minutes to a near-empty chamber on the failures of the Howard Government's industry policies. The former shipwright's thick Irish brogue echoed through the chamber. 'The Government,' he concluded, 'is holding an industry to ransom because they do not have the capacity to make a decision to get it on the road.' The heavy-set Campbell flopped back into his seat; it was getting late and those few senators in attendance just wanted to get home. Senator Brian Greig happened to be in the chamber, and he was surprised when he heard the acting deputy president call on the next speaker – Senator Heffernan (New South Wales), minister and cabinet secretary. Heffernan had earnt the nickname 'the Ghost Who Walks', because he was so rarely in the chamber. 'He was always loitering in the corridors,' Grieg recalls, 'never spent any time in the chamber, and it was extremely rare for him to talk on anything. He was Howard's hatchet man. He wasn't a legislator.' As Heffernan rose, Greig noticed something else: the cabinet secretary was extremely nervous. 'His hands were shaking.'

The Senate was quiet for a moment, then Heffernan began his speech, rattling off his words almost like a machine gun, but at a monotonous level with little emotion in his thin voice. 'The child protection mission statement for any government, institution or parent need be no more complicated than the following statement: all children have a basic right to their childhood and should enjoy an unconditional safe guarantee of passage through their years of innocence.'

What was to unfold was a rather unexciting piece of oratory and a premeditated assault by the most junior government minister on the fifth most senior judicial figure in the Commonwealth of Australia. Heffernan continued:

> I refer to a judge who has put himself at grave risk of blackmail, entrapment, compromise and hypocrisy. This judge has come to the attention of senior police and the Child Protection Enforcement Agency [. . .] a judge [. . .] who indiscreetly, improperly and illegally used Comcar, who regularly trawled for rough trade at the Darlinghurst Wall, who according to

> police statements and interviews regularly played out his fantasies in a fee-for-service arrangement.

Kirby's was the name they dare not speak. The senator rattled on for seventeen minutes without identifying the judge in question, until the coup de grâce in the last five words of his speech: 'The Honourable Justice Michael Kirby'.

This was a carefully thought-out and self-serving strategy. The minister needed the protection of parliamentary privilege to deliver his defamations – what has become known as the coward's castle. In this way he could destroy Kirby's reputation but remain protected from any legal action. This was the same cover Franca Arena had used before her words led to the destruction of David Yeldham's life. Privilege means that MPs can speak freely without fear that they will be sued for defaming someone. It is not expected that they will deliberately set out to defame. In fact, an attack on a sitting member of the judiciary without a substantive motion calling for the judge's removal from office is not allowed under the standing orders of the Senate. As soon as Heffernan mentioned the name of the judge, the presiding officer of the Senate would have been obliged to order him to sit down. The senator had trashed this convention, structuring his speech so that the name of the judge was delivered in the last few words and the deputy president of the Senate therefore could not intervene until it was too late.

Senator Brian Greig was convinced that Heffernan had not written this speech himself: 'Heffernan was inarticulate. I don't mean that in an unkind way. He's a bushy – he kind of bumbles. He's a bit confused, he's a bit eccentric. He did not write that speech . . . it was well crafted.' Greig was sure it had come from much higher up. Such a vicious, damaging and premeditated attack from one branch of government on another had never been advanced like this in the more than one hundred years since federation.

Most of the minister's speech was fairly predictable; some of it involved political criticism of Kirby's judgements. But there were two potentially damaging claims. First, that Heffernan had in his possession statutory declarations by young male prostitutes that would in some way implicate Michael Kirby in wrongdoing – either gross impropriety or criminality. The second allegation appeared equally as worrying. It centred on the log sheet that the Commonwealth car driver had given Heffernan, pointing to illegal use of a Comcar at least, and part of a pattern of procuring underage boys for sex at worst. These claims were immediately and immensely damaging to Kirby's reputation.

On 13 March 2002 Michael woke as he always did at about 5 a.m., at his and Johan's Kingston flat in Canberra. The dinner at the High Court had gone on late and he was careful not to disturb Johan, who was still asleep. By five-thirty he was on his way to work, making the brisk walk along the banks of Lake Burley Griffin to the High Court building that was his daily routine. By 6 a.m. the phones in his chambers were ringing – unusually early, even for him.

First on the line was ABC Radio, asking for a reaction to what had happened in the Senate the night before. It was the first Michael knew of any of it. The journalist offered to send the news clipping, and when Michael read it, he felt disturbed as the enormity of what Heffernan had done began to sink in.

> There was no forewarning, no advice, no due process, no opportunity to put another case before such a thing was done. I was at work early because it was a very big, detailed case concerned with negligence with effluent affecting oyster farmers, so I was trying to get that in my brain. When I saw it was alleged that I had been trawling around with Commonwealth cars, to be completely honest, I thought – knowing that it wasn't true – that anybody who had said this should take a reality check and make very sure that they had accurate evidence before they made such an allegation. If you know you are not guilty then you perhaps naively tend to be a bit dismissive of such things. However, that's not the way things necessarily play out in this world.

Michael's first thought was to get hold of Johan. He tried ringing their flat but Johan wasn't answering the phone. He had made the long drive from Sydney to Canberra the night before and was still sleeping.

> So I had to go into court knowing that he didn't know about all this. So that worried me. I got a phone call from Malcolm Fraser and from David Bennett, the solicitor-general, and a few other people who were expressing outrage and shock. But I just went into court and I sat there and I saw journalists coming in and looking at me and staring at me as I was listening to,

> and asking, lots of questions on effluent and oysters. I always knew the assertion about the use of Commonwealth cars was ridiculous and false. So I just got on with my work. I just concentrated on the oysters and that went on and on – that case lasted I think about four days. Meantime, the drama was unfolding.

As a judge of the High Court, even one with his high profile, Michael Kirby was in no position to enter a public slanging match with Heffernan. While the minister had all the apparatus of government at his fingertips and ready access to the prime minister and the media, the judge could do no more than release one short statement to the press: 'Senator Heffernan's homophobic accusations against me in the Senate are false and absurd. If he has such accusations, he should approach the proper authorities, not slander a fellow citizen in parliament. In so far as he attempts to interfere in the performance of my duties as a judge I reject the attempt utterly.'

Here the personal assault by the senator and the professional slur were wrapped up together. It was hard to separate the two but always at the heart of Kirby's concern was advocating for and maintaining the proper relationships between these great institutions of government: the parliament and the judiciary. What the senator – and, through his tacit acceptance, the prime minister – had done in making this attack on a sitting justice of the High Court was to damage the finely balanced relationship between the two arms of government. One of the foundations of the Australian constitutional system, the separation of powers, where parliament, the executive and the judiciary stood separately, each as a check and balance on the other two arms, would be severely eroded if attacks of this sort were allowed to stand.

One of the things that went through Kirby's mind was the terrible ordeal his friend and predecessor, Justice Lionel Murphy, had had to endure during what had become known as 'the Murphy Affair'. Nearly three years of claim and counter-claim, the parliamentary inquiries into his behaviour, the criminal charges, the court cases and the final acquittal. In Kirby's view, there was no doubt that the years of stress had contributed to Murphy's death from cancer, even though he was finally acquitted of all charges a month before.

> I saw Lionel Murphy during the time that he was under a lot of stress and I saw the impact of the cancer on him. I saw him waste away and ultimately die. But don't forget, his ordeal went on for years – years of stress and pressure. You can't tell me that stress and pressure over a very long time doesn't either trigger cancers or accelerate them if they're latent in the person, because I've seen it in a number of cases.

Heffernan's speech in the Senate on that Tuesday night enraged the Leader of the Opposition, Simon Crean. He saw it as a gross misuse of parliamentary privilege and immediately called on the prime minister to instruct Heffernan to apologise to Justice Kirby and to resign from the ministry. But Howard had nothing of the sort in mind. By the Friday he had hit the airwaves on 2UE, foreshadowing the establishment of a parliamentary inquiry into the activities of the judge – the first step towards Kirby's potential removal from the High Court by a motion of both houses of parliament on the grounds of 'proved misbehaviour or incapacity'. This was the only way a High Court judge could be removed under the Australian Constitution. Howard asked Australians to remember that, in his view at least, 'proved misbehaviour' did not have to amount to criminal conduct. The fact that Howard would not back away from Heffernan was no surprise to Michael Kirby.

> I knew that the prime minister and the senator were quite close allies and I think during Mr Howard's bad years, Senator Heffernan had been one of his supporters and had contributed to his ultimate rise to return to the leadership. So you understand on a human and political level these arrangements. But you've got to think in terms of institutions, and this was not really a good way to go in the relationship between the institutions of the highest court and the parliament. Just to become the judge, jury and executioner and not to involve the police or the ordinary authorities of law is really the definition of the way one should not go about things in serious matters of that kind.

Over the weekend the news media had a field day with the story of Justice Michael Kirby's alleged use of rent boys and Comcars; it was in every newspaper around the country. The tabloids in Sydney were particularly excited, with a front-page photograph of Michael headed 'The Evidence Revealed', and inside a rather smug photo of Heffernan along with an exclusive: 'Senator's Two Pages of Evidence Against the Judge'. On Sunday, 17 March the *Sun-Herald* ran a full-page story reproducing the Comcar docket and quoting from a statutory declaration, both of which Senator Heffernan had provided. The statutory declaration, the newspaper claimed, was sworn in August 2000 by a 29-year-old man, and in part read:

> I have given written statements to the Child Protection Enforcement Agency about my sexual encounters originating from the Wall in Darlinghurst with Michael Kirby. I know Michael Kirby is a judge. On several occasions he took me to a unit in Darley St at the end of the 'Wall' [. . .] At the times Michael Kirby picked me up from the Wall, I was a young male prostitute and heroin addict. I told Michael Kirby this.

The journalist noted that this man's allegations against Justice Kirby had already been investigated by NSW Police in 1998 and discounted as not credible. He had also given similar evidence in the defamation case brought by the high-profile and openly gay solicitor John Marsden around the same time. The judge in that case had again rejected the witness as unreliable. This 'evidence' against Kirby was not new.

The Comcar docket, however, was new and potentially damning evidence. There it was on the front page of the *Sun-Herald*, for all of New South Wales to see. The day in question was 2 April 1994. It displayed a list of jobs, clearly showing Michael Kirby's alleged movements. Heffernan had claimed in parliament that the judge had taken his Commonwealth car to Darlinghurst – a place called 'the Wall', where homosexual male prostitutes work the street – and there picked up a male passenger and returned with him to the judge's home in Rose Bay. The Comcar docket reproduced in the *Sun-Herald* in support of this allegation showed a trip by the judge from the law courts in the city to his home at 7 p.m., a trip taking fifty minutes, and then at 11 p.m. a journey from there to Darlinghurst. Annotation on the log entry showed that the judge did not travel on this last trip and it does not reveal who did travel.

This was the lowest point in the whole saga for Kirby. To pick up the Sunday papers and see a photo of himself on the front pages and to then read the continuing defamation, in lurid detail, was almost too much. It was the thing he had feared his entire adult life. He had seen it played out so many times before – Lord Montagu, Peter Wildeblood, countless other gay men, their lives destroyed through the pages of the tabloids, and all too often it ended in a long prison sentence. This was 2002, not 1952, yet nothing seemed to have changed.

Johan and the whole Kirby family were shattered and angry. David Kirby had feared such an attack on his brother for a long time: 'It was always a concern that people would maliciously and for their own ends seek to discredit him.' Johan was terribly aggrieved, shocked and lost for words. He just kept asking the same question over and over again: 'Why?' Michael's father, Don Kirby, had the day Heffernan's allegations surfaced etched into his mind and he would never forget it: Wednesday, 13 March 2002. He wrote out a poem and sent it to his son.

Michael 13-3-02
If I were hanged on the highest hill,
I know whose love would follow me still,
Father o' Mine, Father o' mine

If I were drowned in the deepest sea,
I know whose love would come down to me,
Father o' Mine, Father o' mine

It was Don's version of the Kipling poem and it showed how far he had come since the late 1960s. At the same time it immediately evoked the memory of Jean (the original Kipling being 'Mother O' Mine'), and summoned her strength and love. Don left the last stanza off his version; perhaps it was too redolent of Leviticus:

If I were damned of body and soul,
I know whose prayers would make me whole,
Mother o' mine, O mother o' mine!

The *Sun-Herald* had photographically reproduced the entire Comcar docket on its front page, and other information on the docket thus came to light. On the same day, in the same car, with the same driver, unconnected entries showed a trip taken by National Party politician Ian Sinclair and, further down the sheet, a trip by Laurie Brereton, who was then minister for industrial relations and transport in the Keating Government. That entry showed a pick-up of Brereton in the city and a trip to Kensington.

Over his Weet-bix that morning at his home in Sydney, Laurie Brereton perused the newspaper. When he saw his name on the Comcar docket he took particular interest – there was something that didn't seem quite right and Brereton smelt a rat. Even his children, who also saw the article, thought there was something amiss. Brereton later examined his parliamentary diaries and they immediately confirmed his suspicions. On 2 April 1994 he had been holidaying with his family in north Queensland. Far from Kensington, he had been on Hayman Island.

The Comcar docket appeared suspiciously like a forgery. It was also now clear the 'signed statements from Darlinghurst rent boys' were, in reality, just one statement and from just one man in particular. And this individual had already had similar evidence, such as it was, thoroughly discredited during the John Marsden defamation trial some years before. The minister's attack on Kirby was now in tatters.

On the Monday, 18 March, everything started to look up for Kirby. Coincidentally, it happened to be his sixty-third birthday. Laurie Brereton held a press conference in the garden at Parliament House in Canberra and after that, Opposition Leader Simon Crean pursued John Howard. If the ALP could show that Heffernan's central piece of evidence was a forgery within twenty-four hours of getting hold of it, how was it that the Government, with all its resources, couldn't deal with the claims much earlier? Why had the prime minister proposed an inquiry with a view to the possible removal of a judge without even the most rudimentary checking of the so-called evidence?

Howard knew when he was on the losing end of a political stoush and he decided to end the matter immediately. He did a doorstop interview, informing the press that he had asked the senator to resign as parliamentary secretary and to make a detailed statement to the Senate and an 'unqualified apology' to Michael Kirby. The next day, seven days after his original statement, Bill Heffernan entered the Senate.

> I want to extend to Michael Kirby my sincere apology and deep regret for the allegations I made in this place: I withdraw them unreservedly. I know that, with the recent widespread media coverage of my speech, his personal standing has been harmed. I do not expect him to accept my apology but, nonetheless, I give it, because I recognise the personal hurt that must have been suffered. I also apologise to the Senate and the whole parliament.

But Heffernan could not control himself, and the remaining six and a half minutes of the speech again trawled over the same defamatory material. Even so, the apology stood. The Senate immediately passed a censure motion against him.

Shortly after the senator concluded his speech, Michael Kirby issued a public statement:

> My family and I have suffered a wrong. But it is insignificant in comparison to the wrong done to Parliament, the High Court and the people. I have been sustained by my innocence, by the love of my partner and family and support and prayers from all sections of the community. I accept [the senator's] apology and reach out my hand in a spirit of reconciliation. I hope that my ordeal will show the wrongs that hate of homosexuals can lead to. Out of this sorry episode, Australians should emerge with a heightened respect for the dignity of all minorities. And a determination to be more careful in future to uphold our national institutions — the Parliament and the Judiciary.

Again Kirby's central focus was not on the damage he had suffered personally but on the damage done to the institutions of government. This was something which, if not repaired, could end up to the detriment of all Australians. *The Age* ran the story on its front page under a giant and very judicial portrait of the judge. It lauded Kirby for stoically accepting Heffernan's apology. *The Australian*'s headline on page one read 'Shamed [Senator] Apologises'. It began: '[The senator's] campaign against High Court judge Michael Kirby has ended with an unprecedented and abject apology from the man who was until Monday afternoon John Howard's cabinet secretary and political enforcer.'

The affair had also further strained relations in the court itself. Only Mary Gaudron had offered her direct support to Kirby during that week and only she had actually taken steps to try to counter some of the clearly false claims. Chief Justice Murray Gleeson refused Gaudron's approaches to publicly release a statement of support for Kirby, even after she had enlisted Kenneth Hayne and Michael McHugh to the cause. Gleeson did, however, speak to the media over the weekend, telling the *Courier-Mail* that use of a Comcar in the way detailed by Heffernan, if it had occurred, was certainly improper. It later transpired that Gleeson had already been informed by officials from Comcar that the dockets Heffernan had were almost certainly fake. Gaudron felt that this information should have been made public immediately, and when that didn't happen, she took the extraordinary step of 'leaking' it. In the end, Laurie Brereton's press conference two days later was a powerful climax to the whole nasty business.

Kirby got straight back to work. He disposed of the oysters and effluent case and started hearing an appeal in Sydney against a decision by the Refugee Review Tribunal. By his own admission it had been a bad week, but he got through it and had already moved on: 'I don't think about it, really. I don't allow it to affect my attitude to parliament or to the Court. But I hope people have learnt from it about the right way of going about things and the wrong way of going about things.'

Nevertheless, many people did not feel quite as magnanimous towards Howard's ex-cabinet secretary as Michael Kirby. Johan in particular remained furious.

> It was a total grab for attention, misusing parliament in the process. Later on he retracted that apology and stated that he had some paperwork wrong – which means that he wasn't really sincere when he made that apology. When he made it I thought, like Michael, 'turn the other cheek and forgive', but later on I thought, 'No, this man didn't regret it at all; all he regretted was that it went that way.' A few times since then he has come up at functions where the camera could have been on him and made apologies again, or comes up with, 'Do you want to shake hands with the devil?'

Many people, especially those in the Labor Opposition and the Australian Democrats, believed that John Howard was the 'brains' behind the Heffernan affair. Certainly nothing important happened during the Howard years that was not first passed by the PM's office, and by his own admission this was no different. Howard ran an extremely tight ship and it seems inconceivable that a close friend and a very junior minister would go behind the boss's back on such a damaging course of action. Howard's motivation in all of this, if he was behind it, would have been simple. It was an opportunity to get rid of a Labor-appointed judge and to replace him with a conservative. Nothing personal.

At the end of the year Michel Kirby's reputation was intact and he was firmly in place on the High Court. *Who Weekly* magazine included Michael in its list of the twenty-five most beautiful Australians for 2002. High Court judges had never featured in such a list before, but his noble and immediate acceptance of the senator's apology after what was such a fierce and unjustified attack was offered as the reason for the listing. Throughout years of public life Michael Kirby had become increasingly highly respected in the Australian community. It was always possible that after his 'coming out' in 1999, that respect might have been dented or diminished in some quarters; indeed, the Heffernan attack was certainly in part a reaction against Kirby's openness about his sexuality. The whole thing had only lasted six days but if the Sunday papers had not reproduced the forged Comcar dockets, or if Laurie Brereton had not seen his name in the list, it could easily have all ended very differently. Michael Kirby has always thought that he has had a very lucky life, and this was another example of his luck holding out.

10

Marching to the Beat of a Different Drum

> Judges of final courts have to think a little bit differently because there's no further appeal. They have to think about the long-term directions. They march to a different drum, in a sense. They know that many of the things that they're dealing with are the same thing as other final courts in other countries are dealing with at the same moment. If they think that they are just an ordinary judge solving a problem, then they're missing both their responsibility and their opportunity in the final court of a nation.
>
> *Michael Kirby*

A documentary film crew arrived at the High Court in Canberra in September 1997. The High Court had never before permitted the electronic media beyond the big glass walls that form its imposing facade, with one exception – on ceremonial occasions the cameras could come in to film the new judge being sworn, but after that they had to go. No judgements or proceedings had been allowed to be filmed. The TV networks and radio broadcasters always set up their tripods and sound gear on the forecourt outside the High Court building, never coming through the revolving doors into the giant atrium and the courtrooms beyond.

There had been a fair bit of discussion in the community about the televising of court cases; the NSW Law Reform Commission had looked at the issue in 1984 and pointed out the obvious educational value and, sporadically, Australian judges had permitted television cameras into their courtrooms. Denis Barritt SM was probably the first, allowing the televising of his decision in the coronial inquiry into the death of Azaria Chamberlain in 1981.

A lot happened in 1981. Aboriginal Land Commissioner Mr Justice Toohey allowed filming of the proceedings of the Kaytej, Warlpiri and Warlmanpa land claim, one of the first under the *Aboriginal Land Rights (Northern Territory) Act 1976*. (Justice John Toohey now sat on the High Court with Michael Kirby.) ABC-TV's *Four Corners* filmed part of the *Social Security Conspiracy* case in the Sydney Court of Petty Sessions, in Hobart news cameras recorded a case on retail trading hours, and in South Australia the trial of a man charged with burglary was filmed, again by *Four Corners*.

Kirby saw television in the courtroom as inevitable and had said as much on several occasions. As far back as 1983, he stated in his Boyer lectures:

> The technology has moved on. If the judges are to remain the great educators of the community they will have, in time, to adapt to it, uncomfortable as that adaptation will be at first.

> In the twenty-first century, the camera will be as common in the courtrooms as the law reporter's notebook is today.

By 1995 he saw no reason to change his view, with developments in the US underscoring his point.

> [When I was in] far-away Lesotho, I saw the trial of a member of the Kennedy clan, on a charge of rape. The trial of Mrs Bobbitt, on a charge of severing her husband's penis, was on the hotel television in Madrid when I was there in January 1994. Now, the trial of the Los Angeles sportsman, O. J. Simpson, is receiving saturation television coverage in the United States. CNN, which provides its global audience with material targeted mainly upon American interests, bring intensive daily reports of this trial with extensive commentary. It is probably true to say that no trial since that of Jesus Christ has attracted so much international attention.

The Americans, with popular shows like Dominick Dunne's *Power, Privilege, and Justice* had made celebrity trials nightly fare for TV audiences. Whether such programs helped or hindered the bringing about of a final just outcome in a particular case was not clear. O. J. Simpson was acquitted when many viewers believed he was guilty. TV host Dominick Dunne certainly did, and made it plain at every opportunity. Perhaps the celebrity status of the accused and the intense media and television interest made no difference to the verdict, perhaps the American system was so robust it could tolerate even the worst excesses of this kind of intrusion by the entertainment industry. Criminologists like David Wiesbrot believed that, if televising of court cases was to become a common occurrence in Australia, then criminal matters should be excluded. Kirby disagreed. 'By what right do we, the lawyers, purport to exclude the people's eyes from a part of the court process of the greatest concern to them?'

After the *Wik* decision in 1996 the High Court had come under intense political attack. Australian politicians seemed to delight in propagating the entirely false notion that somehow, whenever a decision came down that the politicians didn't like, the judges had improperly crossed over from their normal role and function into the political arena. Howard and his ministers slammed the judges and there was no way they could defend themselves. In this heated atmosphere the chief justice, Sir Gerard Brennan, decided that there had to be a way of educating the Australian people about the true role and nature of the work of the High Court. When a Melbourne production company approached Kirby and proposed a documentary film that could screen on the ABC in prime time, it seemed like a perfect vehicle. Kirby passed the proposal on to Brennan, who took the idea to the other judges. John Toohey, Mary Gaudron, Bill Gummow and Michael Kirby sided with the chief justice in favour of the idea. Michael McHugh and Daryl Dawson were not in favour and would not be involved, but would also not stand in the way of the production.

All involved in the filming, perhaps especially the judges themselves, imagined that Kirby, renowned for his media-friendliness, would make himself a major part of the program. As it turned out, he remained in the background. During the shoot Justice Dawson retired and was replaced by another Victorian, Kenneth Hayne. Justice Hayne arrived with the film production well underway and joined the majority decision to cooperate.

All the judges except McHugh were scheduled to appear for a roundtable discussion to be filmed in the judges' meeting room in the High Court in Canberra. This was a significant occasion – no televised panel discussion involving six of the seven sitting justices of the High Court had ever before taken place. On the day, only five judges arrived: Brennan, Toohey, Gaudron, Gummow and Hayne. Kirby, the most media-savvy, the strongest advocate for televising court proceeding, was a no-show. He never offered a clear explanation as to why he could not attend. It was almost as though he had decided to confound his critics both on the court and in the commentary pages of the newspapers. They had formed the view that he was a self-promoter who was incapable of shunning the limelight. On this occasion he would prove them wrong.

Gerard Brennan used the film to make the strong case for judicial independence. He was fed up with the not-so-subtle pressure coming from John Howard. The chief justice was front and centre from the very opening scene of the film.

> We have a society that is ruled by law. The options to being ruled by law is being ruled by power and that can be a source of oppression. But the law can rule only so long as there are impartial arbiters who can enforce the rule of law. It is very important that the public should be satisfied that the judges are not, as it were, working with governments, because frequently the issues that arise concern the exercise of power by

governments. A judge must be independent of any source of power or influence that could impermissibly tilt the scales of justice.

Oddly enough, Justice McHugh, not willing to support the filming, became one of the more interesting characters on the screen. When special leave hearings and constitutional cases involving him were filmed he did not object, and his feisty and humorous exchanges with counsel were entertaining. Justice Kirby, on the other hand, was very much a secondary character in the documentary, but he made his presence felt.

In February 1998 a major constitutional case, *Kartinyeri v. The Commonwealth*, came before the Full Court and for the first time, TV cameras were there to record it. Justice Toohey had retired and given John Howard a second opportunity to shape the court in his own image. His replacement would placate the calls from Howard's front bench for a capital 'C' Conservative. *Kartinyeri* was to be only the second case that the new justice, Ian Callinan, was to sit on. Callinan was a Queensland barrister widely known as the QC who had prosecuted Lionel Murphy. There had been a big celebration, in some quarters, when he secured a conviction of the radical judge on charges of attempting to pervert the course of justice. (Unfortunately for them, the champagne had gone a bit flat when Murphy was finally acquitted after an appeal and a retrial.)

Kartinyeri had its origins in a dispute between developers of a marina complex in South Australia and local Indigenous people.

The Hindmarsh Island bridge was intended to join the sleepy island community 90 kilometres south of Adelaide to the township of Goolwa on the mainland; it was to cost $14 million and was to be funded by the South Australian Government. The prime beneficiaries, however, were developers Tom and Wendy Chapman, who needed the bridge in order for their massive marina complex to turn the greatest profit.

There was community unease over the Chapmans' proposal because it would change the nature of the quiet seaside resort forever. Stage-one work commenced on the bridge in October 1991 but by 1993 there was substantial opposition from a broad-based group, including the Conservation Council of South Australia, the Construction, Forestry, Mining and Energy Union (CFMEU), the Goolwa Residents and Ratepayers Association, Greenpeace, local residents and holiday-home owners, and the Ngarrindjeri Aboriginal people. The issue came to a head the following year, when the federal Aboriginal Affairs minister in the Keating Government, Robert Tickner, made a declaration under the *Aboriginal and Torres Strait Islander Heritage Protection Act 1984* stopping the building of the bridge for twenty-five years. The basis for the ruling was the minister's obligation under the Act to preserve and protect from injury 'areas and objects that are of particular significance to Aboriginals in accordance with Aboriginal tradition'.

A group of Aboriginal elders had presented evidence about their beliefs to Tickner in envelopes marked 'Confidential: to be read by women only'. This was sensitive material that no man could see and it was referred to as 'secret women's business'. A campaign began, circulating the view that the 'secret women's business' had simply been made up by the Ngarrindjeri women. The Keating Government was lashed for being so politically correct and naive that they could be duped by 'lying Aborigines' into stopping important economic development. The Aboriginal women's beliefs were ridiculed by largely white, male politicians and commentators who, by their own admission, knew nothing about it.

By the time Ngarrindjeri elders Doreen Kartinyeri and Neville Gollan took their action in the High Court, Howard had won the 1996 election and as prime minister had introduced the *Hindmarsh Island Bridge Act*. Under Howard's new legislation, Aboriginal heritage protection was made inapplicable in relation to just one thing: the proposed bridge. In fewer than 700 words he excised the Hindmarsh Island bridge from the purview of the original Aboriginal and Torres Strait Islander Heritage Protection Act. The Hindmarsh Island bridge development was simply no longer subject to the law protecting valuable Aboriginal heritage sites. (This was a method Howard would employ again later, excising geographical parts of the Australian nation from the *Migration Act 1958* in order to deny refugees landing on outlying islands full legal rights in their claims for asylum.)

The South Australian Liberals, who had opposed the construction of the bridge, had won the state election in December 1993, changed their position and, under pressure from John Howard, set up a royal commission into the Ngarrindjeri people's religious beliefs. It was to be a farce. The royal commissioner was never told what the 'secret women's business' was, but decided to make a series of assumptions about what it might be and test those assumptions. In a staggering piece of logical contortion, the royal commissioner found that the Ngarrindjeri did not hold the religious beliefs they claimed to hold, even though the royal commission remained unaware as to exactly what they were. By now, the bridge itself was well under construction and the very phrase 'secret women's business' had become a national joke.

Generally speaking, if a justice has already stated his or her opinion on a matter that subsequently comes before the Court then they must recuse themselves from the hearing. Justice Ian Callinan had indeed given advice on this specific controversy; in fact, he had done so on two separate occasions as a QC in Queensland. First, he had prepared a draft of suggested terms of reference of the South Australian royal commission on the Hindmarsh Island bridge, and second, he had written a joint opinion for the Howard Government on the constitutionality of the very legislation now before the High Court. Nevertheless, he did not feel the need to stand aside. Jim Spigelman QC, appearing for Doreen Kartinyeri, thought otherwise. Callinan listened attentively to Spigelman's arguments but rejected them, appearing on the bench with the others on the first day of the hearing. Spigelman then said that if the justice would not recuse himself, he would ask the other six justices to make a ruling. This had never happened before and the idea of such a spectacle – the six brother and sister judges sitting in judgement on one of their own – was unthinkable. Callinan sensibly withdrew.

In 1967 the Australian people had altered the Constitution in the celebrated referendum on Aboriginal rights. It meant that the constitutional prohibition on the federal government making 'special laws' for Aboriginal people was removed. As a result, the federal government could pass legislation like the Aboriginal and

Torres Strait Islander Heritage Protection Act. At its heart, the constitutional question proposed in *Kartinyeri* was very simple. There was no doubt that the removal of the requirement that the Aboriginal and Torres Strait Islander Heritage Protection Act apply to Hindmarsh Island was detrimental to the Ngarrindjeri, but was it constitutional? It all turned on the following passage in the Constitution:

> The Parliament shall, subject to this Constitution, have power to make laws for the peace, order, and good government of the Commonwealth with respect to:
>
> (xxvi) the people of any race ~~, other than the aboriginal race in any State,~~ [as amended in the 1967 referendum] for whom it is deemed necessary to make special laws

Did this mean only laws for the *benefit* of Aboriginal people, or could the Australian Government use this power to make laws to the *detriment* of Aboriginal people? Many constitutional experts, including Justice Lionel Murphy years before, believed that the use of the word 'for' in the Constitution ('for whom it is deemed necessary') meant that the power must only be used *for the benefit*. Until the advent of the Howard Government, the very idea that laws might be made in modern Australia that would be to the detriment of Aboriginal people was not a concept that anyone had ever sensibly propounded. In *Kartinyeri* he sent Solicitor-General Dr Gavan Griffith QC into the High Court to argue that there was no restriction on the race power and that it could therefore be used to the benefit of Aboriginal people or to their detriment.

As the Government presented its case, Michael Kirby began to squirm. He was deeply troubled by the line of argument, and felt angry. He addressed Dr Griffith directly from the bench:

> I mean, it seems unthinkable that a law such as the Nazi race laws could be enacted under the race power and that this Court could do nothing about it [. . .] How would you apply that distinction to the case of Nuremberg-type laws which, after all, were race laws or to land area laws such as were enacted in South Africa? Would they be permissible under this power?
>
> Griffith: Your Honour, they may well be. The races power is inherently a discriminatory law.

It was a simple question: 'for the benefit' or not? But the answers that came back from the six High Court justices were anything but simple. Like crows in a corn field scared by a shotgun, the justices all flew in different directions. Only Kirby and Mary Gaudron found that the Constitution restricted governments to enacting laws for the benefit of Aboriginal people. Only Kirby found in favour of Kartinyeri and Gollan. All the other five judges, including Gaudron, found that the Government's Bridge Act was constitutional, but each for different reasons. It was heartbreaking for the Ngarrindjeri who, like many Aboriginal people after *Mabo*, had come to believe that the High Court was their last refuge in a struggle to uphold their human rights, but it was also mystifying. To the layman it seemed extraordinary that all six justices could come to different findings. The adversarial nature of the law suggests there are two sides to every case; *Kartinyeri* was the clearest example of how wrong that assumption can be. In truth, there are as many sides to each case as there are justices. Kirby's position could not have been stated more clearly.

> The Bridge Act 1997 does not answer to the description of a law with respect to the people of any race for whom it is deemed necessary to make special laws. It is a special law; that is true. But it is detrimental to, and adversely discriminatory against, people of the Aboriginal race of Australia by reference to their race. As such it falls outside the class of laws which the race power in the Australian Constitution permits. No other head of power being propounded to support the validity of the Bridge Act, it is wholly unconstitutional.

The Ngarrindjeri people had to stand by and watch the SA Liberal Government literally bulldoze their sacred sites. In 2001, long after the bridge had been built, they had a Pyrrhic victory when Justice John von Doussa of the Federal Court threw out a damages claim by the Chapmans. 'Upon the evidence before this Court,' he determined, 'I am not satisfied that the restricted women's knowledge was fabricated or that it was not part of genuine Aboriginal tradition.'

Nine years later, in 2010, the last chapter in this tragic saga was finally written when the SA Government acknowledged the Ngarrindjeri people's claims were truthful. The ABC reported:

> Environment Minister Paul Caica says the Government accepts a Federal Court ruling, made in the wake of the royal commission,

which acknowledged that secret women's business was not made up to try to stop the bridge construction.

'The state government of South Australia acknowledges the decision of Justice von Doussa and the conclusion he makes that Ngarrindjeri knowledge was a genuine part of Aboriginal tradition and was not fabricated,' he said.

In a sad coda, Ngarrindjeri elder Tom Trevorrow was left to make comment for his people: 'We may use the bridge to access our land and waters but culturally and morally we cannot come to terms with this bridge.'

Kartinyeri was to be one in a long line of cases where Michael Kirby would be dissenting, often in a minority of one. As time passed he began to look fondly back at his time on the NSW Court of Appeal, where he was a leader, respected and liked by his judicial colleagues and regularly writing for the majority or all members of the Court. As the High Court became, with each new appointment by the Howard Government, more and more conservative, Kirby was to find himself increasingly out in the cold. Justices would openly joke about the very thought of joining with Michael Kirby in a judgement. It was not a happy time.

The close-knit Kirby family were suffering, too. In 1998 Jean Kirby became gravely ill. She had been sick for a decade since a heart bypass operation in 1985 but now lymphoma began to take hold. On 17 July of that year, Michael had to fly to South Africa, but didn't want to leave his ailing mother. Michael wrote to his parents:

Dearest Mum and Dad,
Forgive me for rushing in – snatching just an hour with the people most important in the world to me. This is how I am programmed. Would have been better if I had been a plumber! [Aunt] Glory was right.

I enclose a few photos. I will be thinking of you all week in Sth Africa. Get ready for my return on Sunday.

Love from Your Son #1,
Michael

Michael's brother David had just been appointed to the Supreme Court of New South Wales, and Jean hoped to attend the swearing-in ceremony in August. It was a wonderful occasion for the family, but tinged with sadness that their mother remained at home, too ill to go. Don and Jean had certainly produced some high-achieving children. One judge in the family was a triumph, but for David to now go to the bench as well was an accomplishment neither of them ever expected. Michael sent flowers to Jean, and accompanying the bouquet was a card that read: 'To the mother of 2 judges.' Michael Kirby got back from South Africa in time to sit in the courtroom as his friend and former Sydney University student politician, now chief justice of New South Wales, Jim Spigelman, did the honours. Spigelman himself had only been elevated from QC to chief justice three months before.

> On behalf of the judges of this bench, and on my own behalf, I congratulate you on your appointment and welcome you as a member of this Court.
>
> My own personal position is of much joy, for the simple

> reason that most of my time at the Bar was spent sharing chambers with your Honour, and most of my time on the bench will be spent sharing the bench with your Honour.
>
> From the Court's point of view, the Courts have endured long enough without a Kirby on it.

David Kirby spoke of the debt he owed to his parents, his mother in particular, and his brothers and sister. He modestly claimed no ambition for himself, but instead, rather tongue-in-cheek, put his entire career success at the feet of his older brother, Michael. It was Michael, he said, who had handed down school uniforms to David as he followed in his footsteps to Fort Street Boys' High School, and then on Michael's direction, became a prefect. He pointed out that in forty-five years, nothing much had changed – Michael had graduated from the Supreme Court to the High Court and so David was now wearing Michael's hand-me-down Supreme Court judge's robes and wig and, as with his homework at Fort Street, David was sure, before long, Michael would be correcting his judgements from Canberra.

It was a funny story, beautifully capturing the relationship between the two men and perfectly describing Michael's position in the family, but it took on a special poignancy on this occasion. The smiles all round did not last long; everyone there knew Jean was suffering at home, gravely ill. Jean Kirby died twelve days later, on 24 August 1998, at the Royal Prince Alfred Hospital. The Kirbys, like any family, had had their tragedies and with Jean's death many of the sad moments came flooding back, especially for Don, who had loved only her since he was a boy of just fifteen.

They had been together for more than sixty-six years. He wrote to friends:

Michael and Diana were greatly affected by my wife's & their mother's death. He was at the hospital every day all day helping her with liquid feeding & I slept in the same room & attended to her thru the nights. Diana was the sister in charge on the floor above in the same hospital (Royal Prince Alfred, Camperdown) & would come down every hour to see that she was comfortable. Donald & David realised that she was in great pain & discomfort & accepted her leaving us as a merciful release from all her suffering.

The Kirby children had never known a time without their mother's wise advice, her 'steady gaze' that seemed to look right into their thoughts, or her loving embrace. The memories of loss were powerful: the third son, the twin, David Charles who had died at eighteen months of age, the death of Michael's beloved grandmother, Norma, and the awful loss for David Kirby of his young wife, Marie-Line Hervic, in 1986. She was only thirty-four when she died and had been married to David since the age of twenty.

Johan had formed a close bond with Jean and they truly loved each other. She liked his quiet intelligence, his practicality and his laconic humour, and most of all she knew he was the right person for Michael and for the family. As Don said later, 'They're inseparable, absolutely, he couldn't manage without Johan. I don't think any of us could.' When Michael delivered a tribute at the Anglican service for his mother, he spoke for Johan and his whole family about the vibrant being whom they could hardly accept was no longer going to be there. It was also the first time he would publicly acknowledge Johan by name.

> We, her children, would visit our parents virtually every weekend. Sunday dinner with them both became almost a religious ceremony for Johan and me. They delighted in all of their grandchildren. Though they grieved in loss of Marie-Line, their lives were recently brightened by the arrival of Susanne and Judith and Jessica and Patrick [. . .]
>
> It is far too painful to tell of the last few weeks. But on Sunday, though she could not speak, she took her leave individually of each one of us by gestures and loving smiles. My father and I were there at six-thirty in the morning on Monday when at last she found peace. A passing she had truly wanted and prayed for came quietly to her. It was not without suffering. But, as always, she set an example of dignity, persistence, courage, practicability and care for others. She was a noble spirit. And now that spirit continues in us who are left.

As Michael finished reading his tribute there was a moment of reflection before the service continued. Sitting in that church, Michael felt comforted. The smell of the polish on the wooden pews and panelling, the stained-glass windows, the hushed silence. It seemed only yesterday that he had held his mother's hand as she took him down to St Andrews kindergarten on Parramatta Road for the first time. Now she was gone. He looked at Johan and then at his father, the slightly stooped old man, his sad face. Michael took a deep breath, stood with the congregation and began singing:

Blest are the pure in heart,
For they shall see our God;
The secret of the Lord is theirs,
Their soul is Christ's abode.

The voices gradually faded in his ears until all was quiet. Michael was alone again, sitting in his High Court chambers, the Commonwealth Law Reports lining the walls and the appeal books for his next case on his desk. A ubiquitous cup of hot black tea and a teapot sat next to the books, the steam slowing rising. He looked for a moment to the blue sky out his window and the low Brindabella mountains lining the horizon, then he turned his total focus to the task at hand.

Two criminal cases that came before Michael Kirby in the first years he was on the High Court seemed to reveal a clear and consistent line of thinking on the law of provocation. In *Green v. The Queen* in 1997, Kirby would have refused an appeal from a 22-year-old man who had been convicted of murdering an older man by stabbing him thirty-five times in a frenzied attack. The 'provocation' claimed by his counsel was that the victim had gently placed his hand on the accused's side, bottom and groin. This, combined with the fact that the accused had suffered sexual abuse as a child, was claimed to have provoked the accused to kill the victim. Kirby utterly rejected this thinking. 'In my view, the "ordinary person" in Australian society today is not so homophobic as to respond to a non-violent sexual advance by a homosexual person as to form an intent to kill or inflict grievous bodily harm.'

Justices Kirby and Gummow did not believe there had been any miscarriage of justice in this case, but they were in the minority and the High Court ordered a retrial. At the retrial, Green was allowed to use the defence of provocation and he was convicted of the lesser crime of manslaughter.

In *Osland v. The Queen*, a year later, Kirby again placed paramount importance on the sanctity of human life. The circumstances of this murder were entirely different from those in *Green*. Heather Osland claimed to suffer from 'battered woman syndrome'. She had endured fifteen years of the most, in Kirby's words, 'deplorable' abuse: sexual violence, bashings and psychological violence at the hands of her frequently drunk husband, Frank Osland. Heather's son, David Albion, had also suffered repeated violent attacks at the hands of Frank Osland. Heather Osland planned the killing of Frank by drugging his evening meal, then holding him down while David inflicted a fatal blow to his head. They then disposed of his body together, and for more than three years acted as though he had simply disappeared. In the subsequent murder trials, Heather Osland was convicted and David Albion was acquitted.

On the face of it, there appeared to be an inconsistency here. Years after the initial conviction in Victoria, Osland's appeal finally found its way to the High Court. Dr Jocelynne Scutt led the case for Osland in the High Court and used several avenues of attack, including the notion that Osland suffered from an identifiable condition (battered woman syndrome) and that this meant that she was unable to see any other way of escape from a domineering and extremely violent husband.

Again Kirby utterly rejected the defence offered. He also rejected the idea that there was any inconsistency in the two verdicts: conviction for the mother and acquittal for the son. 'No civilised society removes its protection to human life simply because of the existence of a history of long-term physical or psychological abuse.'

In both of these cases, Kirby was demonstrating his very conservative approach to the fundamentals of criminal law. It was almost as if he was going right back to the Bible teachings: *Thou shalt not kill.* But Michael Kirby's life experience was, by his own admission, very limited. He came from a close and loving family. Perhaps the very notion that a mother could be so tormented by a physically and psychologically abusive man that she saw no way out of the situation other than to kill her husband was something that he could never understand. It was unfortunately a daily reality for many, with a battered or murdered woman the more usual outcome.

There were two things that irked Kirby more than anything else in his long career, first at the Bar and then on the bench. Most annoying were the matters where by some action or omission of his there was an outcome that was less than ideal. The law was imperfect and, like in all human activity, mistakes would be made. But for Kirby, it was a different proposition when there was something specific that he should have done, something he should have realised was necessary but he neglected to do. Second and allied to this was the conflict between seeking a just outcome and applying the law as it stood. Sometimes finding a suitable resolution of these potentially conflicting objectives was impossible. Kirby didn't like the word 'impossible'; it grated.

It was Justice Michael McHugh who first alerted Kirby to the *Mallard* case. McHugh has an eidetic memory, and can recount whole pages of acts and judgements on command. The appeal papers arrived on Kirby's desk in late 2005 and at first they did not ring any bells, but after Justice McHugh reminded him, the memories came back. Eight years before, Justice Toohey, McHugh and Kirby had formed a special leave hearing panel that dismissed an appeal from the same man. At the time the decision was unremarkable. 'Unfortunately the arguments that were advanced related to the refusal of the trial judge to admit a lie detector test,' Kirby later recalled. 'That wasn't a particularly good argument to get into the High Court because they're not really part of our system in Australia. So we refused special leave.'

As he examined the appeal documents a feeling of dread overcame Kirby. It was the same feeling he had had all those years ago, when Mr Corbishley had been taken away in custody. Andrew Mark Mallard, like Glenn Corbishley before him, was a man whose appearance and behaviour could be disturbing. He suffered from mental illness and had spent time in a psychiatric hospital. He had been convicted of the brutal murder, in 1994, of Perth shopkeeper Mrs Pamela Lawrence. He had exhausted every avenue of appeal against his conviction, including the special leave hearing in the High Court that Kirby had sat on in 1997. After eight more years in prison, Mallard had petitioned the governor of Western Australia for a pardon and this had been referred to the WA Court of Criminal Appeal. Again his case had been rejected by the Appeal Court judges. This time, though, his subsequent application to the High Court for special leave to appeal had been successful.

His major avenue of appeal was in relation to a number of important facts that were not disclosed to the defence in his original trial, although they were known to the prosecution at the time. Kirby was disturbed by what appeared to be a pattern of behaviour by both police and prosecutors in this case and he highlighted this with Bret Walker QC, counsel for the WA prosecutors.

> Yes, but Mr Walker, I have often, over twenty-five years in criminal appeals, pointed to my associates and said, you mark that, you mark the way the Crown did that because that was done out of its sense of a duty of fairness, and here we have a catalogue of things that were not put before the jury which do not seem to accord with the standard of the fair presentation of an honest presentation of the case. I have to say that in this case there were things, deleted things, suppressed things not put forward and it leaves one with a real sense of disquiet – it leaves me with a real sense of disquiet and does not seem to conform in its totality with the normal way in which the Crown prosecutes in this country.

Six important matters had not been disclosed to the defence in Mallard's original trial for murder. They included forensic tests police had conducted that did not support the major theory of the prosecution that Mallard had committed the murder with a wrench. They also included evidence from eye witnesses that did not support claims by the prosecution about the dress and the movements of the accused on the day of the murder. In the end, Kirby and the other four justices of the High Court found unanimously that

Mr Mallard must have his conviction quashed. It was a case that would not quickly leave Kirby's mind. Had he missed something in the 1997 special leave hearing? An innocent man had sat in jail for eight long years more. Kirby asked himself the same questions over and over again:

> Did I miss the point that this was an innocent person? If I'd been helped a bit more, if I'd read more carefully myself, would I have picked up a point that was not being urged on us? Of course then you ask the ultimate question: 'What cases have been before me where I have made a mistake which I didn't see was a mistake, that the Court wasn't helped to see the error?' That is a judge's nightmare – to be responsible for somebody being in prison for a very long time or suffering other disadvantage, is a nightmare. But you have to just get on with the next case. You can't just sit there like a centipede, anxious to take the first step the next day. You've just got to start again and do your very best.

Shortly after *Mallard*, Michael Kirby hit rock bottom at the High Court. His only true ally on the Court, Mary Gaudron, had retired in early 2003 and now Michael McHugh was also gone, retiring from the bench and returning to private practice at Wentworth Chambers. While they'd had their professional differences McHugh was personally close to Kirby. They had sat side by side, first on the NSW Court of Appeal and then on the High Court, for the best part of twenty years. Kirby wrote to his friend, 'I find it hard to describe what it is like without you around.'

The Court began to sink into a well-worn path. Bill Gummow and Kenneth Hayne would write the lead judgement in many cases, Chief Justice Murray Gleeson would invariably join them, and then they only required one more to get the majority. Kirby was frequently off on his own. The Murdoch press loved to sideline him as 'the great dissenter' and therefore slightly irrelevant. It was a moniker he hated. 'It's been given to me by media, which sometimes doesn't really fully understand the nature of the judicial task.' It wasn't even strictly true. From 1998 to 2003 the conservative Ian Callinan dissented the most – 30 per cent more frequently than Kirby, with McHugh not far behind. But by 2005 Michael was in a league of his own, dissenting on constitutional matters more than 40 per cent of the time.

> I hope that citizens would understand that a judge has a responsibility to state the judge's own conviction of what the law and the facts require in the particular case. We don't have a court system that is based on Tammany Hall. It's not just for the judges to cook up an outcome simply because that will make everyone happy. We're not there for that, we're there to state honestly our opinion and that's what I endeavour to do.
>
> I have asked myself, 'If you had worked harder at interpersonal relations on the High Court, if you had driven more passionately to get consensus, could you have done so?' I don't think there would've been much of a change, because if you demand space for your opinions, you have to accord space for the opinions of your colleagues, and I did. They had their view on big issues and conflicted issues and I had my view and each

> of us stated our view. That's as it should be. Whether some of my dissents in the future will be vindicated, that is for the future, and it's not something I can predict. The future hasn't done much for me so far.

Kirby's head was telling him that he should be doing something else, perhaps at the UN or UNESCO, where he was respected and, more importantly, where he could make a difference. At the same time his body was telling him, for the first time in his life, to slow down. Late in April 2005, not long after his sixty-sixth birthday, Kirby was admitted to the Royal Prince Alfred Hospital for quadruple heart bypass surgery. Suddenly, early retirement, four years before he would have to, seemed like an attractive option. He even discussed the possibility with Johan and later his friend Gareth Evans, by then no longer active in politics. Johan would support any decision Michael made and was, of course, excited about the possibility of the two spending more time together. Evans had very different advice.

Mark Latham had just lost the leadership of the Labor Party and the veteran Kim Beazley had returned to the job. Evans was sure things were changing on the federal political scene and that John Howard's days were numbered. As the person who had fought hardest to get Kirby onto the High Court, Evans could not in all conscience sit back and let him hand another appointment over to Howard, especially when the Labor Party now had the best chance in years to squeeze back into office. He pleaded with Kirby to hang in there; in eighteen months everything might be different. It took a bit longer, but on 24 November 2007 Kevin Rudd led the ALP back into government, and it wasn't a squeeze but a 'Ruddslide', the third biggest swing since 1949. Howard lost his parliamentary seat – only the second time that a prime minister had lost his seat since federation.

In the last years of his government, from 2002 to '07, John Howard established his credentials as a war leader, taking Australian troops into Iraq and Afghanistan, and became a fervent advocate for tough counter-terrorism laws. His terrorism legislation was unprecedented and was devised in the wake of September 11, when ten Australians died, and the Bali bombings of October 2002, which claimed the lives of eighty-eight Australians. And there was a second change to the laws in 2005 after the London Underground bombings, in which one Australian was killed. The laws allowed for the detention of people, including children, who had committed no offence, who were not even considered suspects, for the purposes of questioning. People could secretly be detained for many days without access to a lawyer or being able to notify their family or friends. The reverse onus of proof applied; under certain provisions suspects were considered guilty until proven innocent. Howard also decided to revamp the laws regarding sedition, which had not been used for fifty years and had been thought by many lawyers to have slipped into obscurity.

The new laws brought back memories of 1963, when a South African businessman, Mr X, spoke at Sydney University about the then-new apartheid anti-terrorism laws. They gave the South African Government 'sweeping powers over the community [providing] for detention of a person, incommunicado, for a possible recurrent period of ninety days, until satisfactory answers have been given to any interrogation, or until such time as the police see fit to release him or her'. They included new clauses on sedition, and placed the onus of proof on the accused.

Howard's anti-terror laws were out of the same playbook, and Michael Kirby was not afraid to speak up from the bench. Jack Thomas, a Melbourne taxi driver and Muslim convert who had travelled to Afghanistan and allegedly trained with al-Qaeda, had been acquitted in the Supreme Court of Victoria of all charges of 'providing support to a terrorist organisation'. Subsequently, the Australian Federal Police sought a control order limiting his movements – not because of what he had done, since he had never been convicted of any offence, but because at some time in the future he might do something, presumably by putting his alleged training into action. Kirby thought the law went too far. 'There are a number of new laws that personally, I would not myself think were useful or particularly effective,' he later commented.

> For example, Mr Thomas, in his control order, was under very strict instructions not to make any contact with Osama bin Laden. Given that the whole world is searching for Osama bin Laden, it seemed a slightly excessive turn of the order and it was ultimately modified. But you can get out of touch with the realities. The world of security forces and sometimes the world of policing, indeed sometimes the world of the law, can get a little bit out of touch with reality. You've got to keep your feet on the ground. But we know we need new powers and we have to respond. You can't be mollycoddling people who are bent on

> violence. Especially intolerant people who are doing it in the name of God – that is an amazing phenomenon. So we need the laws, but we've just got to keep our sense of proportion.

Kirby believed that the greatest decision in the long history of the High Court of Australia was the decision in the *Communist Party* case in 1951, in which Prime Minister Menzies' attempt to ban the Australian Communist Party was found to be unconstitutional. The Court, in a five-to-one decision, had found that Menzies' legislation relied on war-time powers, and that to ban a political party in this way, in a democracy, in a time of peace, was not within the constitutional power of the federal government. Kirby strongly believed those five justices were right to find in the way they did.

> Not because my grandmother's new husband was a communist affected by it, but because it stood up for the principle that in Australia, we punish people for what they actually do. We don't punish them for their beliefs. We don't take their civil liberties for their opinions, however bizarre we may think those opinions to be. That was done by six judges of the High Court in the majority, with horsehair wigs, most of whom had a background in commercial law, but they decided that case. That was a really wonderful thing, when the United States Supreme Court with the great Bill of Rights reached the opposite conclusion. I think it was a great case.
>
> But in *Thomas*, there were justices who suggested that the use-by date of the *Communist Party* case had been reached. The use-by date of the *Communist Party* case has not been

> reached and we must never let it be reached. It's important that it stands there as a symbol for Australians and as a warning and guide for the future judges of the High Court.

Justice Callinan in particular rejected the thinking behind the majority in the 1951 *Communist Party* case. He believed that internal threats in a time of peace, such as the threat of communist subversion in the 1950s or the threat of terrorism now, could justify the use of the defence power, therefore making Menzies' law constitutional and, on the same basis, the current 'control order regime' used against Jack Thomas would also be legal. Of the seven justices in the *Thomas* case, only Michael Kirby and Kenneth Hayne wholly or substantially rejected this approach.

The recent Australian terrorism laws, which the High Court was reviewing in *Thomas*, had been passed as a direct reaction to the suicide bombings of the London Underground in July 2005, where fifty-two people were killed and nearly 800 injured. Yet much of the rhetoric used by counsel and apparently accepted without question by five of the High Court judges had already been repudiated by the British themselves, with comments like this from the UK's Director of Public Prosecutions:

> London is not a battlefield. The innocents who were murdered on 7 July 2005 were not victims of war. And the men who killed them were not, as in their vanity they claimed on their ludicrous videos, 'soldiers'. They were criminals. They were fantasists. We need to be very clear about this. On the streets of London, there is no such thing as a 'war on terror'

> [. . .] The fight against terrorism on the streets of Britain is not a war. It is the prevention of crime, the enforcement of our laws and the winning of justice for those damaged by their infringement.

From the bench, Kirby tackled Solicitor-General David Bennett on how it was that acts of terrorism were so readily and immediately described as acts of war. The *Thomas* case hinged on the nature of the defence power of the Constitution – in its broadest terms, the federal government's power to raise an army and defend the nation of Australia from attack. The Australian Constitution divides all powers between the states and Canberra; the defence power is a federal government power while the criminal law is, by and large, dealt with by the states. Under the Howard anti-terror laws, the federal government had carved out a special area of expanded powers for the Australian Federal Police and other federal bodies, even the armed forces. If the terrorist acts themselves were simply criminal acts of violence, then the defence power would not apply and the acts would be more appropriately prosecuted under the criminal law, probably by state police forces. In the UK, one of the Law Lords had questioned how it was that the threat faced by the nation in 2005 was greater than, or even on a similar scale to, that faced by the nation in 1939–45.

> Kirby: Lord Hoffmann's dissenting speech – none of this is binding on us, but as far as I am concerned it was pretty persuasive. If Britain was not damaged by the threats of the Nazis with their ever-present invasion, you can hardly say that

the nation of Britain was threatened by the type of things that have occurred in the list of activities that you are relying on.

Bennett: The other view is that he was proved wrong by the events in London shortly after the judgement.

Kirby: The nation has gone on. The British nation has gone on. I mean, with all respect, it is pretty unconvincing to say the life of the nation is threatened. It is a wicked and monstrous act; it is dealt with in the normal way by police and by other responses of civilian society. The nation is not affected.

There were two major issues in this case, and in the whole counter-terrorism debate, that Kirby was angry about. The first had to do with the proportionality of the response. The events of 11 September 2001, with the devastating loss of nearly 3000 people, had been invoked to justify two wars, one in Iraq and one in Afghanistan. These conflicts were conservatively estimated to have cost US$3.5 trillion, and up to 1 million people killed (both figures continued to grow on a daily basis). In a further disproportionate act, it now appeared to Kirby that the events of September 11 were accepted by some of the High Court judges as justification for a curtailing of Australian civil liberties unlike any we had ever seen before in peacetime. Kirby had worked tirelessly for more than two decades to help those millions of people all over the world suffering AIDS. When the solicitor-general began to grapple with the issue of proportionality in the terrorism laws, Kirby couldn't turn his back on the obvious. According to Mr Bennett, adhering to well-established procedures and protections apparently was 'what in the United States is sometimes described colloquially as "September 10 thinking"'. This glib put-down generated an immediate reaction from Justice Kirby:

> Yes, but the Americans, with all respect, have become completely obsessed with September 11 and that is not an event that occurred in this country and I think we have to keep our eye on the threats to Australia. I mean, more people die every day from AIDS than died on 11 September.

The second issue in the terrorism debate that Kirby was angry about was the trend for governments like Australia's to do so much damage, as he saw it, to the open democracy most Australians took for granted by the curbing of well-established civil liberties. He believed that in the end, this subversion of democratic freedoms would do the terrorists' job for them. The *Communist Party* case and the *Thomas* case were the same in one vital respect. In both instances the government was criminalising Australians not for their actions but for how they thought; not for what they had done but for who they were. Thus, under Menzies' law, a law-abiding trade unionist who joined the Australian Communist Party would instantly become a criminal, liable for five years' jail. Likewise, Jack Thomas had committed no offences – in fact, he had recently been acquitted of terrorism charges – yet he was the subject of a control order imposed at the request of the Federal Police because they feared he *might*, sometime in the future, do some terrorist act. The repudiation by five of his colleagues of the *Communist Party* case, the greatest decision in the history of the High Court was, as far as Kirby was concerned, a very great loss for Australian democracy.

The famous quote from the *Communist Party* case by (the later chief) justice of the High Court of Australia Sir Owen Dixon came immediately to mind.

> History, and not only ancient history, shows that in countries where democratic institutions have been unconstitutionally superseded, it has been done not seldom by those holding the executive power. Forms of government may need protection from dangers likely to arise from within the institutions to be protected.

Kirby had held those words close from the moment he had first read them, decades earlier. They came from one of the most conservative justices of the High Court and one of the most respected, and his thinking on this occasion, as far as Kirby was concerned, was impeccable. 'In explaining his conclusion that the law was constitutionally invalid,' he says, 'Dixon relied on a broad political and philosophical notion of the rule of law. He treated this as an assumption implied in the Constitution. That assumption helped to determine the outer boundary of federal legislative power which had therefore been exceeded.' Kirby could not believe that any High Court bench, let alone one that he sat on, could reject the great words of Dixon. And yet that was the position he found himself in.

By August 2007, when the verdict in *Thomas* was handed down, Kirby had less than eighteen months more to serve on the Court before he had to retire at the age of seventy. The possibility of the

Court gradually coming round to his way of thinking in any matter now seemed utterly remote. His decision in *Thomas* might have been in dissent but he was not going to allow his brother and sister judges to trash the *Communist Party* ruling and escape unscathed. A significant part of his dissenting judgement amounted to a stinging attack on his fellow justices:

> I did not expect that, during my service, I would see the *Communist Party* case sidelined, minimised, doubted and even criticised and denigrated in this Court. Given the reasoning expressed by the majority in these proceedings, it appears likely that, had the Dissolution Act of 1950 [Menzies' legislation to ban the Communist Party] been challenged today, its constitutional validity would have been upheld. This is further evidence of the unfortunate surrender of the present Court to demands for more and more governmental powers, federal and state, that exceed or offend the constitutional text and its abiding values. It is another instance of the constitutional era of laissez faire through which the Court is presently passing.
>
> Whereas, until now, Australians, including in this Court, have generally accepted the foresight, prudence and wisdom of this Court, and of Dixon J in particular, in the *Communist Party* case (and in other constitutional decisions of the same era), they will look back with regret and embarrassment at this decision when similar qualities of constitutional wisdom were demanded but were not forthcoming.
>
> In the face of contemporary dangers from terrorism, it is essential that this Court should insist on the steady observance

> of settled constitutional principles. It should demand adherence to the established rules governing the validity of federal laws and the deployment of federal courts in applying such laws. It should reject legal and constitutional exceptionalism. Unless this Court does so, it abdicates the vital role assigned to it by the Constitution and expected of it by the people. That truly would deliver to terrorists successes that their own acts could never secure in Australia.
>
> The wellspring of constitutional wisdom lies in legal principle. Its source is found in the lessons of constitutional history. When these elements are forgotten or neglected by a court such as this, under the passing pressures of a given time, the result is serious error. The consequences for the constitutional design, as for individual liberty, can be grave. It must then be left to a future time to return to that wisdom and to rediscover its source when the mistakes of the present eventually send this Court back to the wise perceptions of the past.

Before Michael Kirby was to retire from the High Court, it would go through further changes. Justice Ian Callinan, two years older than Kirby, retired shortly after the decision in *Thomas* was handed down. This gave John Howard another opportunity to make an appointment and he turned to conservative lawyer Susan Kiefel QC, once a junior to Callinan. She had been appointed to the Federal Court of Australia in 1994, and was now only the third woman ever to sit on the High Court.

About a year later, under the new Labor Government, Kirby's

fellow Sydney University alumnus Chief Justice Murray Gleeson left the court and was replaced by Western Australian Robert French. Kirby had played leapfrog with Gleeson throughout their respective careers: Kirby had gone to the Supreme Court of New South Wales before Gleeson but the latter came in as chief justice, and Kirby had first gone to the High Court only to be followed by Gleeson as chief justice. At least now Kirby remained, by virtue of his youth, a few months longer than Gleeson on the Court. Kirby had seen him come and seen him go.

Robert French was the first appointment by a Labor Government since Kirby himself in 1996, twelve years before. The days of big 'C' conservative appointments were gone and yet new Labor prime minister Kevin Rudd's choice was no Labor man either. Justifying the appointment, Rudd laid emphasis on the fact that French had been a parliamentary candidate for the Liberal Party years before, and later, from the Federal Court bench, he had overturned Justice North's original *Tampa* decision. This had allowed John Howard to begin off-shore processing of refugees, contributing to his 2001 election victory.

In the last weeks of Kirby's tenure on the High Court of Australia, the documentary film crew returned. This time they recorded the last time the judge was to sit on a constitutional matter in Canberra, and this time they were there for Michael Kirby alone. They were producing a film about his life, before, during and after his time on the bench. On 2 October 2008 the seven justices filed into the High Court to begin hearing *Wurrigal v. The Commonwealth*.

In one of the last acts before his government lost office, Prime Minister Howard instituted the *Northern Territory National*

Emergency Response Act 2007, also known as the Intervention. The Intervention was justified by Howard on the basis that a recent report in the NT, *Little Children are Sacred*, had found high levels of child abuse in remote Aboriginal communities. The report by Patricia Anderson and Rex Wild QC delivered a scathing attack on both the NT and federal government policies and it made ninety-seven specific recommendations. The report prefaced all of these with one overarching recommendation, considered the most important: 'In the first recommendation, we have specifically referred to the critical importance of governments committing to genuine consultation with Aboriginal people in designing initiatives for Aboriginal communities, whether these be in remote, regional or urban settings.' Not only did the Howard Intervention not implement or even address the vast majority of these ninety-seven recommendations, it shunned the most important one and undertook no consultation with Aboriginal people, and immediately imposed a regime that had severely detrimental implications for many aspects of Aboriginal people's daily lives.

The Intervention had made four major changes that breached Aboriginal control over their own lands. The Racial Discrimination Act was suspended, immediately indicating that the Government's legislation breached anti-discrimination provisions: not for the first time Howard was being challenged in the High Court for making laws to the detriment of Aboriginal people. It removed the permit system whereby Aboriginal people controlled who could and could not enter their communities. It required Aboriginal people to lease property to the Government in exchange for the provision of services and it compulsorily acquired Aboriginal land. Impositions of these kinds have never before or since been enforced over any other racial group within the Australian community.

Wurrigal was a claim in the High Court that the Intervention was unconstitutional in that it confiscated Aboriginal property rights without adequate compensation and that this acquisition was not, therefore, on 'just terms'. Michael Kirby was the only one of the seven justices to allow the appeal of the Aboriginal people from Maningrida. He opened his judgement, the last he was to write in his long career as a judge, with the following words:

> The claimants in these proceedings are, and represent, Aboriginal Australians. They live substantially according to their ancient traditions. This is not now a reason to diminish their legal rights. Given the history of the deprivation of such rights in Australia, their identity is now recognised as a ground for heightened vigilance and strict scrutiny of any alleged diminution.

Kirby could see the racial discrimination so obvious in these acts and he was most appalled that none of his fellow judges saw it the same way. He was further incensed about the way in which the matter was disposed of. The legal term 'demurrer' meant that the Commonwealth never actually had to have a full trial fighting over the merits or otherwise of the constitutionality of the Intervention. Instead, it simply applied for a demurrer – meaning that the appeal by the Maningrida community should be dismissed as a matter of law before any of the facts of the case were argued since, according to the Commonwealth, it could never amount to a successful constitutional challenge. This was a further slap in face for the Aboriginal people: their fears and daily reality were actually not even worth debating. Kirby's judgement continued:

> The legislative provisions in question here are applied to Aboriginal Australians by specific reference to their race. The Emergency Response Act expressly removes itself from the protections in the Racial Discrimination Act 1975 (Cth) and hence, from the requirement that Australia, in its domestic law, adhere to the universal standards expressed in the International Convention on the Elimination of All Forms of Racial Discrimination, to which Australia is a party.
>
> If any other Australians, selected by reference to their race, suffered the imposition on their pre-existing property interests of non-consensual five-year statutory leases, designed to authorise intensive intrusions into their lives and legal interests, it is difficult to believe that a challenge to such a law would fail as legally unarguable on the ground that no 'property' had been 'acquired'. Or that 'just terms' had been afforded, although those affected were not consulted about the process and although rights cherished by them might be adversely affected. The Aboriginal parties are entitled to have their trial and day in court. We should not slam the doors of the courts in their face. This is a case in which a transparent, public trial of the proceedings has its own justification.

Chief Justice Robert French saw Kirby's admonition of the other judges' position as 'gratuitous', and in his reasons bluntly said so.

This kind of heated attack is rarely seen in the High Court and was far from the mannered prose of most judgements. Kirby made his final order, the last he would ever make, in sole dissent, and in favour of the Aboriginal claim:

> The issue for decision is not whether the 'approach' of the majority [the other six judges] is made on a basis less favourable because of Aboriginality. It is concerned with the objective fact that the majority rejects the claimants' challenge to the constitutional validity of the federal legislation that is incontestably less favourable to them upon the basis of their race and does so in a ruling on a demurrer. Far from being 'gratuitous', this reasoning is essential and, in truth, self-evident. The demurrer should be overruled.

Michael Kirby's career on the bench of the High Court had moved a full 180 degrees. He had begun in the *Wik* case, dealing with issues of racial discrimination and Indigenous rights, but he had been in the majority. The court had made a strong statement, it had led to important political change and Kirby had been a part of that. Now on the very same matters he sat alone and shunned, the sole dissenting voice. His judgement was there on the record but he had achieved no change; he was impotent. Wik elder Gladys Tybingoompa was so delighted with the judgement in 1996 that she had danced on the forecourt of the High Court building. Now when Kirby looked out his window, all he could see were Aboriginal demonstrators – a small, dejected group of people, and to one side a team of federal police. It would have been sad if this was to be the only public gathering to mark his departure from the Court.

On the day that the judgement in *Wurrigal* was handed down by the High Court, Justice Kirby sat for the last time. It was usual on the retirement of a judge of the Federal Court or a state's Supreme Court for there to be a retirement ceremony, the bookend to the swearing-in ceremony. Family, friends, fellow judges, senior members of the Bar, Solicitors-General and Attorneys-General would all put in an appearance. On the High Court, however, these ceremonies were reserved for the chief justice's retirement alone. Michael Kirby thought it was proper that there should be a change. He felt a judge's often long service (and Kirby was then Australia's longest serving judge) should be ceremonially recognised. Michael loved ceremonies and he didn't see why he should miss out on one.

True to form, his fellow High Court judges disagreed. If Kirby wanted a farewell ceremony, fine, but he could do it on his own time. None of his fellow judges would attend. The Court would not even allow the event to be entered into the official record. When historians examine the law reports in years to come there will be no mention of the farewell ceremony for Justice Michael Kirby. It was a fairly petty and some might say mean act, but then, for a profession utterly hidebound by an adherence to precedent, perhaps not unusual. As Justice Murphy remarked years before:

> Then there is the doctrine of precedent, one of my favourite doctrines. I have managed to apply it at least once a year since I've been on the bench. The doctrine is that whenever you are faced with a decision, you always follow what the last person who was faced with the same decision did. It is a doctrine

> eminently suitable for a nation overwhelmingly populated by sheep.

Precedent may have been the excuse but there was something else happening here. From where his colleagues sat, they simply saw a man who was trying, as always, to promote himself undeservedly above the team. In that regard he was insulting them, and in particular he was insulting the chief justice.

It was a sad and telling moment that on his last day as a judge, after a long and illustrious career, none of his fellow High Court judges wished to attend his farewell ceremony. How did it come to this? Perhaps this was the one occasion where Michael Kirby should have swallowed his enormous pride and said to himself, 'No, I won't upset my colleagues, I won't elevate myself above all the justices of the High Court who have gone before me. I won't act as though I should have been given the job as chief justice and now, having not achieved it, I will not take for myself one of the perks reserved for that office alone.' These thoughts may have fleetingly crossed his mind, but if so, he dismissed them.

So, on Monday, 2 February 2009, the Honourable Justice Michael Kirby walked into courtroom number 1 in the High Court in Canberra as he had done so many times before. A packed courtroom stood until he had taken his place on the bench. Two of his previous colleagues, Mary Gaudron and Michael McHugh, were there, and the one who was to replace him, Justice Virginia Bell, also attended. The room fell quiet and the TV cameras whirred. The speeches were laudatory and even passionate, from the federal attorney-general, the presidents of the Australian and NSW Bar associations and the Law Council of Australia, and Tom Hughes QC, now eighty-five years old, who had been there when Michael Kirby was sworn in as a judge of the Arbitration Commission almost thirty-five years before. Sitting in the front row of the public gallery were Don Kirby, brothers Donald and David, and, most importantly, Johan.

> On past occasions, when I have come to this point, I have referred to my debt to unnamed 'loved ones'. My fearless sisters-in-law would always dig my partner Johan van Vloten in the ribs to let him know that this was him. He was on. Well, those times are over. Johan has been a great strength to me during my time on this Court and long before. He has occasionally had to absorb unkind blows without complaint: a steadfast rock throughout all my judicial years. Today, I can thank and praise him publicly. And next week we celebrate forty years together.
>
> In the interval between my swearing in and now, many good things have been achieved in Australia, including sometimes in this place, to improve the position in law of those whom I mentioned at my welcome: Aboriginals, women, homosexuals, Asian Australians, non English speakers. Challenges remain and there are new injustices to overcome after today. The noble struggle for justice is never completed.
>
> My departure has permitted me to send a lot of papers to the National Archives. At my request, last month, they gave me access to my ASIO file. I combed through the insubstantial records of long-forgotten, trivial activities in student affairs, in

the Council of Civil Liberties (Mr Murphy) and other innocuous events far away. And then my eyes fell upon a report of an unidentified agent's conversation with my great-aunt, Gloria Boes. She was a friend of Jessie Street. She was, what we would now call, a 'progressive feminist'. She had some communist friends. No doubt that was how she came under surveillance. She died in 1993.

In the conversation, she is reported as having said: 'Michael Kirby is very brainy but he [is] a reactionary.' Somehow this did not seem to square at all with all the talk of a 'judicial activist', 'maverick' and 'great dissenter'. So I thought about it. Actually, my aunt, who was very intelligent, may have been onto something here. You see, I could never get out of my mind the notion that the law of Australia is basically an instrument of justice. That its invariable tendency is to bend towards equal justice for all. That it would not lightly condone a constitutional interpretation oppressive to the 'little people' in Australia. That our law is generally fair and rational. And that where it is not, parliaments or the courts have their responsibility to step in, so far as they can, to make it so. When you analyse them, these are truly very 'reactionary' thoughts. They exhibit a naive and touching faith in Australia's institutions. It is a faith in which I have never wavered these past thirty-five years.

11

Citizen Kirby

> I keep thinking of what Richard Strauss was told by his son: 'Dad, everyone is telling you how good you were. Sit down and do something really noble and grand. Try to do something that is new and different.' And he sat down and wrote the *Four Last Songs*, and they are one of his greatest legacies. I don't know if I've got that in me, but I'm certainly going to be looking around and trying to look into myself for something new, different and grand.
>
> *Michael Kirby*

Johan had never before appeared on camera speaking publicly about his relationship with Michael Kirby. But this was a special time. Michael had retired from the bench and was now an ordinary citizen and Johan thought it was the right time to go on the public record. One Sunday night in 2010, hundreds of thousands of Australians switched on their televisions to see Johan van Vloten, until very recently the private part of Michael's life, speaking frankly and humorously about their long life together.

> We are together now for forty years and a bit. This is the forty-first year. The key of the success would be that both are a little bit hard of hearing; and, frequent absences – that all helps. But definitely we do enjoy each other's company, very much so. We have so many things in common – history, reading. So I'll be reading and tell him about what I've read and he'd tell me his daily stories, which are just as interesting as any historical novel.

If Johan had thought that now Michael was retired he would slow down or that the two of them could take that long holiday they had often talked about, he knew it was a pipedream. When asked about his plans now he was retired, Michael would say, 'I'm busier now than I have ever been.' And he was right. He might have moved out of his judge's chambers in the High Court but it was business as usual down in his new chambers on Macquarie Street, Sydney. A less grandiose suite of rooms than he was used to, but very central and all arranged and renovated by Johan. There was a host of honorary doctorates to receive, a UN job on the cards, a new career in mediation, and a grand farewell tour around the nation – films, books, TV shows, radio and public lectures to sell-out crowds. And overseas trips. In 2009 he spent 40 per cent of the year out of the country, on nineteen trips and 140 days of travel to Bhutan, China, France, Hong Kong, India, Ireland, London, Malaysia, the Netherlands, New York, New Zealand, Thailand and Zambia. He was overseas every month of the year except for February, the month of his retirement. A million frequent-flyer points.

Michael Kirby was the first to admit that he had a problem

with his work–life balance, but he was the last to ever seriously do anything about it. The Monet and Degas exhibitions came to the Australian National Gallery in 2008 and Michael, who walked every day he was in Canberra past the building, 200 metres from the High Court, had not attended. Many films, concert and plays opened to enthusiastic audiences but Michael was never among them. All too often he would arrive home from his Sydney chambers, or a late flight from Canberra, to a house that was empty except for Johan's prowling Abyssinian cat and a note on the table.

Dearest Michael,
Finished all the cooking. Your meal is in the fridge. Top shelf.

The cold water tap needs a new washer (will fix Monday). In the meantime close the tap vigorously (firm).

Love Johan

Exhausted from a day as the third most senior judge on the High Court of Australia, he would flop into a chair to eat a reheated meal alone, to the sound of a dripping tap and the purring cat.

> You'd have to ask Johan how my work balance has affected his life. I think, looking as objectively as I can, that it hasn't been an easy life. He's sometimes said to me, 'I believe I'm in a waiting room, just waiting for you to be there.' That is the truth of the matter. But he isn't Robinson Crusoe; this is very common in most top members of the legal profession, other professions. You've got to be very lucky to have a partner who will put up with you and put up with that, and put up with

> the ego of it and of the obsessiveness of it. Not everybody will do that, but in my life, I've been really fortunate in my tolerant family and partner.

Johan was far from happy about it and he had long since walked out of that waiting room. There was so much he had hoped the two of them could do together after Michael's retirement. They both loved travel; there were plays and films to see – Johan couldn't say when they had last attended something at the Opera House. It had been thirty-five years since Michael and Johan's second kombi trip – the last time they had had a real holiday together. Johan wondered when Michael was going to stop thinking only about number one and realise that there were more important things in the world than the next book review or committee meeting. Who knew how much longer either of them would be around for – surely it was time to give something back to Johan? But Michael was incredibly stubborn. He professed concern about his work–life balance but the truth was that he was never going to really retire until they took him out in a pine box. It was an attitude that hurt the person he loved most.

Three months after leaving the High Court, Michael Kirby was presented with the latest in a long line of awards and honours: an honorary doctorate from the University of Melbourne. In accepting the degree he gave a speech at the graduation ceremony for the law faculty before the students and their families, the dean of law, the acting vice-chancellor, the chancellor and a collection of retired judges. Also in the audience was the former governor-general and

ALRC commissioner Sir Zelman Cowen, and Lady Cowen. Kirby began by describing his first association with the university, in his heyday as a student politician, coming to Melbourne to carouse with the likes of Gareth Evans, who was then Gary, the bearded SRC president. He had attended many similar events over the decades, but there was something very different about this occasion. This time Johan was there as an official VIP.

> I'm proud to be at this ceremony with my partner, Johan van Vloten, a guest of the university. That's a rare distinction that he has been expressly invited to be with me on this day – this wouldn't have happened in earlier times. He has accompanied me through every day of my public life over the past forty years. So things happen, the earth moves, wrongs are righted, the world can be made a better place – international and national law can play a part. Johan joins me today in honouring all the students, the faculty, and the families. So in your presence I hope you'll forgive me if I honour him, a fellow citizen and a life companion, for his contributions to my life. Today is probably the closest to a public affirmation like marriage that we two will ever get, so it's just as well for us to say these things in your presence, out loud, and in a university that has always led, and challenged the spirit of the times.

It is unclear if the many parents, family and friends, or the bulk of the law students themselves, understood the full import of Kirby's speech. That he was affirming his love for his male partner in public in a way that he had never done before. Since 2004, when John

Howard had amended the Marriage Act, it had been illegal for same-sex couples to marry in Australia as, increasingly, they were doing in other parts of the world. The Marriage Act had stood Australians in good stead since 1961 but, mimicking the Republicans in the US, Howard decided he could 'wedge' the ALP by demanding that the Act urgently needed to be amended. Johan and Michael, like many gay (and straight) couples who had been together for decades, had never imagined they would ever get married, but once Howard enacted this discriminatory legislation things changed. Now it had become a political statement to support gay marriage.

At the drinks afterwards there was as usual a great deal of interest. The graduating students were lined up to get their pictures taken with Michael Kirby. These were the scenes that always accompanied his visits to the universities; he was no longer Justice Kirby but the star quality had not faded. The students were like adoring fans with a rock god. One after the other they shook hands, laughed and had their photos taken. Often it was Michael taking the photos for his own collection and all the time in the background was Johan. Things really hadn't changed that much. Johan had always been there in the background; now it was official. But he had his own life and work, and he would not suddenly be attending every function Michael had lined up – indeed, that would be impossible for anybody except Michael Kirby. There was a short window where Johan was available to be Michael's partner-on-show and then it was back to normal. Johan was an intensely private person and he was happy to go back to being an anonymous figure – as much as that was now possible.

Every year Michael and Johan would travel together on so-called holidays. The itinerary was carefully constructed to follow a series of work engagements for Michael. In reality, Johan enjoyed the holiday part of the trip while Michael worked, snatching an evening or afternoon off here and there to be with his partner.

> Can't call it a holiday with Michael, because he always puts in another thousand and one functions and so you do resent that. But on the other hand when you're there, you meet so many people, which is quite interesting, and of course he gives good speeches – most of the time, anyway. Sometimes they are very, very good and sometimes they are mediocre. I'm a very harsh critic in that. But of late he's been very good.

Kirby made one such speech just a few days before his retirement. Delivered on Australia Day in 2009 to the State Supreme Court and Federal Court Judges' Conference in Hobart and entitled 'Fifty years in the Law: A Critical Self-Assessment', he divided his life's work into 'successes' and 'shortfalls'. Few people in public life would ever consider preparing such an appraisal. Malcolm Fraser, the former Liberal prime minister, for example, had recently released his memoirs (which Michael had launched), and in Kirby's words, Fraser 'remained an enigma'. On the one act of his career that brought the greatest disapprobation upon his head – the events surrounding the dismissal of the Whitlam Government in 1975 – Fraser was mildly rebuked by Kirby: 'nothing new was offered'. Kirby, by contrast, was apparently much more open to self-reflection and in this speech he attempted to tackle his own shortcomings head on. It had a kind of religious overtone to it, a confession of sins, but the favoured approach of the judge in the adversarial system also immediately came to mind, where the scales of justice are so finely balanced, with conflicting testimony on either side. There were ten points in each category. It was only a beginning, of course – there could have been so many more added to the lists, but only so much can be done in one speech. Whether the shortfalls should really have outweighed the successes or vice versa would be left to history to decide.

On the positive side of the ledger, Kirby listed his years of independent and impartial service as a judge and the fact that in all the time he had sat on the bench, no one had ever even attempted to unduly influence his deliberations. He spoke of his achievements in creating a congenial and collegiate atmosphere in his courtroom where all was conducive to the task at hand, and nasty, vituperative attacks from the bench towards counsel, common in years gone by, were no longer tolerated. The elevation of the NSW Court of Appeal to a model emulated throughout Australia was on the list, as was the acceptance of the Australian Law Reform Commission as an important and indispensible legal institution. His frequent use of academic sources and international law references had led to a much wider recognition of these within Australian courts, thereby improving the quality of judicial decision-making. Allied to this, he had helped in the move from the 'strict and complete legalism' that had dominated judicial thinking to an approach more prepared to look at the broader context. He cited his willingness to turn to the media to disseminate ideas and the use of language that was clear and intelligible in the expression of complex legal issues as major successes.

Finally, Kirby referred to his personal life with Johan and his openness, particularly in recent years, about his homosexuality. This had resulted, eventually, in many changes for the better, including equal rights for same-sex couples in relation to federal government entitlements. He had been enormously moved by the many letters and communications he had received from people, straight and gay, helped by his frank advocacy.

Kirby then listed his 'shortfalls': the fact that he was not a senior member of the Bar before his appointment as a judge; that his first judicial appointment, as a trial judge, only lasted forty days; and the difficult transition from being the boss at the NSW Court of Appeal to being just one of the seven on the High Court – that is, he never made it to the position of chief justice. Rather than shortfalls, it seems more appropriate to describe these as elements peculiar to Kirby's professional life, not really anything he could or should have changed for the better. Many people would have seen it as a positive that he came to the bench with a life experience that was uncommon for a senior judge. The fact that he never became chief justice of the High Court was a political decision entirely outside his control. Kirby felt acutely some of the criticisms he had suffered from colleagues during his career: that he was unqualified to be appointed to the bench in the first place; that others, like Michael McHugh QC, were at that time more qualified to be appointed president of the NSW Court of Appeal. These barbs had stuck with him to such an extent that, now, a few days before he was to retire as a judge, he felt the need to address them. It was all a bit late; surely he should have let them go years before.

It was not his fault that he had not been appointed chief justice of the High Court, but it was unfortunate that he behaved, at times, as though there had been some mistake, that he should have been in that role. Kirby's mother had observed in her 22-year-old son an oversensitivity and inability to accept criticism. It was these traits that seemed to have come to the fore as negatives during his time on the High Court. He believed he should rightly have been the chief justice, and this conviction coloured so much of his behaviour throughout that time.

Then there were his high rates of dissent, his referencing of international human rights law and his failure to influence the majority of the High Court to turn away from an overly legalistic approach in its decision-making. In each of these areas Kirby had been unsuccessful in convincing his colleagues on the Court to adopt his own views and approaches. He had suffered as a result of his failures in this regard. He had sometimes behaved as if he were the leader of the Court, out in front, showing the way, whereas in fact it had increasingly been the opposite. He would have rejoiced if the Court had seen the error in their ways and turned to him for guidance, but they were never going to do that. He respected their independent judgements on these issues but he longed for it to have been otherwise.

Kirby could have pointed to some direct and pungent criticisms. Many academic commentators, for example, assessed his time on the High Court as a low point in his career overall. Somehow, Michael Kirby had ended up concreted into a position of isolation on the bench. No successful Appeal Court judge allows that situation to develop. It meant that he had become an irrelevancy. Counsel and the other judges would take heed of his views at their peril. Rather than adopting a stance that allowed for others to find room to come even part of the way across to him, Kirby had built a massive wall around himself, impenetrable and repellent. He could imagine that at some future time his dissents might become the majority view, but that was a fantasy. In the Realpolitik of the High Court, all that counted was the outcome on the day.

His seventh shortfall related to mistakes made in decisions. His first example was *Mallard*. Mr Mallard, the poor man who was wrongly convicted of murder in Western Australia, was finally released and compensated as a result of the High Court's intervention, but the fact that he had remained in prison for eight years after Kirby had been part of the special leave panel that rejected his initial application was a bitter taste that would remain with Kirby forever. Like a doctor who loses a patient, a lawyer who is party to a wrongful or unjust conviction, no matter how hard they worked for a different outcome, carries a heavy burden.

The next case was less obvious. In 2007 the High Court had decided in favour of an Aboriginal woman, Vicki Roach, who was serving time in prison. John Howard had changed the electoral laws to prevent any prisoner from voting. Just coincidentally, this had removed many thousands of votes that would in the majority usually go to the Labor Party. Roach was incensed that her right to vote should be removed and she took action in the High Court, claiming that Howard's law was unconstitutional. One relevant point was that the Constitution specifically stated that if a parliamentarian was convicted of an offence that carried a jail term of less than one year, then they were still eligible to sit in parliament. Under Howard's change, a parliamentarian in this situation could claim their constitutional right to sit but would be legislatively prevented from voting in an election. Howard's law seemed incompatible with both the Constitution and common sense. Kirby's judgement in *Roach*, this time in the majority, was to throw out Howard's change as unconstitutional. So why was this on his list of shortfalls? In retrospect, he thought that it might have been preferable if the Court had gone further. He believed that the right to vote was a basic human right, as recognised in the Universal Declaration of Human Rights. Perhaps, then, the existing Australian law, which he had upheld in his judgement in *Roach*, was also unconstitutional. The existing law declared that prisoners serving more than three years in jail were ineligible to vote. Kirby now thought all prisoners should be able to vote, no matter how long their term of imprisonment.

It was a little too neat to offer this example of Roach. He had taken the accolades at the time when he found in favour of the prisoner; now that he was no longer on the bench it was safe to say that, perhaps, he should have taken a stronger line. If he had really believed that, why hadn't he argued the case at the time? After all, it wasn't a particularly novel view – Lionel Murphy had advocated a similar thing years before. The real 'shortfall' here was that Kirby had taken the easy path. When his vote really counted in this matter he'd been absent.

Michael Kirby then turned to his years of commentary in the media, his high profile as a 'celebrity judge'. He acknowledged that over a long career and many thousands of media releases and commentaries, he had made a few mistakes. He had spoken up about political or social issues when as a judge he should have maintained a distance. 'I have made occasional errors. But not many.'

He acknowledged that if he had not been as open about his sexuality and his relationship with Johan, then Senator Heffernan might not have mounted the attack on him in parliament. This episode had harmed the relationship between the institutions of the federal parliament and the High Court. Plus: 'It hurt my family. It damaged my name.' Kirby had recently been to see the feature film *Milk*, in which Sean Penn, in an Oscar-winning role, played the gay San Francisco city councillor who was murdered by a homophobic political rival. 'I saw some parallels in what happened in San Francisco to Harvey Milk. I must, I suppose, at least be grateful that in Australia we do not generally settle our differences with bullets.'

No doubt there would have been those in the audience who cringed at this speech. They would have seen it as another occasion where Kirby had taken the opportunity to focus on himself: Michael Kirby, the great self-promoter. Other judges might make brief comments on their personal lives, for example, perhaps at swearing-in or retirement ceremonies, but Kirby seemed to dwell on this kind of material. What might seem normal and human to an outside lay observer would be read as grossly self-indulgent by many of his judicial colleagues. He did not do himself any favours in this regard by choosing a list of achievements and shortfalls that could easily have been dismissed as self-serving. Criminal trial judges, for example, have to deal with wrongful convictions or unjust outcomes more regularly, and they do not make a big deal about it. Kirby's frequent hand-on-his-heart references to the *Mallard* case wouldn't win him any friends in that area. Why claim achievements in raising issues of international law and a rejection of strict legal formalism and then list those very areas in the shortfall category as well? And the same could be said for his openness about his long-term relationship with Johan – a positive and yet also a negative. Surely he didn't really think that he should never have come out because as a result 'creatures' like Heffernan might attack or damage the institution of the High Court? And yet he appeared to be leaving the door open for that conclusion.

His last shortfall was a work–life balance that was frighteningly lopsided. 'I doubt if, on the deathbed, any judge would regret not being able to rush into chambers to finish writing another decision; to write another speech; or to complete a book review on time.' This was certainly true, but it seemed almost designed to antagonise colleagues. Was he implying that others didn't work hard enough? Or perhaps just grandstanding about his own, almost super-human, schedule. Either way it would not be received well.

In the end, Michael Kirby did not really care about the critics. Of course he could be hurt by snide comments or dismissive attitudes, but he had suffered that kind of rebuke from some quarters all his professional life and it had never stopped him doing or saying what he believed was right. This speech was no different; every word was genuine and delivered with an unusual kind of honesty, and to most in the audience that is how it was understood. It was an introspection of sorts, and about as far as he would ever go in self-criticism, because ultimately Kirby was comfortable with who he was and the choices he had made in his life.

Having finished his speech he did rush back to chambers. As of Tuesday, 3 February 2009, he was no longer Justice Kirby, just plain old Mr Kirby. His days as a judge were now over. Or were they? The UN had contacted him, asking if he would put his name forward for a position as judge on the Appeals Tribunal of the new Dispute Tribunal, which had been established to deal with internal grievances and disciplinary cases within the UN. The new tribunal was an attempt to address allegations of corruption in the UN by ensuring 'that individuals and the Organization were held accountable for their actions'.

Geoffrey Robertson was a member of the UN International Justice Council and it was he who had thought of Michael for the role. Usually these appointments are considered sinecures for national governments to bestow as rewards and political favours. But it would not have been a good look to stack an anti-corruption body with those kinds of appointments. So this time the UN had advertised the positions and Geoffrey Robertson recalls that he was asked to devise an examination to be taken by each applicant: 'I set them a written examination – which rather surprised them. Kirby wrote the longest answer, the longest judgement, as you would expect. He was one of fourteen that we recommended for the top UN court. He was certainly the best.'

Kirby waited with bated breath. To serve as an appellate judge on an international tribunal would be the perfect cap to a career that had taken him to the highest court in Australia. Exactly one month later, the general assembly of the United Nations voted. Twenty-three judges stood for election out of 237 applicants from fifty-five countries and there were twelve places to be filled. Seven judges were elected to the Appeals Tribunal. Michael Kirby was not one of them. He had missed out by twenty-four votes. One requirement was that there be a geographical spread of successful candidates. New Zealand had already taken one of the spots on the Dispute Tribunal so when Kirby's name came up in the second round of ballots for the Appeal Tribunal, delegates chose from another, less represented, region. It was a disappointment for Kirby; he truly would now have to face the fact that he would no longer be a judge. But it was a short-lived regret. He was too busy to dwell on such things.

> Since I left the High Court of Australia, I have been busy in a number of fields. Mediation (where I have a perfect record of achieving settlements in every case attempted); university lectures (where I have honorary professorial rank at twelve universities); public speaking (where I have to beat them off – you have no idea how many conferences are now held in Australia); and international committees (I am on five busy UN and other bodies). I try to juggle all these things and to remember that I have a family and partner. But I have found that outsiders are very intolerant of their demands.

For the next two years Kirby worked as hard and as tirelessly as ever. At the UN he advised on human rights for the Joint UN Programme on HIV/AIDS; he was rapporteur of the Judicial Integrity Group of the United Nations on Drugs and Crime, specifically dealing with the potential for corruption in the judiciary worldwide; and he was a member of the UN Development Programme's Global Commission on HIV and the Law. This commission had been established to counter the growth of laws that extended the discrimination and stigmatisation of AIDS and thereby limited effective controls on the spread of the disease. In 2010 in New York Kirby chaired the

Technical Assistance Group of the commission, in Colombo he attended meetings of UNAIDS, in Vancouver he appeared at the Human Rights Institute of the International Bar Association, and in the Netherlands he joined the board of the Hague Institute for Internationalisation of Law to deal with issues of globalisation especially as it affected weak or fragile states.

In October 2010 he flew to the George Washington School of Law in Washington DC to accept the greatest international honour presented for law, the Gruber Prize for Justice. Johan stayed in Sydney. The prize carried with it a cheque for US$500 000. Kirby shared the justice prize with two other winners: Professor John Dugard, who had been instrumental in the drafting of South Africa's recent human rights laws, and the Indian Law Resource Center, a US body established to promote indigenous rights in the Americas. Peter Gruber, the Jewish philanthropist behind the awards, had fled Hungary as a refugee just before World War II and had spent time in the rag trade in Melbourne before establishing a hugely profitable investment business in New York. Kirby issued a press release:

> I am conscious of the many people with whom I have worked over the years on human rights and justice who are equally deserving of recognition . . . There is also probably a need for a special Gruber Prize for the spouses and partners of Gruber Prize winners. My partner of forty-one years, Johan van Vloten, definitely deserves a prize for putting up with me. Probably the Victoria Cross.

Michael and Johan continued to go to Sydney Street in Concord for a regular Sunday meal with Michael's father, Don, who liked to play host and feed the whole family. They didn't always see Donald, David or Diana, who would often go at a different time on the Sunday. On 17 April 2011 Don, Michael and Johan were joined by Diana and her three children, two of whom had pregnant wives. Don had just got his driver's licence renewed at the age of ninety-five, so there was plenty to celebrate. He cooked up a big meal of vegetables and Michael was relaxed and happy. 'It was a great evening and we had lots of joy and fun.'

Don Kirby loved to drive. As for a lot of elderly people, it gave him a sense of independence, but he was also a good driver. If a guest dropped in, even in his nineties Don was always the first to offer to drive them home, and if home was right across town it did not matter. That was one thing on which Michael Kirby was never going to outdo his father: Michael remained a confirmed non-driver. Don had been a bit nervous about going for the licence again but needn't have worried – he came through with flying colours. But he didn't get to use his new licence that much. Within a few months he was extremely sick with cancer, and on 11 November he died at Wolper Hospital in Sydney. The funeral took place the following week at Rookwood Crematorium.

The house at Sydney Street and its longtime occupant, Don Kirby, were like an anchor for Michael's life. It had been thirteen years since his mother Jean had died and in all that time Don had been the centre of the family. Now there was just an emptiness where the powerful force of Don Kirby's intellect and presence had once been. Don had kept Michael's room as a kind of altar to his son's life. Every single milestone was preserved there: his schooling, his degrees, his judgeships and his awards. The tiny room was full of framed photos, press clippings and mementos. It had not changed in any other way since the day Michael had moved out. The siblings would now have to pack up nearly eighty years of family life and sell the house. Twenty archive boxes arrived at Michael's chambers in Macquarie Street. Don had kept everything – he'd been the official family record-keeper, and this job would now pass to Michael. The Kirby clan would go on but the close and lucky family that Michael always known, with Don Kirby at its head, was gone forever.

One thing Don had taken great delight in was the fact that he had been introduced to Her Majesty the Queen – not once, but twice, first when accompanying Michael during the bicentennial in 1988, and then in 1992 during the sesquicentenary of the incorporation of the City of Sydney. Michael had met the Queen on many occasions during her Australian visits, and in 2011 he had an audience with her at Buckhingham Palace, together with other members of the Commonwealth Eminent Persons Group (EPG). When his father was very ill in September 2011, Michael was required to be in Perth for the Commonwealth Heads of Government Meeting (CHOGM). He asked his father if he should stay in Sydney, but Don would have none of it. He gave his son firm direction: 'You do your duty. Go to Perth. That's what Queen Elizabeth has always done.'

Kirby's work on the EPG was designed to present a plan for the future of the Commonwealth of Nations. Initially the Commonwealth had primarily existed as an organisation of nations that had all once been part of the British Empire. Now that was not even true. Two of the fifty-four member nations had never been connected in any way to Britain – Mozambique, a former Portuguese colony, and Rwanda, colonised by Germany and then Belgium. It was not at all clear why these two African nations had recently decided to join the Commonwealth and, by the same token, why their membership was accepted. Not all former British colonies were now members of the Commonwealth, either. Burma had left, Zimbabwe walked out and Fiji had been suspended because of democratic and human rights violations. Ancient colonies like the USA, Hanover and parts of France had never joined.

There was no doubting his love and respect for the head of the Commonwealth, Her Majesty, but Kirby seemed at best rather ambivalent about his role on the EPG. Forty-one of the fifty-four nations of the Commonwealth had notorious and punitive anti-gay laws that they had inherited from the British. In many of these countries it was not uncommon for gay men to be beaten, harassed and jailed. In Uganda in January 2011 the gay rights activist David Kato had been brutally beaten to death. Gay men in Africa could suffer fates ranging from two years in jail to being stoned to death. On many occasions in his HIV/AIDS work, in a range of international forums, Kirby had had to sit down around the table with people unable to disguise their homophobic attitudes, some of whom belligerently walked out when he raised the human rights of gay, bisexual, lesbian, transsexual and intersex (GBLTI) people.

Wider human rights violations by many of the member states were not uncommon and not limited to matters of GBLTI discrimination. But there was an even more fundamental problem with the Commonwealth of Nations. There was no clear rationale for its existence any more, other than, perhaps, a kind of nostalgia. Commonwealth nations now tended to go to the G20 or the UN to resolve issues. These organisations had been relevant and effective; the Commonwealth had not. Three papers written by Kirby highlighted this existential crisis. For the *Parliamentarian* he wrote 'Commonwealth at the Crossroads: The Eminent Persons Group and the future', and for Geoffrey Robertson's chambers' *Doughty Street Lecture* he asked: 'The Commonwealth of Nations Today: Historical anachronism or focus for universal values?' And for the *Commonwealth Yearbook*: 'Renewal of the Commonwealth: But is there the will?'

The EPG identified many shortcomings of the Commonwealth. Where there had been electoral irregularities in Zimbabwe, they had acted; when Fiji suffered another coup, they had acted. But a host of other breaches of human rights had gone unchecked. Kirby doubted that the Commonwealth would survive on these terms.

> An international organisation that repeatedly proclaims its commitment to core values of human rights, tolerance, respect and understanding, the rule of law, freedom of expression, gender equality, good governance and respect for civil society, cannot indefinitely ignore serious or persistent instances in member states where these values are breached. There is a limit to international tolerance of hypocrisy.

The report of the EPG was delivered in October 2011 to CHOGM in Perth. Prime Minister Julia Gillard hosted the event with the leaders of the UK, Canada, South Africa and many other nations. The Queen presided and opened the meeting. The report formed an important guide to the discussions that took place. Thirty of the EPG recommendations were agreed to and a further twelve were made subject to an assessment of the costs involved. Almost all the remaining recommendations were passed on for consideration by a taskforce of ministers. The BBC described the result as a 'watershed for the organisation'. In a phrase often employed by Kirby, the report stated that 'silence is not an option' when it came to dealing with human rights abuses by member states.

The first recommendation of the EPG was for the adoption of a Charter of the Commonwealth, an idea proposed by the chair, Abdullah Ahmad Badawi, former prime minister of Malaysia. This document would outline the values of the people of the Commonwealth nations. Kirby, now stepping in the footsteps of Eleanor Roosevelt, personally prepared the draft of this document. It called for an adherence to the principles laid down in the Universal Declaration of Human Rights but went further, given the changes in the world since 1948.

He nominated a list of values that were essential if the Commonwealth was to continue with any relevance in the contemporary world:

> International peace and security; democracy; human rights; tolerance; respect and understanding; respect for the separation of powers and the rule of law; freedom of expression; economic and social transformation and development; upholding gender equality and empowerment; access to health and education;

commitment to good governance and respect and protection for civil society.

This first recommendation of the EPG was agreed to at CHOGM. The second recommendation was for the appointment of a commissioner for democracy, the rule of law and human rights. There seemed little point nominating a set of universal values if there was then no way of determining whether or not individual nations adhered to the charter. A commissioner could conduct such investigations and then report their findings. This recommendation was sent to the Secretary-General for evaluation. These recommendations, one and two of the report, assumed great significance. The fact that recommendation two was not adopted at CHOGM led some commentators to describe the exercise as a failure. Michael Kirby disagreed. They may have been small steps, but steps were being taken to make the organisation more relevant and effective. Some immediate and positive developments, especially in relation to containing the spread of HIV/AIDS, were accepted as well. If the Commonwealth could act side by side and in complementary ways to the UN, then it did have a purpose.

Recommendation number sixty was adopted in Perth: 'Heads of Government should take steps to encourage the repeal of discriminatory laws that impede the effective response of Commonwealth countries to the HIV/AIDS epidemic, and commit to programs of education that would help a process of repeal of such laws.'

As with his work in the UN, Kirby had shown that advances in the prevention of the spread of HIV/AIDS, especially in developing countries, were inextricably linked to the treatment of minority groups in those countries, and the protection of their human rights. Many of the Commonwealth nations were particularly bad offenders: having inherited the British laws on 'sodomy', they felt deeply threatened by homosexuality. The acceptance by CHOGM of this recommendation could now pave the way for real action in those forty-one anti-gay nations. Kirby wrote in the *Sydney Morning Herald*:

> Just as sexuality is a special Commonwealth problem, so is HIV/AIDS, which is twice as prevalent in Commonwealth countries as elsewhere in the world. Part of the reason for this may be the difficulty which the Commonwealth has demonstrated in tackling issues of sex and sexuality frankly and openly. In the absence of a vaccine or a cure for HIV, it is virtually impossible to halt this Commonwealth problem.
>
> At stake are the lives of millions of our fellow Commonwealth citizens. If the Commonwealth is truly a value-based organisation, it will act and repeal those foolish, ineffective and counter-productive laws. The Commonwealth has reached a moment of truth.

UK prime minister David Cameron immediately raised the idea of cutting aid to states that did not undertake reform of anti-gay laws. By the following month a global campaign to decriminalise homosexuality had begun, its first action a court case in Belize. The new Human Dignity Trust was to target the eighty-plus countries in the world that criminalised homosexual sexual activities. Over half of these nations were members of the Commonwealth.

A barrister working for the trust cited the 1994 UN decision in the case brought by Tasmanian gay activist Rodney Croome to support their action in Belize.

At the end of CHOGM, Prime Minister Gillard announced that the UK, Canada, India and Australia would inject millions of dollars into polio eradication. And in an issue close to Kirby's heart, but outside the brief of the EPG, the sixteen nations of the Commonwealth who have the Queen as their head of state, including Australia, approved changes to the royal succession. Amendments to a raft of ancient British Acts would remove the requirement that the monarch must be the eldest male child. Now the eldest child whether male or female would inherit the crown. At the same time, the UK Government would remove the bar to the monarch marrying a Catholic. These changes would only apply to the children of Prince William and Princess Kate and their progeny; they would not be retrospective. Gillard liked this significant change: 'You would expect me, as the first female prime minister of our nation, to say I believe women are equal to men in all regards.'

It was most unlikely that the glacial pace of change in the Commonwealth, epitomised by this massively overdue recognition of gender 'equality' in the most elite and discriminatory office in the world, the British monarchy, was going to shoot the organisation into twenty-first century relevance. The media generally had decided to treat CHOGM and therefore Kirby's work on the EPG rather trivially. The two big stories in Australia were that Prime Minister Gillard had not curtsied to the Queen and that David Cameron *badly* impersonated Julia Gillard's accent at a subsequent ritzy London function. 'I turned to the Australian prime minister and said, "Thank you very much, Julia, for allowing us to have this meeting in Australia", and she said (I can't do the accent but I'll try anyway), "Not a bit, David, this is good news for sheilas everywhere."'

In December 2011 Michael Kirby received three letters of thanks for his work with the Commonwealth EPG. Each said a lot more about the author than anything else. The prime minister wrote a formal but friendly letter: 'Dear Michael, I would like to thank you for your contribution . . . The dedicated efforts of the [EPG] were critical to laying the foundation for reform-focused outcomes at CHOGM 2011.' The prose was laden with the current bureaucratic buzzwords but it was warm and sounded genuinely appreciative. Foreign Minister Kevin Rudd dropped him a Christmas card: 'Thank you for your great contribution . . .' Not much substance but relaxed and showy. From the Opposition Leader, Kirby's friend Tony Abbott, he received a brief note. It was all about Abbott. 'Thank you for your recent letter of support. I appreciate your encouragement.' There was little in the nine-line letter about the EPG, other than a broad assertion of the Coalition's support for the promotion of human rights. A handwritten note at the bottom read: 'Thanks for your gracious defence of my very clumsy statement.'

Kirby was unsure what Abbott was referring to, but later realised it was probably Abbott's recent comment to *60 Minutes*. He had told the Channel Nine journalist that homosexuals made him feel threatened. Kirby hadn't exactly defended him when asked about the comment at a State Library of Queensland forum.

> I do not think Tony Abbott was being irresponsible in expressing truthfully his response to homosexuality. It is probably a product of his religious upbringing. Fortunately, that kind of religious attitude is on the wane in Australia today because of the growing knowledge in our community of the science of sexual variation. There may be special reasons in Tony Abbott's seminarian life, when he was training to be a priest, to explain why he felt 'a bit threatened'. Most younger people today do not feel 'threatened' because many younger GLBT peers today are open about their sexuality. They do not waste their time on 'straights' who do not share their feelings.

If Michael Kirby was to find something new and different and grand to do with his life after retirement, it still wasn't clear what that new thing was going to be. In truth, every day of his life had thrown up a new and different problem and a fascinating solution. As he headed towards his seventy-third birthday he could look back over the last three years of his life and see that there had been some changes.

Having left the bench he was just as outspoken about the issues that had always been important to him. He was not any *more* outspoken, but he was appearing much more frequently in media that, as a judge, he had usually avoided: newspaper gossip columns and men's, women's and gay glossy magazines were likely to carry an interview with Michael Kirby. He was also prominent on the internet and he established his own website, providing access to his speeches and press releases. He was increasingly appealing to younger people. The new director of the online social and political advocacy group Getup!, 25-year-old Simon Sheikh, nominated a speech by Kirby as being one of a couple of important events that had changed the direction of his young life.

In July 2001 Kirby had gone to his old stamping ground, Fort Street High School, to deliver an address to the school assembly. He'd spoken about his former classmate, Chinese Australian John Yu, now a highly respected paediatrician, who had just received Australia's highest honour, the Companion of the Order of Australia. Simon Sheikh, who has Saudi Arabian and Indian heritage, was then sixteen and in the audience.

> John Yu must sometimes have felt in a small minority in the school back in the 1950s. I did too. It was whilst I was here at Fort Street, that I discovered my sexuality. I found out that I was homosexual: gay. It was nothing to be proud of, or ashamed of. It was just the way I was. But in those days, it was a source of great shame, fear and secrecy. I thought I was alone.
>
> There are people who still discriminate against others because they are different. Because they are gay. Because they are female. Because they are Aboriginal. Because they are Asian-Australians or Arab-Australians. Because of their religion. Or for other irrational reasons.
>
> Fortians must reject such attitudes. Ours is a public school – a school for equality. Fort Street upholds the dignity, worth and equality of every human being. Ours is a school that rejects irrational and unjust discrimination. We judge people for what they do; not for who they are.

Sheikh saw the parallels between his own feelings of shame about his mother's mental illness with the different shame that Kirby spoke about. Sheikh's father had come to Australia from Pakistan in the 1960s under the study programs for Asian students – the same programs Kirby had championed when he was at Sydney University. Like Kirby and John Yu, Sheikh was also in a minority as an Arab/Indian Australian, and he had struggled with family tragedies and illness and finally, against the odds, gained access to the selective Fort Street High School. Kirby's speech started Sheikh thinking about his own family situation.

But it was not until he saw the Heffernan affair unfold the next year that Sheikh realised how important Kirby's words had really been. He was inspired to embark on his first piece of activisim, writing a letter to the newspaper. In 2011, he told ABC-TV:

> When I saw Bill Heffernan do those despicable things to Justice Kirby, making allegations using parliamentary privilege, I had a moment of realisation that we had to say something in return. That we couldn't allow someone to make these allegations about a fine human being in the way that he did.

Sheikh was then, at twenty-five, the head of one of the most influential progressive political lobby groups in Australia, with more than 450 000 members and a budget of millions of dollars. They had campaigned for refugee rights, a charter for human rights, animal rights, and same-sex marriage. In what became known as the *Getup!* case, they had gone to the High Court, after Kirby had retired, to overturn John Howard's changes to the Electoral Act, which had disenfranchised hundreds of thousands of Australians by closing the electoral rolls early and therefore excluding those who had left it to the last minute to enrol to vote. Getup! won the case and the Howard laws were ruled unconstitutional, giving voters four extra days to enrol before that year's federal election.

Kirby knew that it was the young people who would now have to carry the baton for the many ideas he had championed throughout his career. Television and radio programs were turning to him with increasing regularity. He had done all these things in the past, but now it was with much more informality and often aimed directly at a young audience. He hated the thought that he might only be speaking to the same group, just preaching to the converted. A lot of his commentaries had a serious subtext but on the surface they were tongue-in-cheek, self-deprecating and funny. But he was always looking for the new and the different.

> Because if I look back on the early part of my life, the biggest puzzle for me is this. When I was in the Council for Civil Liberties at the age of about twenty-four, taking an active part, we stood up for Aboriginals and the Aboriginal scholarship and for Asian-Australians in the attempts of the universities at that time to reduce the number of Asian people coming to Australia to the university. But we never spoke up about gays, never once. And we didn't speak up about some of the other issues like climate and the biosphere and so on that we speak about today.
>
> So the real puzzle is, what are the things we do not see today that people in thirty years' or forty years' time will look at you and say, 'How could you not have seen the importance of that?

> How could you be so ignorant? How could you be so unfair? How could you have been so cruel?' And that is the challenge for thinking, conscientious people. And I think that's what you've got to focus on – what are the things your generation is not seeing that will be seen, and you have to contribute to the seeing of it.

There was something that Kirby had taken for granted throughout his life, something he had never given a second thought to, something unkind, cruel and, now he was convinced, utterly wrong. In 2009 he was asked to launch a book, *Animal Law in Australasia*, edited by Peter Sankoff and Steven White. In the last years of his life, Don Kirby had encouraged his son and Johan to eat more vegetables, and by the time of Michael's heart scare he had decided to cut back on his meat-eating. But after reading this book, Kirby realised for the first time in his life the important ethical questions raised by eating animals.

> If the ordinary Joe and Jill in the street knew how bacon comes to be made; how pigs are kept in close confinement in crates, unable to move or scratch themselves; how chickens, which are one of the most sociable of animals, are corporatised and killed on a production chain and pumped with hormones in order to get to the stage where they can be killed quickly; and how animals are pained during experimentation on them and other animals are subjected to terrible conditions for entertainment of human beings in sports, they would really think twice about it.

He agreed to be the patron of the animal rights organisation Voiceless. He determined to stop eating any meat or chicken and went home to tell Johan: 'That's it!' Johan, in his inimitably laconic way, simply said, 'You'll get over it.'

But Kirby did not get over it. 'We now have the complication at dinnertime that he is still a carnivore and I'm not – I still eat fish but not meat or poultry.' The best-known human rights advocate in Australia had now added animal rights to his list. Kirby had spoken up, on a daily basis, for people who did not have a voice in the corridors of power. For people who suffered fear, disease, discrimination, persecution or death and had no one else to speak for them. Now he would give a voice to animals who lived side by side with humans in a world that so often abused and neglected them. Animals that depended totally on humans to speak for them since they could never speak for themselves. To many people, this was not something of priority in their lives. To many people that kind of talk was extremist and wrong; it threatened them. Perhaps Michael Kirby had found that new and grand thing.

> And in the meantime, my ideas have been expressed and are working away in the minds of thousands of people who may adopt some (and reject others). Ideas will be my children. Ideas about reality in the law; the choices faced by judges and how they should be resolved; the link between national and international law; truth about human relationships and sexuality; the importance of secularism and its defence; the need for courage and kindness to one another; the need to consider more actively animal welfare and the biosphere; the

> obligation to search for spiritual meanings to existence and to make the most of every day.

Only weeks from his seventy-third birthday, Kirby was increasingly left to his own resources. Where once he had a full-time secretary and two associates and all the resources of the Court, he was now reduced to one part-time personal assistant. Throughout the beginning of 2012 the photos were still being taken but they piled up, unfiled and unlabelled, and the speeches were written and delivered but few signs of them appeared on the Michael Kirby website. The workload did not decrease. From 25 January to 19 February he flew to meetings in Jakarta, Oslo and Brussels. His appointment book for the year ahead was already filling. It was now hard to find a space for a lecture, conference or book launch well into November.

As his Qantas flight soared into a blue sky so bright it hurt the eyes, Kirby relaxed back into his seat. How many times had he embarked on this journey across the immense landscape below? Certainly there had been hundreds of trips. Vast expanses of western New South Wales seemed to go on forever and were still suffering from a long drought or, looked at another way, simply living the normal life of the Australian continent, shaped by these forces over millions of years. The patterns below were more Clifford Possum Tjapaltjarri than Fred Williams. What did all those Australians down there think of Michael Kirby and his work? Would he be remembered as a great jurist and humanist? Had people already forgotten about him, and if not, how long before they did? These were questions that Kirby could never answer. He just let them hang in the thin air at 10 000 metres.

Kirby would keep moving and keep thinking, debating, explaining and advocating. Since his teacher Mr Goringe first gave him that copy of the Universal Declaration of Human Rights in 1950, so much had changed that Kirby barely recognised the Australia of 2012. Michael Kirby himself had changed in many ways. Novelist Julian Barnes has identified a common trajectory where, as the hair thinned and greyed and the waistline swelled, there was almost inevitably the 'ritual shuffle to the Right'. A comfortable ease into conservatism. For Michael Kirby there certainly would be no shuffling; shuffling was not something he ever did. But perhaps there was a sense of freedom after his retirement. If he had been at all restrained as a judge, constrained in what he might say and where he could softly tread, those days had passed.

Notes

Excerpt from *East of Eden* granted courtesy of Warner Bros. Entertainment Inc.

Passage from Ellis, Bob, 'My Life in the Lower Courts', *Blackacre 68*, Sydney University Law Society Yearbook, reproduced with permission of the author.

Unless otherwise indicated, quotes from Michael Kirby are from interviews with Daryl Dellora conducted on 30 January 2009, 25 May 2009 (filmed) and 27 June 2011; quotes from David Kirby are from an interview on 30 March 2011; quotes from Don Kirby (Senior) are from an interview on 31 March 2011; quotes from Geoffrey Robertson and Johan van Vloten are from interviews for the film *Michael Kirby: Don't forget the justice bit* (Film Art Doco, 2010) on 3 April 2009 and 27 May 2009 respectively.

Unless otherwise indicated, copies of letters and family documents were provided by Michael Kirby, and speeches, addresses, book reviews or other writing (except judgements) can be found at michaelkirby.com.au.

THE YELLOW JACKET

6 'This is a very important night…' Michael Kirby at Victorian Arts Law Week function on 7 May 2007, transcribed from footage recorded for Multicultural Arts Victoria.

8 'intellectual architect…' Russell, Peter, *Recognizing Aboriginal Title: The Mabo case and Indigenous resistance to English-settler colonialism*, University of Toronto Press, Toronto, 2005.

10–11 'Two weeks ago…' Michael Kirby, speech, University of Sydney, 28 February 2009, transcript at sydney.edu.au/news/84.html?newsstoryid=3089.

A LUCKY LIFE

14 'Where, after all…' Eleanor Roosevelt, speech, tenth anniversary of the Universal Declaration of Human Rights, 27 March 1958, transcript at www.udhr.org/history/frbioer.htm.

14 'one of the pleasant customs here' … Eleanor Roosevelt, 'My Day' newspaper columns, 11 September 1943, at gwu.edu/~erpapers/myday/.

26 'by the skin of his teeth' … Sir Robert Menzies, Hansard, House of Representatives, 4 May 1950.

31 'that bright prospect…' Clark, C. M. H., *A History of Australia, vol. 4, The Earth Abideth Forever 1851–1888*, Melbourne University Press, Carlton, 1999, p. 124.

32 'We always used to…' Neville Wran, interview from Dellora, Daryl (dir.), *Mr Neal Is Entitled to Be an Agitator*, Film Art Doco, 1991.

I WAS A NON-SEXUAL BEING

39 'In James Dean...' François Truffaut, quoted in Roth, Sanford and Beulah, *James Dean*, Taschen, Cologne, 1987, p. 60.

41 'Australia's greatest menace' ... Details come from Willett, Graham, 'From Vice to Homosexuality: Policing perversion in the 1950s' in Robinson, Shirleene, *Homophobia: An Australian history*, The Federation Press, Sydney, 2008, pp. 119–20.

41 'smash homosexuality in London...' Details of the Montagu trial come from Wildeblood, Peter, *Against The Law*, Weidenfeld and Nicolson, London, 1991.

46–7 'only 16 per cent of all graduates...' *Australian Yearbook 1958*, Australian Bureau of Statistics.

47 'We both yearn to have...' Bob Ellis at the launch of his book *And So It Went*, Sydney, 19 June 2009, transcript courtesy Film Art Doco.

48 'freshers are to use the day...' *Honi Soit*, 5 March 1956, p. 6.

48 'out and out exam passers' ... Memories of Sydney University in 1956 come from James, Clive, *Unreliable Memoirs*, Cape, London, 1980; and Hughes, Robert, *Things I Didn't Know: A memoir*, Vintage Books Australia, North Sydney, 2006.

49 'Sir, I congratulate you...' Robert Hughes, letter in *Honi Soit*, 26 September 1957, p. 4.

55 'Mary Gaudron's more militant position...' See Brown, A. J., *Michael Kirby: Paradoxes & principles*, The Federation Press, Sydney, 2011, p. 54.

58 'I would rather die' ... Kirby, Michael, 'Fifty Years After Wolfenden: Personal reflections on homosexual law reform', *Meanjin*, August 2007.

59 'the whole thing was shut down...' See Wallace, Christine, *Greer: Untamed shrew*, Pan Macmillan Australia, Sydney, 1997.

61 'We have been bundled...' Hull, Crispin, *The High Court of Australia: Celebrating the centenary 1903–2003*, Thomson, Sydney, 2003.

66–7 *'The General Law Amendment...' Honi Soit*, 30 July 1963, p. 1.

71 'The Freedom Ride to Walgett...' Curthoys, Ann, *Freedom Ride: A freedom rider remembers*, Allen & Unwin, Crows Nest, NSW, 2002.

75 Exchange between Kirby and Ellis recorded at the launch of *And So It Went*, op. cit.

84 'Speech from the Throne', Michael Kirby, reported in *Union Recorder*, 16 March 1967, p. 49.

I COULDN'T LIVE A LIE

87 'Bob appeared at the house...' Nelson, Penny, *Penny Dreadful*, Random House Australia, Milsons Point, NSW, 1995. See also Ellis, Bob (dir.), *The Nostradamus Kid*, Simpson Le Mesurier Films, 1993.

88 Exchange between Kirby and Ellis recorded at the launch of *And So It Went*, op. cit.

89–90 Ellis, Bob, 'My Life in the Lower Courts', *Blackacre 68*, 1968, pp. 48–9.

90 'a travesty of justice' ... Buckley, Ken, *Offensive and Obscene: A civil liberties casebook*, Ure Smith, Sydney, 1970, pp. 196–208.

93 'The picture is one...' Justice J. D. Holmes, *Corbishley; Re Locke* [1967] 2 NSWR 547 (CA), 549.

94 'Sadly, he came before a judge...' Michael Kirby, 'CCL Thirty Years On: We are all civil libertarians now', speech, thirtieth anniversary dinner of the NSW Council for Civil Liberties, 13 April 1995.

96 'Interesting, is it not…' ibid.

100 'The magistrate took…' Chief Justice Garfield Barwick, *Crowe v. Graham* 121 CLR 375 (8 March 1968).

102 'One of the best things…' Kirby, Michael, Foreword, in Campbell, Scott, *History of the NSW Council for Civil Liberties 1963–2005*, NSWCCL, Sydney, 2007, p. 3.

102–3 Roy Jenkins, UK Hansard, House of Commons, 3 July 1967, at hansard.millbank-systems.com/commons/1967/jul/03/clause-8-restrictions-on-prosecution.

105 'anti-war, anti-poverty, anti-greed…' quoted in Hocking, Jenny, *Lionel Murphy: A political biography*, Cambridge University Press, Melbourne, 2000, p. 71.

106 Jim McClelland interviewed by Robin Hughes for *Australian Biography*, Film Australia, 24 January 1995, at australianbiography.gov.au/subjects/mcclelland/interview1.html.

111–12 Ivor Balmain quoted in 'US Servicemen on R&R from Vietnam', *Four Corners*, ABC-TV, 1968.

112 'They would come running out…' NSW Police Senior Constable (retired), personal communication with the author, 18 November 2009.

114–5 'It happened in a secluded restaurant…' Michael Kirby, as related to the author and based on 'Out and about', *Sydney Morning Herald*, 30 December 2008.

115 Demofilo Solera quoted in Kirby, Michael, *A Private Life*, Allen & Unwin, Crows Nest, NSW, 2011, p. 73.

135 Sir Robert Helpmann… Kirby, Michael, 'The Purple Onion', *DNA Magazine*, March 2008.

AN EXPERIMENT IN LEISURE

136 David Kirby interviewed by the author for Dellora, Daryl (dir.), *Michael Kirby: Don't forget the justice bit*, Film Art Doco, 2010.

153 'Sharp. Dedicated. Focused…' Michael Kirby, inaugural Neville Wran lecture, NSW Parliament House, Sydney, 13 November 2008.

154 'Every now and again…' Michael Kirby, 'Memories of Hickson, Lakeman and Holcombe', speech, May 2002, at hcourt.gov.au/assets/publications/speeches/former-justices/kirbyj/kirbyj_memories.htm.

156 Gough Whitlam, Hansard, House of Representatives, 10 October 1972, p. 2296.

157 Don Dunstan interviewed by Jenny Hocking for Dellora, Daryl (dir.), *Mr Neal Is Entitled to Be an Agitator*, op. cit.

158 'For all the faults…' Michael Kirby interviewed by Peter Coleman, *Law in Australian Society*, National Library of Australia Oral History Section, 8 July 1995, p. 49.

161 Michael Kirby, ibid.

164 Sir Garfield Barwick, *Cormack v. Cope* (joint sittings case) 131 CLR 432 (5 August 1974).

167 'The Minister for Labour…' 'Judge not my friend – Cameron', *Sydney Morning Herald*, 14 December 1974.

168 Tom Hughes QC, Australian Conciliation and Arbitration Commission, Sydney, 13 December 1974, official transcript.

THE GREAT COMMUNICATOR

171 'He died at the feet…' Michael Kirby, 'Tradition and Diversity', speech, Supreme Court judges' dinner, Supreme Court of NSW, 12 February 2004.

172 'It wouldn't have been my scene…' Michael Kirby interviewed by Peter Coleman, op. cit, p. 55.

173 Senator Lionel Murphy, second reading speech, Law Reform Commision Bill, Hansard, Senate, 23 October 1973.

174 'I'd only got through…' Michael Kirby interviewed by Jenny Hocking, op. cit.

174 'No, I don't want any of those…' Lionel Murphy as recalled by Michael Kirby, interview with the author, 25 May 2009.

187 'I'm sure that he was…' Michael Kirby interviewed by Peter Coleman, op. cit, p. 60.

192 John Laws interview with Michael Kirby, 2UE, 31 January 1980, transcript.

193–4 'You and the law…' Munday, Rosemary, *Australian Women's Weekly*, 2 November 1977, pp. 24–5.

194 'Should parents…' Kirby, Michael, 'My Week', *Australian Women's Weekly*, 27 January 1982, p. 24.

195 'That was a most…' Michael Kirby, 'Health, Law and Ethics', lecture, Australian Institute of Health, Law and Ethics, first annual conference, Canberra, 15 November 1996, at hcourt.gov.au/assets/publications/speeches/former-justices/kirbyj/kirbyj_kirbylec.htm.

197–8 Michael Kirby, 'The Judges', Boyer Lectures, ABC Radio, 1983.

199–200 'Lionel was a sort of counterpoint…' Michael Kirby interviewed by Jenny Hocking, op. cit.

206 'Murphy Affair'… Hocking, Jenny, *Lionel Murphy: A political biography*, op. cit, p. 289.

HOLDING THE MIDDLE CHAIR

209 'It is vital…' Michael Kirby, 'AIDS and the Lawmaker: The need for a rigorous approach and realistic goals', speech, joint WHO/Australian Inter-regional Ministerial Meeting on AIDS, Westmead Hospital, Sydney, 21 July 1987.

210–11 'Peter's concern…' Michael Kirby, 'AIDS: Return to Sachenhausen?', speech, first international conference on the global impact of AIDS, Barbican Centre, London, 8–10 March 1988.

216–7 'I cannot tell you…' Michael Kirby, 'The Five Commandments for New Legislation on AIDS', speech, third international conference on AIDS, Washington DC, 2 June 1987.

222 'a thoroughly unmeritorious…' Turnbull, Malcolm, Acknowledgements, *The Spycatcher Trial*, William Heinemann Australia, Richmond, 1988.

223 'the greatest adventure…' ibid.

224 Gough Whitlam quoted in Turnbull, Malcolm, ibid, p. 151.

226 'Civilisation as we know it…' Michael Kirby quoted in Bevins, Anthony, '"Spycatcher" judge condemns British official secrecy', *The Independent*, 9 February 1993.

229 'Some people – based upon…' Kirby, Michael, 'Reflections on Constitutional Monarchy', in Hudson, Wayne and Carter, David, (eds), *The Republicanism Debate*, NSWU Press, Sydney, 1993.

232–3 'I'm perfectly content…' Michael Kirby quoted in Wild, Dorian, 'His Honour's Honour', *Ita*, 1994.

237 Kirby's report, 'Cambodia: A parting assessment', 1 April 1996, at lawfoundation.net.au/ljf/app/&id=4E7B74498AA7928BCA2571A800006D07.

246–7 Jeff Kennett, Rob Borbidge and John Howard quoted in Dellora, Daryl (dir.), *The Highest Court*, Film Art Doco, 1998.
248 'What about former …' Franca Arena, Hansard, NSW Legislative Council Debates, 31 October 1996.

THE DEVIL MADE ME DO IT

261 Michael Kirby, 'The Legal Protection of Same-Sex Relationships in Australia', speech, King's College School of Law, University Of London, 3 July 1999.
262 'As chance would have it…' Kirby, Michael, 'Riverview: A modern morality tale', *Quadrant*, vol. 44, no. 5, May 2000, pp. 19–25.
264 Brian Greig interviewed by the author, 20 October 2011.
266 'situational paedophile' … Michael Kirby, *Ryan v. The Queen (2001)*, 206 CLR 267.
267 Bill Heffernan, Hansard, Senate, 12 March 2002.
268–9 Bill Heffernan, ibid.
269–70 Brian Greig, op. cit.
279 For Heffernan's apology, see Hansard, Senate, 19 March 2002.
280 Only Mary Gaudron… See Brown, A. J., op. cit, pp. 340–4.

MARCHING TO THE BEAT OF A DIFFERENT DRUM

285 '[When I was in] far-away Lesotho…' Michael Kirby, 'Televising Court Proceedings', *University of NSW Law Journal*, vol. 18, no. 2, 1995, pp. 483–92.
286 'By what right…' ibid.
287–8 'We have a society…' Sir Gerard Brennan in Dellora, Daryl (dir.), *The Highest Court*, op. cit.
289 'secret women's business' … See Maddox, Marion, *God Under Howard: The rise of the religious right in Australian politics*, Allen & Unwin, Crows Nest, NSW, 2005, pp. 124–37.
293 Exchange between Justice Michael Kirby and Dr Gavan Griffith QC, *Kartinyeri and ANOR v. The Commonwealth of Australia* A29/1997 [1998] HCATrans 13 (5 February 1998).
294 Michael Kirby's judgement in *Kartinyeri v. Commonwealth* [1998] 195 CLR 337.
294 'Upon the evidence…' Justice John von Doussa, *Chapman v. Luminis Pty Ltd* (No. 5) [2001] FCA 1106.
294–5 'Environment Minister Paul Caica…', ABC-Radio 891, 7 July 2010.
296–7 Chief Justice Jim Spigelman, swearing in of Justice David Kirby, Supreme Court of NSW, 12 August 1998, transcript.
298 'They're inseparable…' Don Kirby (senior), interviewed by the author for Dellora, Daryl (dir.), *Michael Kirby: Don't forget the justice bit*, op. cit.
300–1 *Green v. The Queen* (1997) 191 CLR 334; *Osland v. The Queen* (1998) 197 CLR 316.
300 'In my view…' *Green*, ibid, p. 408.
302 'No civilised society…' *Osland*, ibid, p. 375.
304 'Yes, but Mr Walker…' Michael Kirby, *Mallard v. The Queen* [2005] HCATrans 679 (6 September 2005).
311 'London is not a battlefield…' Cited in Lynch, Andrew, 'A Case Note: Thomas v. Mowbray: Australia's "war on terror" reaches the High Court', *Melbourne University Law Review 32*, pp. 1182–1211, 2008.

312–314 Michael Kirby and D. M. J. Bennett QC in *Thomas v. Mowbray & Ors* [2007] HCATrans 76 (20 February 2007).
315 Justice Owen Dixon in *Australian Communist Party v. Commonwealth* [1951] 83 CLR 1 (9 March 1951).
316–7 Michael Kirby's judgement in *Thomas v. Mowbray* [2007] HCA 33 (2 August 2007).
320–2 Michael Kirby's judgement in *Wurrigal v. The Commonwealth of Australia* [2009] HCA 2 (2 February 2009).
323–4 Justice Lionel Murphy cited in Williams, George, 'Lionel Murphy and Democracy and Rights', in Coper, Michael and Williams, George (eds), *Justice Lionel Murphy: Influential or merely prescient?*, The Federation Press, Sydney, 1997, p. 63.

CITIZEN KIRBY

333–40 Michael Kirby, 'Fifty Years in the Law: A critical self-assessment', speech, State Supreme Court and Federal Court judges' conference, Hobart, 26 January 2009.
342 'Since I left the High Court…' Michael Kirby interviewed by Greg Callaghan, 'Q&A', *Weekend Australian Magazine*, 2 April 2011.
344 'It was a great evening…' Michael Kirby interviewed by Margaret Throsby, ABC Classic FM, 18 April 2011.
347 'An international organisation…' Kirby, Michael, 'Renewal of the Commonwealth: But is there the will?', *Commonwealth Year Book*, 2011.
348–9 'International peace and security…' Michael Kirby, 'The Commonwealth at the Crossroads: The Eminent Persons Group and the future', *The Parliamentarian*, 2011.
350 'Just as sexuality is…' Kirby, Michael, 'Ending sexual apartheid', *Sydney Morning Herald*, 25 October 2011.
351 Julia Gillard quoted in Hudson, Phillip, 'PM Julia Gillard to voice fears on European debt', *Herald Sun*, 25 October 2011.
352 David Cameron quoted in Pearlman, Jonathan, 'David Cameron's imitation of Julia Gillard "worst Australian accent ever"', *The Telegraph (UK)*, 15 November 2011.
353 'I do not think Tony Abbott…' Kirby, Michael, 'Kirby Takes the Stand for Gay Rights', *Insight: State Library of Queensland Magazine*, issue 8, winter 2010, pp. 6–7.
355 Simon Shiekh interviewed by Virginia Haussegger, 'One Plus One', ABC-TV News24, 3 June 2011.
356–7 Michael Kirby, speech, ANU Law Students Society, 13 October 2008, from transcript of filmed lecture, courtesy Film Art Doco.
357–8 'If the ordinary Joe…' Michael Kirby quoted in Dwyer, Lynne, 'A late-life epiphany for Michael Kirby', *Sydney Morning Herald*, 17 December 2011.
358–9 'And in the meantime…' Michael Kirby interviewed by Greg Callaghan, op. cit.
360 'ritual shuffle to the Right' … Barnes, Julian, *Nothing to be Frightened Of*, Vintage Books, London, 2009, p. 79.

Acknowledgements

This book would not have been possible without the support and assistance of Michael Kirby himself. He provided access to many never-before-released materials, including private letters. He also made himself available for lengthy interviews. I am also indebted to Johan van Vloten, David Kirby and the late Don Kirby (Senior), all of whom were interviewed.

A. J. Brown (author of the comprehensive *Michael Kirby: Paradoxes & Principles*) and Geoffrey Robertson generously provided their time and valuable insights for the film *Michael Kirby: Don't forget the justice bit*, which was the starting point for this project. I also thank Sue Maslin for her enthusiasm and encouragement, Penny Chai for invaluable research, and filmartdoco.com for kindly providing access to all its archives.

Donald Kirby (Junior), David Kirby, Ian Wansbrough, Gary Dellora and Jenny Hocking all read the manuscript at different times and gave important feedback. Ian Freckleton and George Williams both provided insightful observations. Thanks go to Janet Albrechtsen, who was interviewed during the production of the documentary, and Brian Greig and Bill Heffernan, who also spoke to me for this book. Dr Beth Spencer has been a good friend and an inspiration in all things literary, and John Hocking, my brother-in-law and one of Kirby's first two associates at the NSW Court of Appeal, was the person who first introduced me to the judge.

My appreciation goes to all those at Penguin, including publisher Ben Ball and editor Jo Rosenberg; and, in particular, I must credit the foresight of Bob Sessions – the very idea of the book was his alone.

I thank my family for their love and support – my parents, Peggy and Geoff, and siblings, Estelle, Maree and Gary.

Finally, my greatest debt in all things, but particularly the writing of this book, must go to my partner, Jenny Hocking, and our son, Carlo Dellora.

Special note on the Mabo *case:* Most Australians had never heard of Eddie Mabo until the High Court brought down its famous decision in 1992. I was aware of him and his case as early as 1980. Barbara Hocking, the mother of my partner, was the first barrister briefed in the *Mabo* case and we would often see large lever-arch folders labelled 'MABO' stacked around the house. We had no idea, for a long time, what these four letters meant. I must thank Barbara Hocking for helping to generate in me a layperson's interest in the wonders of the law.

Index